"[An] animated history of American eating habits . . . Food is a conduit to our innermost desires and fears, and Tisdale, as adept at scintillating interpretation as at solid research, brings it all to the table for our perusal."
—*Booklist*

"[Tisdale] applies her considerable intelligence and curiosity to the notion of appetite itself, the ways we both indulge and deny that appetite and what food means now [and] draws on an impressive, eclectic bibliography. . . . *The Best Thing I Ever Tasted* accomplishes what Tisdale does best: It takes a topic and explores it unhurriedly, through history and myth, advertising and imagination, always asking, always striving for connections."
—*The Philadelphia Inquirer*

"Elevate[s] the recently burgeoning genre of food memoirs. . . . *The Best Thing I Ever Tasted* takes a sharp look at the history of food and consumption in America. By inserting a smattering of her own experiences into the narrative, [Tisdale] illuminates the origins of certain culinary tastes and national attitudes toward food."
—*Book*

"Weaving together childhood memories of Fritos and Orange Crush with meditations on the history, psychology and economics of food, she explores the complexities of how we satisfy the most basic of human needs."
—*Chicago Tribune*

"An appetizing critique of modern food culture, spiced with gourmet phrasing."
—*Kirkus Reviews*

"Tisdale, who has written on such monolithic subjects as sex and home, here examines a subject close to everyone's hearts and mouths. . . . Lively, smooth prose and witty interpretations . . . Her honesty makes her especially likable."
—*San Francisco Chronicle*

"At once forlorn and apologetic and elegiac . . . Tisdale waxes lyrical about junk food, waxes grim about the decline of community at the family table—which she sees as having become a dust-specked Edward Hopperesque vision of a bus station diner counter at 4:30 a.m., waxes elegiac about a much-decorated restaurant called Fiddleheads in her home-city of Portland, conceived in tribute to Native American cuisine. . . . Tisdale can be, often is, a marvelous writer."
—*The New Orleans Times-Picayune*

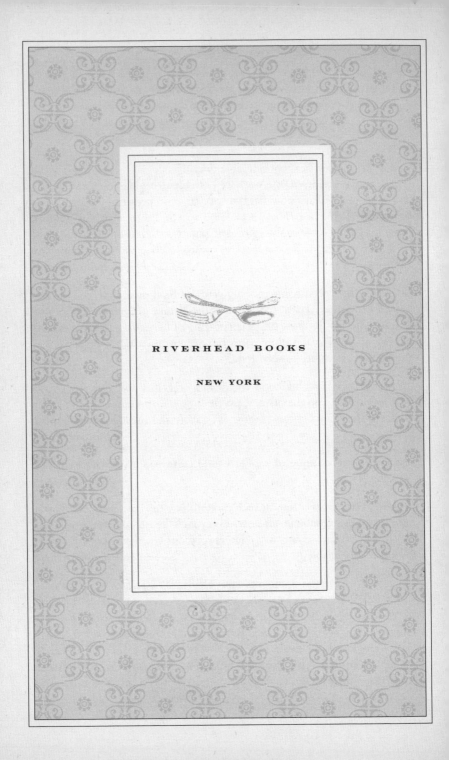

RIVERHEAD BOOKS

NEW YORK

THE
BEST
THING
I
EVER
TASTED

THE SECRET
OF FOOD

Sallie Tisdale

RIVERHEAD BOOKS
Published by The Berkley Publishing Group
A division of Penguin Putnam Inc.
375 Hudson Street
New York, New York 10014

Copyright © 2000 by Sallie Tisdale
Book design by Marysarah Quinn
Cover design by Jess Morphew
Front cover photograph by Alese Pickering

First Riverhead hardcover edition: January 2000
First Riverhead trade paperback edition: January 2001
Riverhead trade paperback ISBN: 1-57322-853-2

The Penguin Putnam Inc. World Wide Web site is
http://www.penguinputnam.com

The Library of Congress has catalogued
the Riverhead hardcover edition as follows:

Tisdale, Sallie.
The best thing I ever tasted : the secret of food / by Sallie Tisdale.
p.   cm.
ISBN 1-57322-130-9
1. Food—History.   I. Title.
TX353.T53   2000   99-048383 CIP
641.3'009—dc21

PRINTED IN THE UNITED STATES OF AMERICA

10 9 8 7 6 5 4 3 2 1

ANNIE ROSE,

that she may be brave and full of appetite

ACKNOWLEDGMENTS

I am haunted by the vast literature of food waiting to be digested; I have been able to taste only a little of it. I am indebted to a number of scholarly writers of history, sociology, and culture, many of whom are quoted in these pages.

Thanks to the many friends with whom I've shared meals over the years. Thanks especially to Megan McMorran, for friendship and praise when it is needed; Steve Tyler, for reading this in an early form and for listening patiently while I went on and on about it; Maria Dolan, friend, writing companion, underwater buddy, and research assistant; Kim Witherspoon, my blunt and loyal agent; Chris Knutsen, my meticulous and attentive editor; Chuck and Barbara Ryberg, excellent dinner companions and good friends; Carlton Grew, for his lovely words and open heart. I am grateful for the help of the staff of the Betty Crocker Test Kitchens.

Special thanks to Bob, who eats almost everything I cook.

INTRODUCTION

WHEN I WAS NINE YEARS OLD, I DECIDED TO make acorn meal the way the Indians did.

I lived in a small town in the high, dry reach of far-northern California, where the summers are hot, the winters are cold, and most days are full of sun. It was a kind town in many ways, nestled in a bowl of soft hills near the maternal majesty of Mt. Shasta. I attended the small elementary school, with a playing field as large as the buildings themselves. At one end was a playground of swings and climbing bars over a bed of sawdust, then a half-acre of asphalt covered with the arcane white circles and lines of childhood games, and beyond that, an endless field of grass. Along one edge, oak trees grew.

That fall, my fourth-grade class studied Indians. We did this almost every year, one way or the other—studied "the Indians," who seemed to be a single, exotic, lost tribe. There were children of several tribes in my class, but it was much later before I even learned the tribal names: Kurok, Hupa, Yurok, Modoc, Tolowa. And Shasta. Perhaps the distant figures we studied were as foreign to them as they were to me. Such things were not discussed.

We were required to do a short report on these imaginary Indians. All that was really expected, I think, was a trip to the library and a few slightly digested paragraphs from the *World Book Encyclopedia* cobbled together with a photo out of an old *National Geographic*. But I took the assignment to heart. On any given day, I planned to be a firefighter or a film star or a nun. But I would have liked greatly to be an *Indian,* the Indian of my imagination. Encyclopedias had nothing to do with it.

So here is an autumn day, and the rough, arid land has grown brown from the long, panting summer, and the curved, old hills that form my horizon are alive with dry grasses and dying thistles waving in the cool wind. The tough, squat oaks with their papery bark and dusty leaves have dropped their acorns. I know from my earnest research that acorns taste bitter and can make you sick, but I also know that the tribes depended on them for flour, cereal, oil. Their days revolved in part around working with these hard, ovoid, olive-green nuts with their squat brown caps. The labor of the acorn was the labor of the tribe.

I gather acorns—alone in the cold, gray autumn day, intimate with the native ghosts around me—and listen to the drumbeat of multiple-layered times. I take them home and do my best, but it is a bitter day. I work for hours, crushing, shelling, boiling again and again, roasting the nuts to get the tannin out. Only then can I hope to grind meal for bread, make cereal or stew. I have no idea, of course, how much work food requires. How could I? The food I eat every day seems to come from the air, free of sweat and roots—

from the pantry, the grocery store. Easy, ordinary. Making acorn meal turns out to be endless, painful work to do, especially to do alone—pounding the nuts with my father's hammer, crushing them with my mother's rolling pin, boiling and boiling until my hands are raw, and getting for my effort only a chewy and terrible paste.

A faint wind of loneliness blows through most people's lives; it has certainly blown through mine. I had a glimpse that day of how much more than food a food could be—and of the disappointment waiting when inchoate dreams don't come true. I see now that the things I wanted to be were marked with the quality of sacrifice. Sacrifice is a most seductive prospect when seen from far away, when seen from a life that doesn't seem to require it. Each of these things is marked by, made by, a community, intrinsically part of something greater, and meaningless alone. That autumn, I felt as though a secret was being kept from me, would always be kept from me. It was not the secret of acorns but of that shared daily labor of the community; it was the secret of men and women and girls and boys murmuring, singing, laughing together while they worked. It was the secret of something stable and traditional and lasting. I wore myself out that fall, grinding acorns in my mother's fluorescent-lit kitchen, longing for a tribe of my own.

WHAT DID YOU EAT FOR BREAKFAST? FOR lunch, for last night's supper, as an afternoon snack? What did you eat, and why? We think we choose food consciously, deliberately, rationally. We think about calories, price, time, convenience, cholesterol and fat and protein and other people's opinions, even as we mull over our desire. But what we choose to eat, even what we *want* to eat, is dictated by forces far beyond our reach, by tiny tides we do not see. Whether we want to believe it or not, we eat what we eat for a thousand reasons. We eat to settle our nerves, in joy and despair, in boredom and lust. We comfort ourselves, make ritual, find delight. What we choose makes us *naughty* or *good*. Food fills many empty spaces. It can be symbolic, mythic, even archetypal— and nothing special. How we feel about food is how we feel about our own lives, and so I am concerned with the central human *experience* of food—the intimate, universal, common experience laced with personal meaning and shared with every stranger.

Last night I made spaghettini with a sauce of fresh chopped clams, new sweet onions, and a little cheap white wine from the corner store. I served it with a green salad and a side of sautéed apples and pears. Why? Many reasons. I felt like cooking. I had time. I found myself near a good market with my checkbook in hand. I wanted the harvest of apples, the sea taste of clam flesh, and I live where apples and clams grow big and sweet. Other days, other needs, other meals: frozen pizza thrown in the oven at the last minute, macaroni and cheese out of a box, tortillas with a warmed-over can of refried beans. Canned soup. Frozen peas. How rarely do we stop to wonder why we want what we want, why we choose what we choose—why we don't take what we want when we can.

In the kitchen, nostalgia and rebellion meet. On any given day, my refrigerator holds chocolate milk, tofu, homemade mayonnaise, Philadelphia cream cheese, cilantro, frozen low-fat enchiladas, rapidly wilting lettuce, Kalamata olives, fermented fish sauce, imitation maple syrup, and a jar of salsa. In the cupboards are Asian spices and Mexican chilies, a half-dozen kinds of dried beans and several packages of Ramen noodles, expensive olive oil and aged balsamic vinegar, Grape-Nuts, and a big bag of Doritos. On the shelf is the 1971 *Joy of Cooking, Italian Country Cook Book, Thai Cooking Class, The Cook's Bible, Regional American Cookery*, and *Betty Crocker's Picture Cook Book*. The lists I have just made are the outward signs of centuries of change across the globe, sliding through me and my life here.

I'm a decent cook—not a great one. I can pull off a good red curry, a decent soufflé, an excellent piecrust. I can cook for large groups if necessary, and I can cook for two. There's no clear rhyme or reason to the way I cook except the rhyme and reason of myself. I cook erratically and unpredictably, like most Americans who cook (and most Americans don't cook much at all). Surveys show we largely don't know at four in the afternoon what we'll be fixing for dinner, and few of us spend more than half an hour on preparation once we decide. I cook like this sometimes, and other days I spend hours. I have no specialty, but cover the globe—badly. I cut corners. I snack on a spoonful of cookie dough and then spend two hours on a composed salad.

For all that, I cook more than most people and usually with pleasure. If you eat and cook at all like I do, you know what it is like to get to know a recipe, to get to know a food itself, to take it to heart, pamper and coddle it, threaten and cajole it. You know the vocabulary and the distant, considering gaze of *what to make*. You also know, like me, the frustration of not having enough time to cook properly and of being under pressure to serve something, anything, to feed the separate hungers of other people. You know the bleak, petty despair of a dirty kitchen after a bad meal, after small disappointments.

American cuisine is an oxymoron, but so are Americans. Here

we have National Pork Month, National Pizza Month, and Chocolate Awareness Month all at the same time. Here we eat too much and too little of just about everything. We consume more good food and more bad food than any other group of people in history. We have at our disposal a greater variety of food than most people ever could have imagined seeing—yet most of us eat the same thing day in and day out. (Several billion served.)

What we want and expect from our lives today, what we desire and accept, even what we imagine our lives should be, is the product of the past. It is as much a part of the expectations, desires, and dreams of the past as it is of actual events. The last century and a half—brief, dramatic, stressful years when everything changed—ripples through our days. Everything changed—from the kinds of work people did and how chores were shared in the home to how people defined their own identities and what they called happiness. Why I made the meal I cooked last night—why I *wanted* it—how I came to associate its tastes and textures with those desires—how its ingredients were available to me—all these are products of another time. The tools I used, the fuel with which I cooked, the methods, the means, are products, too. What I mean by "cooking dinner" is a product of dinners served for more than 150 years.

How much does a cuisine reflect its place and time? What does any cuisine mean in an increasingly global society? More than most people, Americans are constantly inventing new combinations of ingredients and methods of cooking—a phenomenon that is either fertile evolution or ugly mutation, depending on your point of view. (In a way, the sum of our culture *is* its pieces; its wholeness can be found only in the fact that it isn't whole.) Our fragmented, contradictory, stitched-together cuisine certainly reflects a fragmented, contradictory, and stitched-together society. Perhaps nothing reflects us better. We are an incoherent society; we *fail to cohere*, we do not gel. But in an unexpected way, our food does. The tensions of class, the economies of scale, the nuances of social status, and the death of leisure time—everything we experience as Americans—are blended together when we sit down to eat . . . whatever we eat.

My own generation is the one whose grandparents and great-grandparents tried to leave the past behind in the process of making things brand-new. They left behind the simmering stewpot and the garden hoe—in some cases, because the pot and hoe were wrenched away—and they walked, however reluctant and uncertain, into the future. What we call tradition now is startlingly new. The ritual of Thanksgiving, that pumped-up store-bought turkey, is for most of us as antiquarian a food as any we knew in childhood.

I was born three years after Swanson's first television dinner appeared—turkey with dressing, peas, and whipped potatoes—and grew up eating good food and bad. Both my parents were teachers, and during the school year we ate "tamale pie" made with hamburger and cream of tomato soup, scalloped potatoes and Spam, canned spinach, iceberg lettuce leaves big as plates with a dollop of reconstituted ranch dressing on top. In the summers, my family spent weeks at a cabin beside the Scott River in the northern California mountains—weeks in the virgin forest, without electricity, drawing our water from a cold spring, with the occasional fresh trout for breakfast. But mostly my brother, Bruce, my sister, Susan, and I spent our days on the beach with bags of Fritos and cold, wet cans of Orange Crush, sticky drops splashing on our Spiderman and Archie comics until the pages stuck together. I ate food as old-fashioned as yesterday's slang, food that at first glance is without history—heavy food, but with no real weight. For a long time I assumed that I had been born into a shiny, slick world like the one in the pages of magazines. I seemed to have no history; my cultural roots looked to be no deeper than my own feet.

One of my surprises in the last few years has been to discover how much that world in which I was raised was the logical product of a very long past. I discovered how much that world I came to disdain and turn from was a world many millions of people had desired and worked to create. What a happy dream my childhood meals were—they were dreams come true. I know now that this *is* my history, this hoped-for world of reheating and frozen individual portions. The food I grew up eating (and the more expensive and sophisticated forms of that food we still eat) seems to be a ghost. Spam and powdered salad dressing are like bodies sucked as dry as shadows, the essence gone and only the shells remaining. But so are pasta primavera and fish tacos ghosts of a kind, homeless foods. When I look more closely, I see that a lot of the roots for which I still long are there after all, simply hidden and tangled and waiting to be found, and not at all what I thought they would be.

For all our nostalgic tendencies, Americans aren't particularly comfortable with the idea that the past has made us who we are. But the future is always made up of local ideas, small mistakes, and long-dead trends. I have thought a lot about food over the last twenty years, but only in the last few years have I begun to think about a few other things: the invention of the tin can, the proliferation of the electric stove, the loss of aboriginal foods, the shift from stone to porcelain mill rollers. To understand why I eat what I eat—why I want what I want—I have to consider such things. I have to remember fourth grade, Columbus, Indians, and acorns.

When I started this book, I began with my mother's *Betty Crocker's Picture Cook Book*, a first edition from 1950 I've used since I was very young. The midcentury world of Betty Crocker seemed both intensely familiar and deeply foreign to me as I grew up. As a young adult, I viewed the cookbook as a kind of anthropological artifact, a set of clues into my mother's life. But as I looked more carefully, with more objective eyes, I began to understand that it wasn't simply an artifact of her life, but also of mine—that this seemingly distant world was mine as much as hers, marked my generation as much as it did hers. It was *in* me. I'd absorbed this world and been driven by it in subtle and subconscious ways. The question I pose—"Why do I eat this today?"—has many parts. To answer it means asking why I grew up eating what I ate, why my mother cooked what she cooked, and so on. I found myself traveling farther and farther backward in time to see what had led me here, in order to know where I was going and why.

I found myself looking at patterns and cycles much larger than I expected. Many cooking trends—such as the shift from heavy, complex dishes to light, simple ones and back—are much older than one might imagine. I found that I couldn't write about food without writing a little about money and class, about gender and the uses of leisure time. I couldn't write about eating without writing about the dance of relationships, about appetite, pleasure, and the multiple uses of the body.

This isn't a work of scholarship, a treatise on health, a memoir, or history, though it partakes of all these things. Certain forces have had a particular influence on my country and my culture, and I wanted to get under the surface and see how they entered my own individual life in ways I'd never seen before. I start with the large international exchange of food across continents that began with Columbus, and the rapid technological and social revolutions of the nineteenth and early twentieth centuries. I look at the assimilation of immigrant cuisines and our patterns of serving and eating together. I look at the peculiarly new thing we call the *housewife*. We have all, no matter what we eat, been touched by the recent shift from classic cooking to nouvelle cuisine to what we now call fusion.

Other forces have influenced not only my national culture but my private self in direct and powerful ways. This is one reason I dwell on the natural-foods movement and the new politics of food as a global issue. Because that movement was vital to forming my concept of how to eat, because even that didn't save me from the self-hatred of chronic dieting, I wanted to look closely at its consequent decay into our obsession with fitness and appearance. Finally, I consider our particular modern confusion, made up of equal parts materialism and loneliness, because it is a confusion I cannot escape in this place and time. It is everywhere I turn, and expressed continually in how we, as a culture, eat——and how I, as part of that culture, eat.

One force in particular informs my life. For many years, I've been a Zen Buddhist, and in many ways this is a matter of going against the tide of larger cultural forces around me. This is a gift—— but going against tides is hard work. Part of my religious practice involves cooking and eating in a deliberate way, different from the way the culture cooks and eats. At retreats, for example, we eat in silence, formally and carefully. Sometimes we are hungry for a long time before a meal, and have no choice in what we eat. Meals are simple; the chores of chopping, stirring, cleaning are done with special care. One learns to pay attention, with time, to everything about the table. Buddhism is comfortable with paradox—apparent or real—and the chronic uncertainty most people feel. I've learned, in particular, to notice the many extremes in my personal experience of eating, in all the messages about food with which I am surrounded. Ours is a culture of hunger as well as greed. Part of my religious practice has been to learn—and keep learning—what it means to have enough and not want more.

My religion teaches a responsibility for oneself that can be frightening in its demands. I settle into a retreat, and then I leave that setting and walk into an American supermarket or the food court at a mall. I walk out into a world of endless choice, hunger and waste, speed and noise, competition and sorrow. My world. It is up to me what I make of it.

I was born in 1957; I am part of the enormous cohort called baby boomers, the 80 million Americans born in the brief time between 1946 and 1964. The baby-boomer relationship to food is fundamentally ambivalent. We are the most well-fed, sheltered, educated, wealthy generation of all time, the luckiest and most powerful mass of people seen on this planet—and we are *always* hungry. We don't always hunger for food, but hunger is our defining experience. I don't think it's a coincidence. Our confused relationship to abundance and hunger, the fact that we are ashamed of both desire and gratification, is a marker of our lives. We are a groundless generation; every wheel we invent is the first wheel. Our great-grandparents forgot how to cook and how to farm; we tried to learn again, mostly gave up, and joined a gym instead.

"There was a time when the phrase *this is the best thing I ever tasted* came to people as naturally as sneezing," wrote Sheila Hibben in 1947, a decade before I was born. Hibben, who started the *New*

Yorker's restaurant column, had a quixotic concern with the disappearance of authentic American foods into the supermarket of convenience. "Often *the best thing* was spoken of reminiscently. 'That,' my mother would declare, describing a delicate Madeira jelly eaten with thick, yellow cream, 'was the best thing I ever tasted.' Or a visiting bishop would recall a certain pigeon pie as the best thing he ever ate, in tones that made it sound realer and infinitely more desirable than the Life Everlasting. Tucked far, far back in everybody's mind—behind all the sorry experiences with Jiffy-Mixes—there must be a warm memory of something that was best."

An orange float in August twilight. Fresh persimmon pie in October rain. A slice of old Amsterdam Gouda, smooth as glass. These are the things that were best—are best. Pleasure of this kind is utilitarian, safe: that's what we want, after all—warmth, the reproductive act, tribal harmony. Pleasure is healthy, not only because it keeps us kind to one another. Taste is not a single sense, not separate from its fellow senses, from aroma, texture, shape. The qualities of taste are entwined, wildly complex. Describe olives, cheese, apples. No word, no image, no simile will do. Such things are instead words, images, and similes themselves. Apples don't remind us of fall—fall reminds us of apples, tastes like apples, smells like apples. Eating is the sum of many things, multiple events, unrepeatable combinations. What we call taste is unbounded, profound; it is really this complexity itself, all the layers and finishes, halftones and shadows, contradictions and surprises, all the aftertastes and memories. "Wouldn't it be great," a woman says to me, "if we could taste with someone else's mouth?"

Today I live—and cook and eat—in a world marbled with nostalgia and iced with irony, because sometimes that warm memory, that best thing, *was* the Jiffy Mix; it was Mom in her new all-electric kitchen defrosting the exciting new TV dinner; it was Pop out back, nipping one with the bishop after the god-awful pigeon pie. It is hard for us to know why we are so filled with longing, why we seem to have no ground, no roots. The dashed ideal of home and family this century has fed on was bred by mass fantasy. It has become an industry complete with mail-order catalogs. We *are* a culture of some kind, a culture with thrice-daily meals and multiple snacks flavored by a kind of metamorphic nostalgia.

On summer evenings, when the sky begins to pale and the crows fly singly and in pairs across its white face, I can still taste hand-cranked vanilla ice cream, every other mouthful flavored by tiny drops of salty water. On cold winter nights, my face dry as papyrus near the hearth flames, I can feel the smooth cream of tiny marshmallows melting into Swiss Miss instant cocoa. And this on cool spring days: slices of canned mandarin orange that seem like the best thing I've ever tasted. The bright light sweetness tinged ever so slightly with a hint of aluminum explodes gently in my mouth as I suck the small cells open one by one. I am sitting in a puddle of sun and watching my mother stir soup. She is making my favorite: Campbell's cream of mushroom.

1

MY MOTHER WAS A FIFTH-GRADE teacher. Sometimes Bruce, Susan, and I walked to school, and sometimes we drove with Mom in the big tan Chevrolet Impala, a majestic boat sailing the wide, shady streets and sliding slowly up the crest of the small hill and down again and rolling into the faculty parking lot. If I didn't feel like walking home after school, I would wait in her classroom, running a finger through the chalk dust, rummaging through her desk drawers until she was ready to leave, and together we would slowly sail home.

In that serene pause before dinner in her otherwise hectic days, she would pour a cup of coffee and light a cigarette, turn on *The Mike Douglas Show* or Merv Griffin, and collapse with an audible huff into her armchair. Douglas and Griffin were plump and avuncular, almost accidental celebrities, and now and then there were cooking segments. My mother and I rarely cooked together, but week after week for several years, we watched celebrities cook on daytime television. She'd smoke a cigarette and do a few desultory isometrics with a rubber-and-spring gadget bought from an ad in the back of *Good Housekeeping* while the nice people on television ate what they'd cooked, and then read her latest romance for a while as I watched *Lost in Space*.

My mother also did all the housework, laundry, grocery shopping, and cooking for a family of five. She was up before the rest of us each morning, bringing my silent father a little hair of the dog in their dark, stuffy bedroom, frying eggs and pouring out cereal, pouring coffee, and lighting cigarettes for herself. When we still attended the primary school a few blocks from home, she often came home from work to meet us for lunch—fried Velveeta-and-Miracle-Whip sandwiches with Campbell's chicken noodle soup, or Vienna sausages still glistening from the can.

Memory is often a matter of the convenient falsehood— chronologies invert, characters combine and reorient. The questions change, and our minds tend to make up answers as we go along. Childhood especially is like a silent film with the subtitles removed—a jerky, dramatic story unfolding again and again before our eyes, the words lost, the meanings misconstrued. Even names become confused. After a time, memory and imagination weave together so tightly it's impossible to tell which is which. Why is that person laughing? Who is speaking? Whose hand is that, holding mine?

But this I remember clearly: how she would at last sigh in the late afternoon and put her book aside, and take a last sip from her coffee mug. "Well," she would say, rising heavily from her chair, "I guess I'll get started on dinner." Then she would go quietly into the kitchen, moving without complaint between one unending task and another, day in and day out.

I HAVE NEVER DONE ANYTHING LIKE THIS. I have not cooked three meals a day, day in and day out. I have not been uncomplaining. I have not been silent. I love to eat, both in the bonhomie of the table and as a solitary delight. I love to cook, too, in rituals followed step by step, transformation, the merging and marbling of raw ingredients into something finished and new. I like this, though I was never taught how to cook by my mother or any-one else. In fact, one reason I like to cook is that I've never done it routinely for long, ever wary of creating the wrong impression, ever a bit unsure about how I want to fit into a kitchen.

When I've gone away from home, I've sometimes felt strained to the point of breaking. To sort out the varied and often conflicting requirements of my life, of all our lives, is a major part of my reli-gious practice, even when it seems that following a religion creates conflict. One makes room for it and tries not to leave anything out, in a world of fragments and multiple demands. In my family, I've refused to act as though I had to fill a role, as though it was my duty to do so, even when guilt and uncertainty poisoned the freedom on which I insisted. I've been bound, in fact, more by my resistance to the traditions that bound my mother than by the traditions them-selves.

At forty-two, I see how my own relationship to food and eating, to cooking and my place in the kitchen, has changed greatly—only to change back, and change again. So many choices. When my mother went shopping, she had to choose between two markets, two bakeries, and one butcher. I have a dozen specialty markets in my neighborhood. She served roast beef every Sunday. I try to decide between Thai curry and fettucine Alfredo and fresh tomatillo chutney. She was bound by routine; I'm bound by change.

When I remember childhood meals, I remember how much the same everything was. Now and then there were sudden infusions of sharp, dramatic tastes: large trout fried over a wood fire just after dawn, in sight of their icy river; beef tongue cooked in a steaming kitchen for hours until it sliced like cream; fresh rhubarb baked into a tangy, sticky pie. But these were brief, almost shameful tastes in a world of instant mashed potatoes. We ate fritters now and then, and pickled pigs' feet and a bit of sauerkraut, but not much else you could identify with a given people, place, or time. It's no coincidence that the good, sharp tastes I remember best were those of fresh, wild things just killed, newly picked, full of the earth. The wild game and garden produce was at least as much a matter of economics as desire, in the strange equation that associated fresh food with poverty for a long time. When I was young, duck à l'orange was the ultimate urban sophisticate's dish. We sometimes dined on freshly killed ducks only a few hours out of the sky, and I loved their wilderness blood, their robust and masculine taste, their dark, fat flesh. But I *wanted* duck à l'orange, which I thought must be something special, indeed.

Sometimes, in the midst of the urban variety in which I shop now, I feel a strange obligation—to partake, to use up, try it all— not in joy but with a weary sense of duty. I think I must buy the baby asparagus because it is there, undeniably and aggressively there at the little produce market around the corner from my house—right there, the treat my mother waited for most of the year. My mother seemed to cook the same seven meals over and over—roast beef on Sunday, and Thursday-night hash. I seem never to have cooked the same meal twice.

When I was about ten, my father remodeled our small kitchen. My beefy, unpredictable father could miter a corner to perfection in one hour and pass out on the couch the next. He taught industrial arts at the high school and was an electrician on the side, a bit of a carpenter, a good draftsman. He had a shop behind our house, which smelled of beer and sawdust and was filled with lovely, lethal hand tools hung on a Peg-Board marked with each tool's outline in black felt pen. The floor held a maze of beer-can pyramids and piles of *Popular Mechanics, True,* and *Argosy,* and the walls were decorated with old calendar pinups, leggy and breasty girls in swimsuits and halter tops, prone on bales of hay and leaning on fences in gator-bait cutoffs. Near the ceiling hung his old balsa-wood plane models, spinning slowly in the brief eddies of air.

The kitchen was a cramped and narrow room. We were always going in and out, and so we were always shoving our way past each other to the refrigerator or the stove or the sink. The counters were crammed—coffeemaker, blender, toaster oven, soft loaves of bread, boxes of cereal, medicine and vitamin bottles, storage jars filled with sugar, crackers, and stale flour. The front door of the refrigerator (inside, more cramming—iceberg lettuce, Miracle Whip, ketchup, bologna, Velveeta) was covered with lists and reminders. On top and on the shelves beside it were draped piles of paper bags, plastic wrap, and placemats. The cupboards held everything from pots and pans to BBQ tools to TV trays, Dad's liquor stash, and Mom's cookies. So much, too much.

My father took my mother's kitchen apart and put it together again, to please her. America was on fire with its imaginary bounty, its tinned fantasy of postindustrial success, and she wanted some, too. He started at the top, with white ceiling tiles and fluorescent lights circling the room behind opaque blue plastic panels. He put in a garbage disposal, cupboards with knubbly blue plastic windows, and a white Formica countertop flecked with gold. The room was still too small. My mother picked out a ridiculously tiny round glass table and two uncomfortable wrought-iron chairs for one corner. She sewed curtains with blue trim and put up blue cornflower wallpaper and bought a new refrigerator, a burly beast that seemed the height of sophistication to me because it had an ice maker. For the rest of the years I lived in that house, a periodic mechanical squeal would erupt from the kitchen without warning — the tray of hardened ice turning over on its automatic arm and raining cubes into the freezer bin. It never worked quite right. I learned to open the freezer with care, prepared for an avalanche of ice falling onto my feet, hard as rocks.

The last grand addition in my mother's new kitchen was a double oven with a microwave on top. She bought one of the first ones on the market, which must have taken all the spare money she had.

I say the remodel happened in the late sixties, but in fact I'm not sure exactly. No one in the family remembers for sure — memory is such a slippery thing. My childhood is a dream to me, but it was my mother's clearly remembered past. When I wanted to know about something that had happened when I was young, I asked my mother. After I moved away she wrote me cheerful letters in her neat handwriting, telling me the news of so-and-so getting married, divorced, pregnant, dead. She sent newspaper clippings and the occasional recipe, and tips on getting my kids to eat right. When I was thirty, she died, and the news stopped.

For a long time I was drawn to simple stories, the kind with obvious narrative devices and clear morals. But a lot of my questions can't be answered at all now, and in the end, that has to be the story. I remember my mother vividly—her voice, the tilt of her head— but I will never be sure if what I remember is her, or only my misshapen belief in her.

I want to know exactly when we got the microwave because I want to know when her endless labor of cooking ceased. The microwave changed everything—though everything was bound to go, anyway. It was the beginning of real change for my thrilled, my gleeful, my silently guilty mother, who was more than ready to plunge into this particular shiny, beeping future.

As a child, I was required to come to the table when called and join the family circle for dinner. We looked, arrayed around the table, like all the families in all the magazines she read—the ones in the advertisements for new appliances and cars and vinyl siding—Mother at one end and Father at the other, Big Brother and Little Sister and me on either side, the golden retriever sleeping on the rug. But dinner was the dread hour of my day, tense and demanding in ways I could hardly stand. As soon as I was old enough to get away with it, I ditched the dinner hour and snacked my way through the day, and Mom didn't try very hard to stop me.

Our freezer gradually filled with little pizzas and tamales and individual-serving-sized boxes of pasta, tubs of ready-made macaroni and cheese and pepperoni pizza rolls and uniformly chopped stew vegetables and chicken pot pies and lots of neatly ordered TV trays of spaghetti-and-meatball dinners and Salisbury steak dinners and fried chicken dinners. Meatloaf was my favorite, with its perfectly symmetrical piece of chopped, formed hamburger in sweet tomato syrup, the neat cubicles of buttered peas and calm mashed potatoes, a place for each, and each in its place. As time went by, I seemed to eat more and more of my meals standing up in the kitchen, reading in my room, going out the door—elsewhere, as my own children have done in their time.

Mom even learned to make peanut brittle in the microwave. After weeks of gooey, syrupy messes and the rank smell of burning peanut butter, she got it right. That it took her far longer to figure out how to make her favorite candy in the microwave than it would have taken her to do it the old-fashioned way was irrelevant. The microwave was a labor-saving device, she was saving her labor, and the facts were less important than the dream. They always are when we're dreaming.

I found a recipe for microwave peanut brittle a few years ago. My adolescent daughter helped stir the goo as it grew hotter and hotter and began to bubble alarmingly. My towering son and his tac-iturn girlfriend arrived and decided, with much whispering, to wait for the results. I spread the candy out to cool and we stood there, waiting, silent, afraid to break the spell, the thin and delicate spell. When we finally broke off big chunks and chewed together rumi-natively, I realized I couldn't remember the last time we'd eaten the same food from scratch, eaten at the same time, in one room.

2

THE HOTTEST THING IN OUR KITCHEN was my father's temper. When I left, I left hungry, wondering for a long time what it was I wanted to eat. When I began to cook myself, I stuffed emerald-green poblanos with cheese, threw slices of Anaheims green as grass into corn soup. I tried chicken mole, pasta puttanesca, pico de gallo, chipotle, kung pao. Most of all, I wanted heat, but under that straightforward urge I wanted what Elisabeth Rozin calls the "flavor principles," the "unique and characteristic tastes" that define a cuisine. What defined my childhood cuisine? For a long time, I didn't know.

Can we speak at all about "American" cuisine? Is there such a thing as "American" food? (As "Americans"?) It's an old question, asked many times by historians, sociologists, cooks. But I eat, and I want to ask and answer the question that way.

Sidney Mintz, an anthropologist, sets out to define the elusive

concept of "cuisine" and ends up with this: "people using ingredients, methods, and recipes on a regular basis to produce both their
everyday and festive foods, eating the same diet more or less con-
sistently, and sharing what they cook with each other. . . . [An]
ongoing, active producing of food and producing of opinions about
food, around which and through which people communicate daily
to each other who they are."

In Mintz's definition, there may be small, isolated pockets of
people in the United States who have what he would call a genuine
cuisine, but the country itself has nothing like that, and Mintz
mourns this fact. Americans do, however, eat in remarkably predictable ways, which means we have a cuisine of some kind or other
even if we need to stretch the definition a bit to find out what it is.

New ingredients are always entering cultures; the foreigner
passing through always leaves traces, no matter how small.
Coherence in a cuisine is a relative concept. Many food historians
have made it clear that the global diet we consider one of our most
modern, quintessentially American inventions is very old hat.
Massimo Montanari calls the cuisine of medieval Europe a "gastronomic *koine*"—that is, a lingua franca marked by "common traits,
recurring foods and flavours, and trading and borrowing between
different regions." In 1577, a man wrote to his family that "Paris provides an abundance of everything that can be desired. Goods flow
in from every region."

When I say American food, I mean the food of the invaders, not
of the aboriginal people. We have not inherited more than a frag-
ment of that broad original menu, but rather the more limited menu
of medieval peasants, European explorers, and colonists. These
more skeptical cooks disdained the native cuisines and usurped

and tamed the cuisines of immigrants. This process has continued without ceasing, continues still. We may not want to believe it, and those of us who can afford to go to a lot of restaurants or cook for pleasure generally don't believe it, but much of today's American menu is dictated by big corporations working hand in hand with a mass media of seductive images. (Restaurants and cooking for pleasure, of course, are central products of this marriage. The very notion of food "trends" makes this fact clear.) Underneath the fashions, the exquisitely rare ingredients and expensive condiments and exotic sauces, is a menu based almost irrevocably in highly industrialized food processing—a gastronomic koine of vertical integration and control.

Sheila Hibben addressed the question of what was meant by American cuisine head-on in her excellent book *American Regional Cookery*. To Hibben, the real American menu consisted of foods that were relied upon, foods that people knew well over time—local and largely native foods, dishes passed through generations, made from scratch.

American Regional Cookery was begun in 1936, interrupted by the war, and finished in 1946. A lot changed in that decade, enough to alarm Hibben even more than she'd been when she began. . . . "In ten years much innocence has fled from our kitchens," she wrote in midcentury. "Only too often an ancient 'rule' for an apple pie has been modernized to include a topping of marshmallow, and here and there an impious hand has even added raisins to the proud austerity of hasty pudding." Hibben wasn't interested in modernity or science in the kitchen; in fact, she thought them dangerous to the art of cooking, in distinct contrast to the sleek conventions of her time. "Indeed, this *is* the very nick of time for recording honestly the dishes to which Americans once sat themselves down in happy anticipation. . . . If the changing world is not to be flavored by the dreary synthetic foods which manufacturers have thought up with, I suspect, less interest in our survival than in their own, our palates must be awakened to old and simple pleasures."

What are these uniquely American pleasures she praises? For one thing, a kind of variety lost to midcentury, mainstream American cooks. At a time when most cooks had been taught that "sauce" was a synonym for "white," she offered sixteen pages of possibilities, Egg Sauce to Raisin Sauce, Tarragon Sauce to Coffee Custard Sauce. Yet her dishes are simple, unadorned, direct. ("Never be deluded," she writes without fuss, "into thinking you can improve upon broiled pompano by cooking it with almonds or a fancy sauce.") She is utterly without apology for the ordinary and plain, for the fresh and straightforward, for the endless possibilities in food derived solely from what is found in our own back yards. "Creamed codfish and succotash are no less our heritage than terrapin and roast turkey with oyster stuffing, and in the hands of loving cooks the solid honesty of grits and okra and blueberry muffins and salt pork can be counted to our honor and glory." Almost all of these foods are indigenous to the continent, truly 'native' foods. Local and native are not coincidental qualities in beloved foods; until very recently, foods known through generations, foods that became the base of a real cuisine, *had* to be these things.

No cookbook has made me want to cook the way Sheila Hibben's fifty-year-old little book did: Spider Cake, Eggs Purgatory, Cabbage in Sour Cream, Gooseberry Fool, Dilsey's Cornpone—even the names delight. The ingredients are easy to find, and rarely more than a half-dozen to a recipe. The demand is for time—for preparation, stewing, simmering, roasting, resting, waiting, anticipating food, and enjoying the anticipation. In this kind of cooking—ordinary cooking—the waiting is part of the making, because the making never really stops any more than the eating does. One meal merges into the next, one leftover becomes the base of the next dish, tomorrow's stew is begun before today's bread is done. Cooking, eating, and thinking about cooking and eating are part of the ebb and flow of one's daily life, instead of events that loom large on the horizon and then disappear.

Saveur, a food magazine devoted to the source of foods and cooking techniques, answers the question of an American cuisine a half-century after Hibben rather differently. Colman Andrews, the editor, writes that over several years, his staff has "found a breadth and depth to American cooking that even we, at our most optimistic and chauvinistic, scarcely could have imagined." The recipes in their collection, *Saveur Cooks Authentic American,* define "American" broadly, happily using everything from matzo balls to radicchio, gnocchi, and gingerbread—because, as Colman points out rather glibly, "we are all immigrants here, or the children of immigrants—even those 'native' Americans whose ancestors walked down from Siberia." (Of course, that means the entire human race is immigrant, not an entirely inaccurate idea, but of little use in defining cuisine. Somebody has to be there at the beginning.)

Not many dishes we eat today are truly "American," in the sense of being invented on this continent. Not apple pie, not jelly doughnuts, not the hamburger. Is clam chowder American? It doesn't appear in the form in which we know it in other cuisines. Waverley Root, one of the century's leading food experts, claims the Native Americans made clam chowder and that the recipe was taught to the colonists along with cranberry sauce, "Boston" baked beans, and steamed lobster. Raymond Sokolov, a food writer and for a brief period in the 1970s food editor at the *New York Times,* is particularly interested in clam chowder. He thinks it might be a bastardization of French fish soup—a profound bastardizing, since the French didn't use milk or potatoes in their fish soup. Perhaps an expatriate Frenchwoman longed for that remembered soup of home, made do with what she had, and invented clam chowder. Perhaps someone who'd never been to France and knew nothing of French fish soups was just trying a few things out one day. Either way, the use of the potato begs the question; that's not French. Clam chowder is probably a newly invented dish, as history goes. But is clam chowder American? It is as American as you and me.

ITALY: PASTA AND TOMATO SAUCE. MEXICO: shredded beef and chicken and pork, topped with cheese. India: curry laced with chilies. Switzerland: chocolate. These images, these associations, feel embedded to us, permanent. But the Mexicans had no beef or pork, no chicken, no cheese, until Columbus arrived with these dubious gifts. There was no chocolate in Europe until sailors brought it back from Mexico in the 1500s; even then it was considered odd, and didn't become popular for hundreds of years, filtering through several countries as a drink. Solid chocolate didn't appear until the 1800s. Chilies didn't arrive in India until the 1500s; until then, curry was made hot only by black and white peppers. The Italians discovered both pasta and the tomato late in the game; pasta with tomato sauce has been a common dish in Italy for only a few hundred years. There were lots of "new" foods after Columbus: Avocados, peanuts and cashews, vanilla, pumpkins, blackberries and blueberries, pineapples, lima beans, turkey, sweet peppers, chewing gum, and more all followed the explorers back to Europe, and on to Africa, Asia, the world.

The river of food ran both ways. Europeans brought oranges, rice, sugar cane, coffee, peaches, lettuce, lentils, carrots, and beets to this country. Slaves brought okra, watermelon, and black-eyed peas. The culinary revolution Raymond Sokolov calls "post-Columbian" was rather slow, as revolutions go, but no less devastating a change for all that. No one escaped; a thousand foods slowly crossed the globe. Some of them slipped into established foodways as though they had only been away on vacation. Others, like much of the traditional Native American menu, were long objects of suspicion and rumor.

Some historians think all people are prone to reject new foods. This is based on the records of technologically developed and urban people who travel to new cultures or meet travelers with different tastes—those people, that is, who keep such records. Nomadic people and cultures living largely off the local bounty are careful about new foods, but receptive to change; they have no choice. They have to accept newness in the midst of the old.

When Europeans arrived on this continent, they found a population of several million mostly healthy people. Many Native Americans ate better, fresher, more balanced diets and a greater variety of foods than did Europeans of almost every class. They ate insects, reptiles, and amphibians as well as domestic dogs and wild game and fish. They used salt and honey. They knew how to preserve as well as cook and bake in a variety of ways. Deficiency diseases like scurvy and beri-beri were almost unknown to the Native

Americans. The conquerors brought smallpox, measles, and vene-real disease, and they brought a world of poor nutrition as well.

These conquerors were a suspicious lot when it came to food. Our cuisine is marked by what Waverley Root calls "the instinctive American rejection of any foods incorrigibly foreign to the eating habits imported from the British Isles." Colonists rejected a lot of Native American foods completely and for good, as well as im-portant agricultural and cooking techniques. "The first settlers had come upon a land of plenty," added Root. "They almost starved in it."

In several cases, the new Americans didn't accept native foods until they had been exported to Europe and returned in the course of things. The potato is native to this land, but the colonists rejected it almost out of hand. Francis Drake took the potato to Europe in the 1500s, where it was grown largely as a decorative plant until the 1700s. Only after it had been taken to Europe and slowly—over centuries—found a niche as a staple food there, and then was brought *back* to North America—as the "Irish" potato—did Americans accept it (and learn to like clam chowder).

Maize, which we call corn, was a vital foundation in many regions of North and Central America. Maize was—is—a mirac-ulous food, as good for people as for livestock, edible both green and ripe, raw and cooked, roasted and boiled—and, unlike a few other excellent sources of nutrients, corn tastes good, so good it provokes rhapsody. Corn is easy to store, both whole and as flour. The crops are high in yield and easy to cultivate, even by a single person. The seeds come neatly bound in protective ears, and even the silk and husks are peculiarly useful. No wonder a lot of people thought corn came directly from God. "Corn to the Inca was embodied in Manco-Paca, son of the Sun and founder of the dynasty of the Royal Lords of Cuzco," writes Betty Fussell in her book on the subject. "Corn to the Totonac of Central America was Tzinteotl, wife of the sun. Corn to the Aztec was the goddess Xilonen and the god Quetzalcoatl. Corn to the Chippewa was Mondawmin. Corn to the Pawnee was the Evening Star, the mother of all things, who gave corn to the people from her garden in the sky." Corn to the Mayans was, in a sense, everything. It was one of the ingredients of human flesh, says the Popul Vuh, "and so they were happy over the provisions of the good mountain, filled with sweet things, thick with yellow corn, white corn . . . It was staples alone that made up their flesh."

Corn is the earliest cultivated grain in the world; cultivated corn nearly 7,000 years old has been found in a cave in Mexico. The Native Americans had more than 200 varieties in crop. Because growing corn didn't require a lot of effort, a culture based on it had a lot of labor free for other work. Without corn, Fernand Braudel believed, the stunning cities of the Incas, Mayans, and Aztecs would have been impossible.

To the first colonists, corn was only "frighteningly foreign," an enormous grass with eerie giant kernels. They ate it only when there was nothing else to eat.

Columbus took corn to Europe in 1493, where it was largely used as a landscaping or home garden plant rather than as a commercial crop. The upper classes didn't much like it, but the peasants appreciated its ease of cultivation and high yield. Corn slowly replaced barley and millet, and in the process became ever more distinctly a peasant food, while wheat became more distinctly the province of the rich. But the Europeans didn't know how to use this

new food correctly. The people who created the amazingly successful corn cultures of Central and South America balanced their diet
with beans, avocados, and tomatoes, and processed the corn with
various forms of alkali, all of which compensated for corn's deficiency in nicotinic acid and vitamin C. When corn became a staple
food in Europe, the vitamin deficiency known as pellagra spread like
an epidemic. In a classic case of blaming the messenger, pellagra was
long called "corn sickness," blamed on the grain itself even into the
twentieth century. European scientists thought it was proof that so-
called "Indian corn" was inadequate food, and therefore corn-eating
people were vulnerable and weaker than wheat-eating people.

Americans have admitted new foods more readily in recent
years, but even now, each is admitted only in a peculiarly American
way. Some foods are misunderstood, in a sense—their meaning
misapprehended. Others are absorbed until their identities disappear. *The Questing Cook,* published 1927, has an undeniably colonial
attitude. "Here are one hundred and twenty-eight recipes ready to
be plundered by any buccaneering cook . . . the booty that one
casual adventurer in foreign kitchens found practical to bring
home . . ." This unique ability of the American to appropriate anything he touches is one of our oldest traditions. "In 1938," notes the
historian Harvey Levenstein, "Wesson Oil advertised that Chef Otto
Gensch of Casa Manana (location unidentified) used its product to
fry his specialty, 'New England Codfish Cakes a L'Aurore.'" After
all, the colonists took pumpkins and made pie. Europeans used corn
eventually, but they didn't use corn like the Mayans did, or chili peppers or tomatoes as they did, either. Given chocolate, the skeptical
European ended up with truffles, not mole.

One quality of traditional foodways is a certain kind of coherence. The changes history has brought to northern Italian, to East Indian, to Thai and Italian and Spanish cuisines have been largely slow, gradually developed ones. They are dealt with logically. New foods, received bit by bit, are considered by many different domestic cooks over time, with the intelligence of long kitchen experience. The new ingredients enter and change the tradition in ways that clearly work to the tradition's benefit, because they work to the benefit of individual cooks, one meal at a time. Thus, the tomato found its way inevitably into pasta sauces and bean stews. The chili pepper entered curry. In coherent cuisines, new foods are never just fashion. They are evolution.

A buried xenophobia was the inevitable inheritance of the grand brand-name revolution of the twentieth century, so much a part of the American philosophy it can hardly be separated in strands. We can see only its facets: repeated references in cookbooks to "exotic" foods from "foreign" lands like Canada and England; recipes of the 1920s with names like Dago's Delight and Wop Spaghetti (the last was "boiled spaghetti baked with grated cheese, onion, and canned tomatoes thickened with flour"); the cherished belief that modern American dishes like chop suey, cioppino, vichyssoise, and chili con carne are traditional foreign foods; a 1957 advertisement for one of the most modern foods of the time, a frozen Rosarita Mexican Style Dinner—"Rosarita frozen or canned foods are not too hot—not too bland—just right with a *true* Mexican flavor your whole family will enjoy."

We cosmopolitan Americans are, in fact, rarely exposed to truly foreign cuisines. What we are exposed to are cuisines removed from their true roots—physically, demographically removed, taken away from any hint of poverty, compromise, conquest, limitation—from real foreignness. After this removal from the source (preferably to a nice neighborhood with good parking) the foreign cuisine is then defined by trademark ingredients. Our love of the new and foreign, so prevalent now as we prattle about the World Wide Web and a global economy, is almost always protected by the filters of the mass media and secondhand exposure. The exotic is not a blunt instrument here, but a soft touch, successful to the extent that it entertains without real challenge. Trademark ingredients ease the way. Once upon a time, pineapple meant Hawaiian food no matter how it was used—and no one eating at Trader Vic's seemed to notice that pineapple wasn't even a native Hawaiian food. In the sense of fundamental flavors, lemongrass indicates Thai, olives mean Mediterranean, the combination of soy and ginger implies a variety of Chinese bases. But lemongrass can be a kind of synonym for Thai food, too, the way soy sauce is for Chinese food—the way a dewy flower is a synonym for cleanliness in a soap ad. Simple association. Thai food uses lemongrass routinely, but outside of Thailand such a core food has a different meaning, precisely because it *is* outside its source. Foreign ingredients are no longer endemic qualities but have become literary referents, and the cuisines they evoke are not so much Americanized by our changes as we have made them ours simply by eating them. We have achiote powder and durian fruit and sea cucumber sushi at our fingertips now, but we use them—we *meet* them—as Americans. What else can we do? We can't eat tik 'n' chik the way a Mayan born in the southern Yucatán eats it. We can only find the achiote powder and make a dish that has the same ingredients. The Big Mac served in Paris is not exactly a Big Mac, either. The food itself is slightly different—everything from the fat content of the meat to the kind of oil used in the frying are different. The soil, the water, the sun are different. But more important, the meaning has changed. The mouth that meets it has a different tongue.

Foreign cuisines are first transplanted, then assimilated. The food writer Clementine Paddleford found immigrant influence everywhere she went in the United States—Russian, Jewish, Mexican, Austrian, Peruvian, Polish. (She never mentions Africa, a significant and often-ignored influence.) After assimilation comes transformation. A lot of the "favorite family dishes" she collected in the 1940s and 1950s have names like "Grandmother's bean soup" and "Mama's kuchen." They have by midcentury been transmuted into something else, into shadows laced with frozen vegetables and canned fruit and cake mixes. I felt ghosts haunting my own mother's "tamale pie," which bore no resemblance to a tamale or a pie. There are ghosts in the Ritz cracker casseroles of a Florida trailer park just as there are in Aunt Flora's apple tart. (The apples aren't even the same anymore.) When we speed up the tart baking with the miracle of ready-mix apple filling, something else happens. After a single generation, we forget how a real apple tart tastes. The shadow becomes the real thing—the real tart, the authentic kuchen, for that generation—the only tart it knows. The twin steals the real king's throne; the ready-mix tart takes the real tart's place. It is the one we remember—the one invested with power. In time, it is the real tart. When I want tamale pie, I want it made with Campbell's cream of tomato soup because that's what the tamale pie I remember *is*. (Way deep down, it is what I know most about tamales themselves.) If you loved Aunt Flora's apple tart, if you want to re-create it, you will need the ready-mix filling she used, not apples. It is a crucial ingredient, and that's one reason giant discount bakeries and freezer cases can fill us with memory. There, everything is made from ready-mix, everything lingers in the mind.

Certain ethnic foodways have been cast in a suspicious light by both nutrition scientists and social workers from the beginning of the century. Hot foods such as chilies were associated with "hot" ideas, like anarchy. All kinds of spices were thought to make people crave alcohol and sex. Garlic, too, was an object of suspicion, a mark of social inferiority. (I read in this morning's newspaper that local Italians are complaining that the good Italian restaurants in town use too much garlic now; the restaurateurs do it, they explained apologetically, to please the Americans.)

"One whiff of the pungent air in the tenements or a glance into the stew pots was enough to confirm that the contents must wreak havoc on the human digestive system," the historian Harvey Levenstein wrote in *Revolution at the Table*, his recent study of American food habits. "'Still eating spaghetti, not yet assimilated,' noted a social worker after visiting an Italian household." Nutritionists believed that mixed foods were harder to digest than separated dishes, and much European peasant cooking was based on stews, soups, and casseroles. Polish immigrants, who ate mixed food from one bowl, were in particular danger.

One of the unseen disadvantages in this effort at dietary assimilation was that many immigrants were better nourished than their middle-class white American benefactors. They ate scratch cooking, lots of vegetables, whole-grain bread, home-canned and pickled foods. Many immigrants at first rejected not only the new types of food but the forms of the food—industrially processed and commercially baked. When they finally shifted their diets, their nutrition shifted, too. Levenstein writes of a project in the 1920s designed to teach American "homemaking" to Mexican-American girls in southern California: "A prime objective was to convince them to abandon the traditional Mexican sauces (whose tomatoes and chilies provided vitamins and whose nuts and cheese provided protein, calcium, and vitamins), in favor of only two sauces: White Sauce, consisting of flour, butter, and milk, and Hard Sauce, mainly sugar and butter." It wasn't long after this rush of Americanizing that industrial food processors responded to new public concern with nutrition by figuring out ways to put back the nutrients processing had removed—the same nutrients that many ethnic foods had in abundance.

The belief that mixed foods were harder to digest was a peculiarly apt metaphor for the dangers of miscegenation. American togetherness has always been about carefully separated strands. Children know that there's nothing exactly wrong about the gravy getting in the fruit salad; it's simply gross. The fruit salad and the gravy each have their place. This is another quality of the American cuisine we've inherited: It is not so much about blandness as it is about incorruptibility and control. Immigrants poured in by the hundreds of thousands, stinking from the ships' holds and smelling of unknown things. They were messy and disheveled, sensual and confusing, and they came to a place brimming with canned beef broth and tinned carrots sold in standard packages with familiar labels. Modern America was to be a place of large machines, long distances, open space, neat niches, and science. Immigrants wanted to eat the same casseroles and stews they'd always eaten, out of a single shared pot, and they lived crammed incomprehensibly close

together in small rooms. This was undeniably exotic behavior—
alien. Americans like things neat, and they like things clear—especially our famous diversity.

So the "melting pot" led, inevitably, to marshmallows in butter-
scotch fondue and the school cafeteria tray. Assimilation meant
merging many parts into a single whole, making different things
alike—"one nation, indivisible." But within that whole, we've made
careful containers. White American social workers, nutritionists,
and domestic science teachers may have distantly known that assimilation doesn't mean that the disparate and threatening elements
will remain in neat packets any more than the fruit and gravy will.
But to an amazing extent, they succeeded in one mission—not in
keeping things apart but in making them so much alike that we no
longer cared if they got mixed up.

Attempts to turn people away from their ethnic diets for political, nutritional, or economic reasons failed. The poor just kept on
stubbornly eating what they liked and were used to eating and had
learned to eat from their parents. So domestic science targeted the
classroom, and there cooking was taught as a rationally derived science instead of the messy, emotional transmission of tradition
within a family.

The assimilation of immigrant diets didn't happen through
deliberate education. It happened through lack of time, increased
economic security, the desire for upward mobility, and, largely,
through children growing up American. The final blows came in the
school cafeteria, where immigrant children learned what real
American kids ate. *That* worked. Second- and third-generation
immigrants to the United States tended to reject their ethnic cuisine, anyway. Children were actively recruited to white bread and

chicken croquettes in the cafeteria line as surely as their parents were recruited to factory work and electric stoves. Mexican and Italian children begged for peanut butter on white bread, for turkey and mashed potatoes, for the food they were served in school. Today's schoolchildren line up for a hodgepodge of burritos, enchiladas, tacos, spaghetti, and pizza that bear almost no resemblance to the namesake dishes left behind by the past.

IS THERE SUCH A THING AS AMERICAN FOOD? Sidney Mintz suggests that our true cuisine may be more behavioral than culinary, defined not so much by what we eat as by how we eat it. He notes the combination of poor nutrition and our obsession with health, part of which comes from the coupling of diet foods with rich treats. He cites the continual, fickle sampling of foreign foods and trends. Certainly Americans demonstrate behaviors around food that are more coherent than our chosen flavors— coherent because, unlike flavors, eating behaviors cross class and ethnic barriers that hinder some of the diversity in our food. It comes down to this: Americans want eating to be easy, they want to eat a lot, and they want to eat it fast.

"We know that people decide what they're going to eat for dinner in the car on the way home, after a full day of work," Marcia Copeland, director of the Betty Crocker Test Kitchens in Minneapolis, told me a few years ago. "We know that people are saying, 'Nutrition tomorrow night.' They are 'assembling,' stopping to buy vegetables that are already cut up for a stir-fry, buying chicken that's already boned, making brownies from a mix. Consumers want fresh, good-tasting food hot on the table in fifteen minutes or less."

Food scientists call this last "speed plus" cooking—food that is at least partly "freshly cooked" rather than simply heated up, but food with no more labor required than the combining. People don't feel guilty cooking this way anymore, Copeland adds. "Ten years ago, there was still a fair amount of guilt about preparing a meal that way. But today, people feel resourceful."

Americans have always felt resourceful using time as efficiently as possible. We're loafers, but we have no leisure ethic; many of us would rather spend time figuring out how to avoid working than spend the same amount of time playing. Unlike other cultures, we've never developed a ritual of leisurely eating. (The only truly leisurely meals in our social lives are those intended for seduction.) Lingering and unhurried meals large and small, special and quotidian, are part of almost every culture, including most of the European cultures the conquering colonists left behind, but they are not part of ours because we have too much to do—too many places to go, room to fill up, things to build and buy. Anything that smacks of waiting, no matter how inaccurately, bothers the impatient American. We snack more than any other culture and feel deprived if snacks aren't included in the day's routine—but snacks are eaten even more quickly and crudely than we eat our meals. Waverley Root is talking mostly about nutrition when he says that "the American contrives to combine deficiency with excess," but he could as easily be talking about the entire state of mind with which we approach the table itself.

World War II soldiers ate—or were encouraged to eat, if they could—eleven pounds of food a day, about 5,000 calories' worth. They even gained weight in boot camp. Americans are gluttons for everything—hungry for big platters and big servings, for space, land, invention, change, as well as the familiar. In 1957, the year I was born, the American government's display of economic and technological superiority at the Zagreb Trade Fair was a fully stocked supermarket.

Excess of one kind or another is clearly a marker of how we eat now—excessive indulgence, excessive denial. Our copious appetite was so unusual in the worldly scheme that "virtually every foreign visitor who wrote about American eating habits expressed amazement, shock, and even disgust at the quantity of food consumed" and the waste left behind after every meal. Americans, however, were wont to brag about the same thing.

Everything's big in America. All that food has made us bigger and taller than ever before, bigger and taller than most people on the planet. We're fat, we're muscular, we're *big*. All these big people demand ever bigger food: Ultimate Burgers and Big Macs and Big Kings and Macho Burritos and Deluxe Doubles and Big Gulps and Super Big Gulps. We are drawn to the corpulent, the inflated, the exaggerated—especially when it's a bargain. Big, cheap, and fast—*Speedy Fast, Extra Fast, Hot and Now*. Even the tiny, beautiful, expensive portions of nouvelle cuisine were perfected here, where everything is done to excess. What is more American, after all? When we run races, we make them marathons.

If there is an American cuisine of fast, plentiful food, then Thanksgiving is the American meal. We shred the big primitive bird, cooked whole in its own skin in fine medieval fashion, with an electric carving knife. The canned green beans are sauced with cream of mushroom soup; the sweet potatoes are coated in brown sugar. The cranberry sauce quivers, still rounded from the can. The white mashed potatoes groan under their pale coating of gravy. The cousins, aunts, uncles, and grandparents line up with one eye pinned to the football game on the big-screen television a few feet away, fill their plates, and begin to eat without waiting, without saying grace, and when they finish, take their seats in front of the television again until it's time for pie—bakery pie with spray-on whipped "topping." We are eating our native foods, the turkey and cranberry and pumpkin, mixed with a world of other ingredients, all of it processed together thousands of miles away in the grand democratic leveling out of multinationals. There is too much to eat, far too much, and we've eaten deliberately extravagant portions in the clear knowledge that there is too much and that we will eat it all too fast. We slide effortlessly into a single day of gorging and sloth, a day when all we have to do is reach like our medieval ancestors for another joint in the pile.

I take my plate, the gravy already mixing with the fruit salad against my will, and think of all those construction-paper turkeys I made in school—all those teepees I drew and the Indian headdresses with autumnal paper feathers cascading to the ground, the hard winter ground cobbled with unharvested acorns—and all those cut-out *Niñas* and *Pintas* and *Santa Marias* sailing sedately across the empty sea of my schooldesk with Columbus at the helm, looking out. Looking forward, and beyond.

3

A FEW YEARS AGO, I WAS AT A dinner party where each person took a turn describing his or her roots: Scottish, Italian, Jewish, French-Hawaiian, and so on. When it was my turn, I laughed and said, "We're white trash." I meant poor white folks. I meant hillbilly, a word not uncommon among hillbillies. I meant I was one of millions of Americans whose desperately poor ancestors came across the sea from England, Ireland, Scotland, and northern Europe in the coffin ships. My family spent generations in Missouri and Kentucky and other parts before working their way across Canada and the midwest and onto the Oregon Trail, and arrived in the Pacific Northwest by the latter 1800s in time to benefit from the Homestead Act and get in on the last of the Indian Wars. My family on both sides was always poor or middling, mostly Protestant with little formal education, until the most recent few generations. They were what they were;

I've often wondered how people could feel either shame or pride in their ancestry, which none of us has a hand in choosing.

A friend was offended at the term I chose. "Don't say that!" she exclaimed. "It's an insult." The writer David Shields suggests that "white trash" is the equivalent of "good Negro"—"its meaning derives from the racist assumption that 'black trash' or 'bad Negro' would be redundant." Such a use never occurred to me; it has always been a self-referential statement of poor roots. To me it meant only bluegrass music and my great-grandmother, a certain lilting vocal rhythm, and corn fritters.

I love corn fritters. On my birthday, the only day of the year when my mother consulted me about the dinner menu, I chose fritters, a simple concoction of flour, eggs, milk, and corn. She dropped heaping spoonfuls of batter into the deep-fat fryer, where they turned golden brown and puffed up to the size of baseballs. We ate them soaked in maple syrup, with bacon and scrambled eggs on the side. I still eat them once or twice a year, soft luxuries of dough and sweet corn and warm velvety oil that seems to come from a world out of time.

I listen to Irish fiddle music, too, to Irish itself sung over the uilleann pipes and tin whistles. I know part of this is that familiar longing for a tribe—my own parents listened to Percy Faith and Mantovani. But part is a deep recognition of something shining forward from long ago. Certain music, like certain food, seems to tickle the back of my American brain with the promise of a different world, a barely forgotten intimacy of past places.

I went to Ireland in the 1970s when I was barely out of my teens, drawn by that tickling need, by the certainty that something of me belonged there. I traveled restlessly all across the Republic by train and bus, often hitchhiking, sometimes alone and sometimes with an American woman I met in Dublin. We were on a lark, but it was a serious lark, as all Irish larks are. We were "bold girls," said the farmwives who came out to talk to us when we rested by their fences, by way of inviting us into their warm, close kitchens for scones and marmalade and tea—bitter, black, oily tea. For months I ate cabbage and drank tea in those kitchens, ate stew and corned beef and drank tea, ate Scotch eggs and drank tea, ate soda bread with fresh-churned butter and drank tea, noting the tea bags hung on clothespins to dry by the woodstove, saved for another day. Gloria and I would find ourselves drinking syrupy port in a rural pub where outsiders rarely ventured then, and lone women were an especial surprise. We were made to sing for our drinks. The only song we both knew was "When the Saints Go Marching In," and we sang it many times and were serenaded in return by polite, laconic, drunken farmers whose only real Irish was in their songs.

We made friends with a fellow named Brendan who had something of a career as a melancholic Irishman. He often shouted out poetry when he was drunk, and hinted at a failed artistic career. Brendan took us to pubs where women still had to sit behind doors in small booths called snugs and wait for the barman to open the discreet little window and take our order. Brendan worked in a desultory way as the gardener for an up-and-coming Dublin businessman who thought all "big houses" ought to be kept "at work." (He also kept horses no one ever rode, because there was a stable.) No one in the family liked vegetables, so Brendan's job involved raising the produce and then throwing it away. He saw nothing strange in this—he didn't like vegetables, either. I tried to cook for him in his tiny kitchen, at the cold linoleum table speckled with years of dust, but he didn't much like the soups and casseroles I made. As a parting gift, I gave him a copy of *The Vegetarian Epicure*. In return, he took my paperback poetry collection out of my hand. "Here," he said. "Give me the pen, here." I sipped lukewarm tea and he wrote his favorite saying inside the cover: *Marbh le tae, agus marbh gan é*— "Killed with tea and dead without it."

WHITE TRASH COOKING, WRITTEN BY ERNEST Matthew Mickler and published in the early 1980s, was dismissed as camp. But Mickler was born and raised in north Florida, a bastion of trailer-park hillbilly history. To him, White Trash—always with capital letters—means people who "never failed to say 'yes, ma'm' and 'no, sir,' never sat on a made-up bed (or put your hat on it), never opened someone else's icebox, never left food on your plate, never left the table without permission, and never forgot to say 'thank you' for the teeniest favor." This I recognize.

My great-grandmother Addie Mae Tisdale Gentry Barrett was a polite, tough woman. When I was little, she lived in a small, dim wooden house with a wood-burning cookstove and a rough wood kitchen table, plain curtains, and a high, narrow, hard bed. Hers was a clean stove, a clean table, and the bed was always made—and we children weren't supposed to sit on it. Into her healthy ninth decade, she was a courteous gentlewoman, largely self-educated, who wore housedresses and aprons and liked to watch me run across the scraggly lawn to climb her ragged fruit trees. My vocabulary is still filled with the language of these roots, cut off though the words are by drifting thousands of miles away from their home. I grew up saying, "I drug the wagon here," and "We brung the soda pop," because that's how some of the adults around me spoke. Even my mother, who grew up in California and had five years of college, liked to sit by the "far" when she was "tard." "You're jumping out o' that fryin' pan into the far," she'd say, and go back to her book.

"Just how can you miss with a dessert that calls for twenty-three Ritz crackers?" Mickler asks. The food he describes is meant for satisfying appetites and budgets, not dietitians or trend makers. It's about social competition in the style poverty allows, and socializing in the way poverty sometimes fuels because you can't afford any other form of entertainment. The recipes have plenty of room to shift and grow: They call for "more or less" of something, tell you that "canned will do in a pinch," and so on. I learned in Mickler's book that it wasn't my own children, after all, who invented the peanut-butter-and-mayonnaise sandwich. This trailer-park clodhopper food was, is, oddly contemporary, too—fluid, creative, full of unexpected ingredients and convention-smashing combinations. This is food based largely in the cheap and available, and in its willingness to try something new and see what happens, poor food can be pretty hip. Backwoods fusion. But this is disappearing now, too—it's archaic, lost to upscale nostalgic diners and a sea of corporate mergers making the very notion of "at hand" a lost one.

MY FAVORITE SANDWICH AS A CHILD WAS toasted cheese, the way Mom made it: Velveeta and Miracle Whip on soft slices of white bread, fried in margarine. Each element was essential to the whole, but the bread was the foundation—the soft, airy, cloud-white bread so fragile that a slice larger than my hand could be compressed into a ball smaller than my thumbnail. It was simple, fun, the consummate modern food. And that was all I knew of bread for many years. I thought those long, floppy, machine-sliced loaves in their slick plastic bags were universal.

I've baked bread on an irregular schedule since I was a teenager. I still bake bread the way women have done for many centuries—or so I believed until recently. I had always believed bread to be an ancient thing. It is—but not the bread I've baked. Yeast bread baked at home, rising in the family kitchen, is new.

Europeans have always loved wheat. The Romans loved wheat. For many centuries, the peasantry of Europe ate rye, oats, barley, bran, beans, and lentils, more often as cereals and soups than in bread. But they chose wheat when they could get it—which wasn't often. Wheat was the upper-class grain, and wheat bread a luxury food. Wheat is one of the grains hardest on the land. It quickly depletes soil and so is often in tenuous supply; that's one of the things that makes it luxurious. Leavened wheat bread (called "soft bread" sometimes) in particular was the food of the wealthy everywhere—"the privilege of a select few," in Massimo Montanari's words. This was true for a long time—in Europe, leavened wheat bread wasn't widely available until the mid-1800s.

Wheat was brought here by the first English immigrants, but it was slow to be established in the American colonies. Because of its low and undependable yields and susceptibility to disease and weather, it was rare and precious on this continent for a long time, the center of the crop moving ever westward with the frontier. Most Americans ate corn, rye, oats, and barley as their grain well into the nineteenth century. These grains were served both as cereals and in quick breads—cornmeal mush and oatmeal; many kinds of fritters and pancakes; thick, flat loaves of rye bread baked in coals; and porridge.

Wheat flour was common only for the wealthy here, as in Europe. Cookbooks offered dozens of recipes for leavened breads and cakes, but they were special treats, holiday foods — desirable, even romantic, but out of reach for most people on a regular basis. A number of factors were involved besides wheat. Until the latter part of the 1800s, neither commercial yeast nor baking powder was available. Stone-ground wheat flour spoiled quickly and was treated as a perishable. To make wheat bread, cooks not only had to buy or grind a special batch of fine flour, they also had to make their own yeast or keep a starter. There were no precise measuring cups, spoons, or scales yet made for the home, so all baking was based on eyesight and experience. Until the oven was common, fine "baking" was done over the fire like everything else, a tricky process requiring constant vigilance.

But the dubious miracles of white flour and white sugar were on their way throughout the nineteenth century. When the primary quality of a product is as insubstantial as color, the color itself must have significance. Whiteness has always had peculiar power in the value of bread. The long chain of economic hardship in both Europe and the United States was in part reflected in a line of increasingly dark and heavy breads and grains. In the United States, the justification for both white flour and white sugar also came to be based on class. White flour wasn't something a person could make for himself. It was a *corporate* product by nature, more expensive, more rare. White was better, too, because it was cleaner, finer, "nicer," "fresher," literally more refined, more modern, more "developed."

In medieval times, sugar was a food of the rich and used largely as a kind of spice, a flavor used sparingly. Honey had always been more important than sugar because it was easier to obtain, and when sugar was used, it was usually brown. Sidney Mintz, in his history of sugar, writes that sugar was one of the first imported foods upon which a whole class became dependent—when the British came to require sugar with their tea. (Of course, they'd already become dependent on their tea.) Sugar was an important crop in the colonies, partly because the syrup was used in making rum, and became widely used only after industrialization, when companies began to see the marvelous opportunities it represented.

The Mason jar, which allowed home canning without reliance on large amounts of vinegar, salt, and sugar, wasn't perfected until the late nineteenth century. By then, the United States had the sweetest cuisine in the world because of its heavy use of sugar in condiments, sauces, and preserving. Even though huge quantities of sugar were being used, the price of sugar dropped steadily through the 1800s, as did profits.

Oh, the marvels of marketing, an infinitely perfectible art: First, people had to be convinced to abandon their local supplies of honey. Then they had to give up the cheaper coarse brown sugar used for everyday cooking. Then they had to be convinced that white sugar was worth the higher price. They had to believe sugar was a staple— a necessity—when it never had been before. And all this was achieved in the last few decades of the nineteenth century.

For centuries, sugar was thought to have medicinal value. Writes Mintz, "The whiter the sugar, the more effective it was supposed to be, medically." But for sugar sellers, whiteness had practical value, too. White sugar has less moisture than brown, so it keeps longer and is easier to bag and transport, and it also happens to be less sweet. This is a tidy package for a manufacturer. White sugar cost more than brown to buy in the first place, and the cook had to use more of it for the same effect. People clearly preferred to use white sugar when they could, partly because it was rare and expensive— a sign of wealth and status. But until the nineteenth century, few were willing to buy it for everyday use.

The sugar sellers decided to convince people that brown sugar was harmful—dirty, adulterated. The most effective campaign involved large pictures of a "formidably organized, exceedingly lively and decidedly ugly little animal," an insect purported to live in brown sugar in "exceedingly great" numbers and not in white sugar at all. That this was a lie didn't stop it from working. What kind of mother would buy such a food for her children? The campaign against brown sugar was one of the early examples of negative advertising and part of a rising fear of hidden dangers in food.

Creating a mass market for white flour was more complicated than making a market for sugar, and took longer. White flour was first promoted widely in the 1830s, after the British Corn Laws had severely reduced English wheat imports and American millers found themselves with surpluses. But a great change in attitude was required to open the slowly emerging middle class to the rich man's way of bread and cake. The success of this quite deliberate campaign to change the lifestyles of millions of people was the result of a complex give-and-take among technological developments, marketing strategy, and the centralization of farming and industry. Invention and society are wound together—and bound together. Rye and cornmeal and rough wheat gradually disappeared from the average American table. As one author put it, "A flood of white sugar and flour spread over the land . . . [and] the nutritive value of the diet of millions changed . . ."

The wheat surplus of the 1820s motivated millers not only to market their product but to improve and centralize the technology. Automatic milling first began in the late 1700s, and has become steadily more automated and centralized ever since. The original "low" milling was replaced around 1870 with "high" methods—progressively closer grindings that removed the wheat germ and bran. When the oil contained in the germ was removed, the flour's shelf life lengthened and the flour whitened a bit, and grew whiter and more durable with each successive removal of bran. But the big selling point quickly became not fineness or shelf life but *whiteness*.

Whiteness everywhere. Immigrants declared their foreignness in their preferences for the homemade and the whole grain in life, because whiteness was everything in the United States—white refrigerators and scrupulously polished white stoves, white clothes for babies and maidens and brides, white houses for the wealthy, white sauce on white fish, white bread on the table with mayonnaise and cream and powdered sugar for toppings.

The almost unconscious attitude toward whiteness we've inherited in this century is obvious in James Gray's laudatory history of the General Mills company, *Business Without Boundary,* written in 1954. The Minnesota mills faced particular difficulties with their hard spring wheat. In traditional stone milling, loose bran was mixed with the flour, and the middlings—coarser flour with flakes of bran—were left behind. "A method must be found to treat the middlings in a second process to purify them of contamination from bran," wrote Gray of the mills' early days. That bran was a *contam-ination* is telling; its only flaw was that it wasn't white.

Flour naturally whitens a little about twelve weeks after milling, but no matter how finely ground, it remains a bit creamy. Thus, a difference even between white flours—bleached and unbleached. In the 1800s, some millers used alum, a toxic ammonia product, to whiten their flour, with some unfortunate results. For a brief time in 1904, millers thought they could use electricity to bleach flour by binding nitrogen and oxygen, but the government, which was in the process of passing the Pure Food and Drug Act, declined to approve. These days, bleached white flour is treated with benzoyl peroxide or chlorine, and sometimes both.

By midcentury, iron rollers first introduced in Hungarian mills replaced the stone rollers of the past. Rolling was more powerful, more efficient; by 1860, flour milling was the leading American industry. But iron rollers quickly gave way to porcelain rollers, because porcelain made even finer, whiter flour, and was easier to clean. Within a few more years, porcelain was traded for steel—a far less subtle milling method, much more degrading of the grain, but even more efficient than porcelain for high-volume production.

Small mill owners couldn't repeatedly refit with new rollers. Middlings purifiers were another big cost—fans that blew the flour through giant sieves of different meshes to sort out particles, a complex and automated system far beyond the capabilities of a local country miller. (Air classifiers of today are capable of sorting particles a micron across.) Small mills simply went out of business. About 75 percent of the mills in this country closed in the two years between 1884 and 1886, and large mills formed "flour trusts"—

huge cooperatives bent on price-fixing and unfair competition. "Traditionalists complained bitterly for a time that milling had lost all its picturesqueness," wrote Gray, without irony. It had certainly lost forever its local character, and so had flour and bread.

In 1876, there were twenty mills in Minneapolis, shared among seventeen companies. By 1889, four corporations controlled 87 percent of the business. General Mills wasn't formed until 1928, but its conglomerate form was simply the meeting of four big concerns that had already, in their turn, absorbed many smaller concerns: Washburn Crosby, the Sperry Company, the Kell conglomerate, and the Larrowe Company, an animal-feed business. When the papers were signed, General Mills held property in Minneapolis, New York, Missouri, Kentucky, Oklahoma, Texas, Michigan, Utah, Montana, Wyoming, Kansas, Washington, and more. The increasing monopolization of mills and the increasing processing of wheat were not coincidental patterns of growth; they were deeply connected. One led, inexorably, to the other.

Several decades after General Mills prospered, in part by convincing women to buy white flour and start baking fancy cakes and yeast bread, the company had another success with Bisquick and dry cake mixes, specifically intended as a shortcut to that baking. They won both ways.

CHANGE IS THE OLD STORY. THE RATE OF change is something else. Human history is largely a matter of events taking place at walking speed, walkers passed eventually by galloping horses and wind-blown ships. Neither goods nor knowledge ever moved faster than the people who carried them. Never, that is, until everything moved at once, until the time when people, products, and information suddenly began to move at the speed of trains and steam engines, moved in flight, moved at the speed of electrons, all in the matter of a few decades, until the very nature of our relationship to time and space was transformed. (Clocks were rare until the mid-1800s, because communication was so local that keeping time over a distance was impossible.) The huge territory of North America took on a false reality in the nineteenth century—all of it seemingly close at hand, connected by thousands of miles of rail and telegraph wire, all of it seeming to fill with factories, farms, and ranches too big to comprehend, on a scale disproportionate to any one person's life. These changes came abruptly, the way wars come, and plagues.

In profound historical logic, what changed the most in the years surrounding the Civil War—those most influential, most provident years—was the notion of *change,* our ability to bend to change, to stop resisting. Ice cutting and storage, canals and rail lines, faster trains, boats and clipper ships, and tin cans were dramatic new technologies. More dramatic still was the fact that distant technologies and unseen inventions could combine into a new economy of daily life, a new economy of food. And most dramatic of all, the greatest change was how readily these dramas were absorbed.

Technological change, in fact, gradually merged with the expansion the changes created like sine waves, canceling each other out into flatness. Changes like trains and tin cans promised a new variety, and often delivered on that promise. But what that variety led to was a remarkable sameness, a homogenized cuisine as frothy as the powdered Milkman milk my mother shook up in her old Miracle Whip jars. The opportunity to vary one's life endlessly with new products was matched by a simple human need for the reassurance of the familiar, for stability and repetition. Variety excited; habits calmed. The unpredictable and the known, like the future and the past, lived precariously together and proved to be a remarkable combination for the making of fortunes based on the tiniest of differences, on nothing more than a brand name.

The advent of packaged food, itself the result of faceless new technologies, had profound effects on how people experienced the world. As the rail cars and tin cans came to dominate produce, so did standard packaging dominate dry foods: crackers, cakes, and cookies in boxes where there had been only barrels before. The small bulk merchant disappeared and was replaced with self-serve markets offering shelves of dried, canned, and frozen things never before available. It was also in the latter part of the nineteenth century that the Shakers marketed a premeasured pancake product requiring only water or milk, anticipating Bisquick by fifty years.

These new choices were at the same time a new set of restrictions all of us have come to share. The opening market of new products channeled behavior, self-image, and expectations into a narrower and narrower bed—the river of the twentieth century, running faster and harder with each passing year. What people ate reflected a much larger world of change than the world they moved in, and seemed to hint at the cosmopolitan and exotic. Packaged foods were more expensive, of course, but that only helped to propel the image: They were promoted relentlessly as more "modern," more sophisticated, than homemade food. Processing was swank. The central irony is with us in television commercials today: The good mother serves her family bowls of steaming, nourishing soup—the kind made by the millions of cans by So-and-So Company.

A great deal of what people ate was exactly like what everyone else ate. The grand machinery of the food business intended just that dissonance.

An ad for the *Brand Names Foundation* ("a non-profit educational foundation") in 1957 says, "Always the same . . . today, tomorrow and tomorrow. Stable as the alphabet! Go out today and buy any product of any manufacturer's brand . . . ask for the same thing tomorrow, or weeks from now . . . match 'em up, and they're uniformly good, or *better*. This uniformity is no accident . . . Want <u>uniformity</u>? Patronize the dealer who provides your favorite brand." Implicit in this paean to sameness is a paean to difference—a tantalizing combination of familiarity and variety. The differences are minute, just enough to distinguish one brand from another without undermining the consumer's desire for something known.

Advertising was as essential to this transition as it was influential. As food became more and more processed and our enormous number of choices was celebrated in every form of media, the differences between those choices disappeared until the only clear variable was the label, the logo, the slogan on the can. Food became an economy of competing homogeneity. But brand names didn't just appear in response to confusion. Corporations, growing larger by the day, actively conspired with and against one another, the government, and the scientific community to flood a tense, newborn century with brands by the hundreds—and then the thousands. Nutritional labeling was seen as a threat to competition. As Harvey Levenstein points out, "If the government guaranteed that the quality of the contents of two different cans was equal, why should consumers pay more for the brand-name product?" Why, indeed? Only advertising could tell.

The tin can was patented in the United States in 1825. It was used first for the same products that had been packed in glass jars—meat, condensed milk, and produce. But the advantages were obvious, even before assembly-line tinning did away with the artisans. Soon one could buy sardines, horseradish, and sauerkraut, and then whole meals like spaghetti and soup in cans. In the 1860s, people living in the Rocky Mountains paid more for a can of soup than we do today. Canned hams followed, and more, more, more. Civil War soldiers in the American southeast had dined on canned fruits and vegetables from California. (At the same time, Californians, writes Waverley Root, began "complaining that the land was being buried under heaps of rusted cans.") The Borden, Armour, Campbell, Van Camp, Franco-American, Kraft, and Heinz fortunes all began with the tin can. I try to imagine a world without the can, and I find it hard to do. I prefer to cook from scratch whenever I can, but my recycling bin is full of cans every week or two. Cans are insidious, essential, impenetrably important, irreplaceable, and very new.

Until the mid-1800s, getting fresh milk in New York City required sending a deliveryman into the country to bring it back. Most New Yorkers drank only "swill milk" from city cows raised in brutal conditions and fed mash from local distilleries. (Fresh milk wouldn't be sold in closed containers till late in the century.) When the Erie Railroad was finished, all that changed; within a few years, millions of gallons of country milk came into New York City, stirred by big tin tubes filled with ice. Produce and other perishables began to follow in refrigerated rail cars, both in and out of season—from California by 1869, from the South in the 1870s, from the Midwest to all parts west and east. In one of the more telling changes of that changing time, farmers began to plant crops beside the railroad and married themselves to the trains. The smaller farmers and orchardists were already doomed. Their very diversity was going to kill them in the age of farming conglomerates to come. This was the new direction of American agriculture, the new philosophy, repeated time and again for many decades—"Get big or get out." Most farmers got out, willingly or no, and left the field— literally—to the growing corporations.

By the 1860s, a Bostonian could buy tomatoes year round; Chicagoans could eat Maine lobsters and California grapes; New Yorkers could eat game shot in Ohio. As railroads brought a bounty of distantly grown foods to urban populations, they spelled the end of less popular varieties of fruits and vegetables. Small farmers stopped diversifying, or disappeared altogether, replaced by the beginnings of agricultural conglomerates who saw profit in mass production. Iceberg lettuce—all I knew of lettuce for many years, just as all I'd known of bread was Wonder—was a new variety developed to withstand the shocks of rail travel. It quickly supplanted the delicate, softer greens people had routinely eaten in season, and "almost single-handedly redirected the path of the modern American diet," according to Harvey Levenstein. In just this way the promise of choice limited possibility.

So much food of so many seemingly different kinds began appearing late in the nineteenth century that a new way of shopping was inevitable. Bulk foods kept in bins, and the clerk who reached up to the shelves behind him as the customer chose her raw goods, were as doomed as the family truck farm. The supermarket was a playing field for a competition of equals, a stadium of attractively, almost hypnotically designed packages, containing essentially the same food and each brand promising essentially the same experience. There were almost 500 A&P supermarkets open by 1912, and a new one was opening every three days. Little more than half a century later, American supermarkets had grown so large they often contained more than 12,000 different foods. The truly remarkable thing is how little there was to choose from in that enormous pile.

By the 1920s, the Campbell Soup Company was selling many millions of cans of soup every week, mainly condensed concoctions of beef, vegetables, tomatoes, and peas. These were used almost as often for sauces and casserole bases as soups. Cream of mushroom soup came out in the 1930s, and has ever since been one of the top-selling brand-name products of all time. (The company claims that Americans consume "2.5 billion bowls" of Campbell's cream of mushroom and Campbell's chicken noodle soups a year.) They represent as well as anything the emerging dream of modern food processing—raw materials grown in large, centrally managed operations, transported to a central processing plant, and then shipped out, back to the region where they were grown and to all other regions, too, meeting the buying public equally, without prejudice. Cream of mushroom soup might as well be the national bird, the national fish, the national flower; it is infinitely versatile, tied to nothing, freed of meaning and association with anything but itself.

In the early 1930s, Clarence Birdseye performed his own marketing miracle on frozen foods, long disdained as a way to disguise inferior quality. Birdseye froze good-quality food and called it "frosted," and made the packaged results appear to be a newly invented modern convenience. Frozen foods were rapidly accepted, and soon were marketed as "fresh"—fresh, that is, compared to the canned foods most people had begun to eat in quantity.

Frozen foods meant freezers, and then refrigerators. A modern mechanical refrigerator was in more than half of American homes with electricity by the 1940s. But they were anticipated well before that. Refrigerators were supposed to make it easier to shop and plan meals, because you could buy more food at one time. Technological advances often were sold as increasing convenience, but convenience really meant faster meals—bigger meals—faster, bigger lives, a gradually jading appetite expecting ever more speed, ever more change.

One of the first really new foods—invented all-American foods—was Jell-O, released just before the turn of the century. Jell-O was easy to prepare, comfortingly sweet, and had a chameleonlike character that allowed it to be both dessert and salad. In the early 1900s, 15 million Jell-O recipe booklets were distributed every year. (In contrast, *The Joy of Cooking* has sold about 15 million copies in fifty years.) Immigrants coming through Ellis Island were offered free samples of Jell-O beneath a sign reading WELCOME TO AMERICA.

Jell-O was followed by a river of new foods flowing toward the same bland, sweet, salty, convenient ocean perfected in the foods of midcentury. General Mills, the home of Betty Crocker, was responsible for "Brown 'n' Serve" rolls, Wheaties, Cheerios, instant oatmeal, Bisquick, and Hamburger Helper. (Their big moneymaker, instant cake mixes, appeared right after the Second World War.) There was Crisco and the first frozen dinner; refrigerator dough, powdered milk, and presliced processed cheese; Metrecal (the first diet shake) and shelled frozen beans; pre-sauced frozen vegetables, fruit cocktail, Spaghetti-Os, Velveeta, dried gravy, Miracle Whip, Spam, Stove Top dressing, Cool Whip, and Tang—and my mother bought them all. She bought them just like everyone else bought them. "New goods almost sold themselves," wrote Warren Belasco. To food technologists, Belasco adds, the mid-twentieth century was "the golden age to which they constantly referred and hoped to return."

The rise of supermarkets was paralleled by the rise of the chain restaurant. The idea of a standard menu and recognizable decor was partly a response to the fear of contamination that took such hold of people in the early twentieth century. But the existence of chains helped fuel the homogenization of food by allowing the excitement of change to clash with the desire for the familiar at an unimagined national level. Howard Johnson, one of the first true restaurant entrepreneurs, chose to emphasize not the taste but the sameness of the food his restaurants served, and highlighted the speed and visibility of food preparation. He boasted of his central, mass-preparation facilities and the low labor costs of simply heating food up instead of cooking it to order. One after the other, Johnson's competitors learned to promote *sameness* as a value. The chain restaurant was a place devoid of anxiety or fear of the unknown; it was secure against invisible contamination, against the cheating of foreigners, against newness, against surprise. "The clam strips were outstanding," a friend who grew up eating at Howard Johnson's tells me. "And I liked the blue and orange." Of such things are memories made.

By the mid-1920s, the same people who had been patronizing

chain restaurants were complaining about the disappearance of fresh, regional cooking. Food was gradually becoming a nationalized commodity. People complained that processed foods weren't as good as fresh food even as they demanded more processing. Advertisers and food conglomerates were listening; the era of mass-produced freshness was on its way.

Right there, in the twenties, a crucial ancient equation of food turned over. Fat had always been a quality of wealth, a symbol of abundance and power. But suddenly youth became the leading value instead of experience, slimness and activity the fashion instead of virtue and achievement. Since the 1920s, fat has been, for Americans, a quality of the poor. This is widely understood as a matter of image and marketing. But it had a deeper, nearly invisible effect as well. The desire to be young, new, and lean combined with the desire to be fast, modern, and efficient. Instead of creating a fashion for fresh and simple foods, a grand rejection of mass processing, the combination became the wedge needed to put processed and convenience foods ahead for good.

Restaurants served several purposes: They provided the working person's lunch or supper away from home, the occasional elegant meal for the upper class, and more recently, the family meals needed by people traveling a growing network of highways. But fast food for a fast world was inevitable: McDonald's, Dunkin' Donuts, Jack in the Box, Kentucky Fried Chicken, Burger King, Shakey's Pizza, and Pizza Hut all arose before 1960. Each name suggested a specific quality, a particular taste just a little different from the others, utterly dependable and distinguished more by the nuances of marketing than by reality. McDonald's succeeded because when Ray Kroc bought the system in 1954, he saw that the future lay in suburbia, and that's where he built. McDonald's continued to thrive later on, when suburbia fragmented, because Kroc took his chain back to the city in pursuit of single adults who remembered it as the taste of their childhood. Predictability was paramount in fast food: From town to town and state to state, from season to season and year to year, the food could be counted upon. My family's occasional trips to A&W were as ritualized as Easter morning service at the Lutheran church—the same slow ride along the same streets, the same bouncy girl bringing the same food to the car window— the same burgers, the same root beer floats, the same appetites, satisfied the same way, while the world outside that bubble grew ever closer, noisier, tighter.

SIDNEY MINTZ POINTS OUT THAT WHAT WE EAT today can be traced to particular historical forces such as immigration, colonization, and mobility. But we shouldn't view these only as remote or historical forces—they all are at work today. We are still immigrants, from more places than ever before. We still colonize cultures, if not countries, and usurp everything from food to clothing to music. We are also, in turn, being colonized by global corporations, which hold more and more of the means of production—not just of food but of everything we buy. And we never stop moving.

Throughout the late 1800s, new states entered the Union, one after the other, and each came complete with its own peculiar bounty, its own regional specialties and crops and ingredients, its own niche. The huge continent was a patchwork of regional foodways passed from neighbor to neighbor, from mother to daughter.

Almost all of them were imported, immigrant ways of one kind or another, marked by local festivals celebrating everything from clams to onions to pickles and smelt. Such festivals, along with ethnic and national celebrations like Oktoberfest and Obon, have never ceased. But they are nothing to the massive flood of new foods. This also was no accident. Bland, standardized food was the central product of processing, which attenuates flavors and textures. But it was promoted relentlessly as a national cuisine of great variety, promoted by every food processor in the country, by every newspaper food page and magazine cooking columnist. This expression of gradually nationalizing tastes fed its own growth. The only way so many millions of outrageously different people could eat as one—indivisible—was for them to eat the same kind of food, food as inoffensive and vaguely defined as possible.

A world of extraordinary possibility turned upon itself. The medieval poor of Europe routinely used at least seven spices, not counting salt and pepper. In 1939, the enormous and nearly exhaustive *Prudence Penny Cook Book* lists two dozen kinds of cheese, from Camembert to Brie, and more than two dozen herbs and spices in its suggested ingredients list. A number of common spices, like saffron and sage, disappeared, lost in the European conflict. But the significant fact is that these spices never came back into common fashion. In 1950, the only forms of cheese Betty Crocker knew were "American (Cheddar) and White cream cheese." She listed two kinds of mushrooms: canned and white. There are six herbs "basic to all seasoning"—mint, thyme, sage, marjoram, rosemary, and basil, one fewer than the medieval peasants had.

This battening down of culinary hatches took place in thirteen years—war years, when hundreds of thousands of young men and many women traveled around the world. War always expands horizons, one way or the other, but it's a common misconception that World War II opened the eyes of Americans to ethnic cuisine. What it really opened their eyes to was the intriguing comfort of simple abundance. A lot of veterans came home wanting the dinner table to look just like the trays in the mess hall, trays physically divided between big portions of meat, starch, and vegetables, and always followed by fruity desserts and a tall glass of milk.

In the 1950s, an inevitable point was reached, one toward which many roads had led: the point where taste became the least important criteria in how people chose what they would eat. Status, nutrition, convenience, symbolism, newness and price all were more or less important, trading places from year to year in priority, but always ahead of capricious individual desire. By then, consumers and even food critics seemed no longer to recognize the difference between fresh and processed food, between cooking and heating things up.

This was, in fact, the dream realized. Montanari has made a particular study of the cycles of famine in European history; in this long lens, "canned, vacuum-packed and frozen foods are precisely the solutions which our ancestors sought." Lots of people have eaten the same food over and over, much of it dried, smoked, salted, fermented, and pickled to a point of unrecognizability—bland, repeated flavors of peasant food, the same meal day after day for months after the harvest. What we in the 1990s fervently desire— the taste of fresh, local, seasonal food—was until recently "a form of slavery," says Montanari, a gigantic dependence on nature fraught with insecurity and even terror.

Of course, what is near is always ordinary. To me, the acorns were the miracle—the bland, tough, difficult acorns that surely became tiresome by midwinter. The endless cans and packages were mundane to me. My desire for sacrifice and community was bound up in the visible work involved, the expressive work of food which cooking from scratch provides. But those who work all day over the basics find convenience pretty compelling.

In *Betty Crocker's Cooking American Style*, the editors extol the virtues of this seasonless, borderless menu: "Alaskan crab is very much at home in Missouri, and some of the most ephemeral berries travel all over the country both in and out of season." The food writer Clementine Paddleford wrote in 1960, "Now, modern transportation and cold storage and freezers make a joke of the calendar." It was a joke eons in the making.

Paddleford, blessed with a most writerly name, traveled all over the United States from 1948 on, writing about regional cooking for *This Week*. Her oddly telegraphed essays, thick with recipes, were released in 1960 as *What America Eats*. These are stories of lobstermen, maple sugar farmers, pumpkin home canners, sheep ranchers and genteel southern lady cake bakers—people, mostly women, who love to cook, who are renowned in their small towns and social circles for a particular torte or chowder or barbecue sauce. All over the country they made Paddleford coffee and invited her to stay and dine, and the author captures well the homey touches of small towns and unsung people. She is celebrating tradition, region, and variety, and she does it in a most revealing way.

Paddleford defined three kinds of American cooking: the truly regional; the foreign dishes brought by immigrants; and the new. This last was "strictly today's, making use of completely new products—the little Rock Cornish hen of recent development, the

time-saving ready mixes, the instants, the quick frozens. Modern
meal planners want the quick and easy, but with the plus of their
own distinctive touches. Women have great need, in this automatic
world, to express themselves creatively."

This juxtaposition of tradition and convenience is just what
Paddleford considers "authentic." She describes the "beautiful place"
that is Mrs. Pigford's kitchen after her husband's retirement.
"Cooking is no longer a duty—a job. She works with sure hands and
a high heart . . . [on] menus with an Old South flavor." But Mrs.
Pigford is no fool. Her "beautiful place" is a well-stocked pantry and
her Old South flavor is that of canned beans and canned crab and
canned tomatoes. In the chapter on Massachusetts, Paddleford dis-
cusses at length the many uses Native Americans made of pumpkin,
and then offers an "honest-to-goodness 1953 pumpkin pie" calling
for canned pumpkin. In her section on Virginia, she has a "traditional" pound cake calling for "three packages commercial pound
cake mix." In Oklahoma, Margaret Fisher's Asparagus consists of a
can of asparagus, a cup of "cheese-flavored cracker crumbs," a can
of cream of mushroom soup, and a tablespoon of butter or margarine.

Nowhere is the loss of variety more visible and poignant than in
the tomato, partly because tomatoes are so overwhelmingly visible.
A great many kinds of tomatoes exist—many more are extinct. But
most Americans know tomato as a single taste. Most of the tomatoes in Paddleford's book, in any midcentury cookbook, are canned.
Betty Crocker's 1950 cookbook goes one step further, noting that
if one doesn't have canned tomatoes, it is acceptable to substitute
fresh ones. In that postwar world, clinging to a blind belief in the
American's right to bounty at all times, canned tomatoes were a

quotidian miracle of industry. Fresh tomatoes meant stoop labor, rationing, fear, dirt under the fingernails. Of victory gardens, Betty Fussell wrote, "We couldn't wait for the war to be over to get back to the security of our cans."

The tomato, cultivated since ancient times throughout Central and South America and the Caribbean, was taken by a Spanish botanist to Europe in 1544. The plant traveled slowly, famously scorned for causing gout and rumored to be an aphrodisiac. Like the potato, the tomato eventually returned to the colonies, properly endorsed by Europeans at last, but it remained primarily an exotic taste for the wealthy until well into the 1800s.

The tomato is now one of the most beloved and widely used foods in the world, having traveled farther in a few hundred years than perhaps any other vegetable or fruit in history. Tomatoes have been embraced by every cuisine they have encountered, and are now essential to many. In the United States, they are the "number-one source of nutrients among all fruits and vegetables in our diet," according to Raymond Sokolov, not because the tomato is so nutritious but because we eat so many of them. But we eat them mostly out of cans and bottles, twice as many processed tomatoes as fresh, and more than half of them in the form of ketchup and chili sauce. And what we are eating is not exactly a tomato.

Tomato flavor is largely dependent on volatile chemicals, fragile molecules that disappear literally into thin air and are destroyed by cold. A true tomato must be vine-ripened and fresh, not as a matter of epicurean snobbery but because otherwise it ceases to be essentially *tomato*. Picked early, put in storage, transported any distance, the tomato becomes something else again—a tomatolike object, a mockery, a cheat.

As far as I can remember, I never ate a vine-ripened tomato as a child. They appeared on our table as canned tomato sauce, as ketchup, in Campbell's tomato soup, which doubled as the sauce for my mother's tamale pie. "Fresh" tomatoes were great beefsteak globes, hard as apples, shiny red and sliced thickly for summer hamburgers or quartered to sit on top of iceberg lettuce leaves for salad. Those tomatoes were colorful, wet, tough, and tasteless, and I largely ignored them.

In 1971, when I left my parents' table for college and entered, without knowing how important it would be for me, the newborn world of organic gardening and enthusiastic vegetarianism, I found the tomato waiting. I remember biting into a slice of fresh, truly fresh, tomato at a round Formica table in the dormitory cafeteria— biting, and stopping in the middle of a sentence, stunned. Since then, the hope of and the wait for tomatoes has become one of the seasons of my body, a way of telling time, climate, place.

On the 4th of July this year, I stood in line at the weekly farmer's market, held incongruously in the parking lot of my local bank. I was waiting, with several other cheerful people, to buy a pound of the first local vine-ripened tomatoes of the slowly emerging summer. The sign announced that they cost $2.50 a pound. Once I would have thought that a shocking price, but it was only half what the dismal so-called vine tomatoes cost in a nearby gourmet grocery store. It was a warm, overcast day, and a bluegrass fiddler played while people pulled red wagons from booth to booth, gathering the early crops of lettuce and the late crops of peas. When the farmer handed me my bag, he said, "Sorry for the wait." But I'd waited most of a year and didn't mind a few more minutes at all.

Today, even "locally" grown fruits and vegetables bought in a neighborhood grocery store are likely to have gone through quite a few hands and storage facilities before they appear under the flattering lights and misty sprays of the produce department. I buy tomatoes from Mexico sometimes, and avocados from Florida, but I have trouble finding local cherries because they've all gone to Japan. A hot meal at a nearby restaurant might very well consist of warmed-over ingredients grown, chopped, precooked and frozen at a great distance to be thawed, heated, and mixed with a ready-made sauce or dressing in the restaurant kitchen. So it has been for a long time; these days, good restaurants will point out that they actually do their own baking.

Tomatoes, lettuce, and so many other delicate gifts of the earth have been largely lost to us precisely because we wanted and were told we could have them all the time. They were destroyed by the belief that we deserved to have them without the cost of labor or patience. And so now most of these delights are limited to expensive grocery stores and occasional farmers' markets and the backyard garden where they began: "heritage" foods from the past, newer than new.

"Alaskan crab is very much at home in Missouri, and some of the most ephemeral berries travel all over the country both in and out of season." But Alaskan crab is not at home in Missouri. How could it be? And ephemeral berries are just that, ephemeral. When crab appears in Missouri, it is Missouri crab, which is something different from *Alaskan* and not exactly *crab*. Neither are the Mexican mangoes you buy today in Ohio really the same as the mangoes people eat on the dusty corner of a Mexican town square, nor is the "fresh" mahimahi you buy in New York City anything like mahimahi off the coast of Peru where it was caught. We celebrate diversity, embrace our proliferating differences, until these things prove uncomfortable or inconvenient—until difference means limits. Then we celebrate our global body, embrace our Jet Age closeness. The nation's foodways have for many decades been based on the belief that time and space have no significant meaning when it comes to food. To claim this is to claim a communal delusion—one each of us knows to be false, but toward which humanity has been driving for a thousand years. It is a delusion that each of us chooses to pretend we believe, ad copy for our lives, public relations for the modern world.

4

COOKING IS A LEARNED SKILL WITH many smaller skills within—and as with all complex skills, the most important part is gaining experience over time. Cooking has always been a local, slow affair, a personal effort peculiar to a moment and a place. Cooking was intimately tied to the cook's locale, to the cook's space—to the cook. And then, just like that, it wasn't.

The common definition of cooking began to change around the turn of the century. Cooking no longer meant the measured preparation of available foods by hand. Fewer and fewer people knew how to do that, anyway. First men, and then women, began to work away from the home, even as relatives lived farther and farther apart in smaller and smaller units. There was no one left to teach a person how to cook—and often no one home to learn. In a society of people increasingly dependent on anonymous manufacturers and experts, the tin can, refrigerator rail car, and electric stove were the first great equalizers. By the 1920s, the United States processed a greater quantity and variety of food than all the rest of the world, which brought about an erosion of quality and nearly extinguished inimitable, local flavors.

That this equalization often required a significant decline in the quality of food people ate was not exactly relevant. Lack of quality was merely a challenge to the emerging art of the advertiser. The consumer had to be convinced that "choice" and "variety" were what they were buying—buying with increasingly busy and stressful lives. Where this led, with everlasting irony, was to a time when a hundred million Americans ate the same food every day.

In the early 1970s, *Redbook* did a survey of 85,000 women on what they cooked and ate. (It appeared in an issue with the cover headline: *The Perfect Diet! Get Well, Feel Great, Lose Weight! Safely, Surely!*) These women, the granddaughters and great-granddaughters of the women who first began cooking by brand name, cooking for speed and convenience as much as anything else, covered a wide range of class and lifestyle. The editors were "totally taken aback" to find very few differences in what they cooked and ate. Most felt they didn't have enough time or help in the kitchen, and very few had help from spouses. When they entertained, it was informally: "A typical dinner was red meat and vegetables . . . most families have salads only three or four times a week. Poultry was served once or twice a week; fish, less often than once a week; and the family only very occasionally substituted beans, eggs or cheese for meat." They bought a lot of canned soups, for making sauces. They used canned and frozen vegetables routinely. "Only 18 per cent said they used fresh vegetables most of the time." Noting how many owned barbecue equipment and large freezers, the editors added, "Obviously these are people to whom food matters."

"Now! Get '4-hour' spaghetti sauce flavor . . . in 10 minutes . . . *while your spaghetti cooks*. French's Spaghetti Sauce Mix." Another product: "Chef Boy-Ar-Dee Ravioli is made to tempt appetites by a Chef who knows the secrets of fine Italian cooking . . . It takes many days to make ravioli like this. But it's ready in minutes for you!" "When you're hungry for soup that tastes like the oldtime slow-simmered kind . . . it's nice to know you can enjoy it in mere *minutes* with Lipton Soup Mixes . . . There's such a difference in soup that's fresh home-cooked. You must taste Lipton soon and see!"

I have no way of knowing whether anyone ever believed these claims, exactly. But they believed the promise beneath the words, the promise of not having to do what always had been necessary to do, the promise of a future where, in some way or other, things would be easier, better, kinder. Maybe no one believed it, but when you go long enough (a whole life) without tasting homemade sauces, you tend to forget what you're missing when you reconstitute a powdered one.

That the rise of processing led to a disdain for both raw food and the labor of plain cooking is no surprise. The disdain was carefully constructed by marketing departments and advertisers. It has been broken now and then in this century by a fashion for a kind of special-occasion cooking that's been granted particular social status. But from the last century to this, cooking from scratch for one's daily fare came to seem stodgy, a waste of time better spent elsewhere in a world full of possibility. The home cook was often portrayed as frumpy, out of date—even unpatriotic. This was true even in the 1950s, when the housewife was a central image. That house-wife was a modern consumer, not an old-fashioned drudge. Cook-ing without recourse to the miracles of food processing was seen as quaint at best.

This has shifted a little at the end of the millennium, but not much. Now so few people have the time—are willing to give the time—for cooking that a meal made carefully from scratch is often a sign of prosperity. Cooking can take hours—days—and time is a far more expensive commodity than it ever has been before. Most people feel they have little choice but to rely on processed food on a regular basis. Many have no idea how to cook even the most ordi-nary dishes. Almost a hundred years ago, the woman who insisted on simmering her stew over slow heat was made into the symbol of those unfortunates who were stuck in the past. Today, again a rarity, she represents the end result of all that forward motion. She is the lucky woman who has escaped the grind.

PRESERVING CHANGED, TRANSPORTING CHANGED. Kitchens changed, so houses had to change, because lives changed—one giving way to the next like dominoes pushed by unseen hands. So cooking changed. Before the 1100s, Europeans cooked over open, central hearths. The ancient art of baking known to the Romans was lost in the Dark Ages, and everything was roasted on the fire. The historian Jean-François Revel believes that the lack of a good fuel source is one reason Chinese cuisine became so sophisticated; stir-frying seems to have developed as a kind of nomadic or battlefield solution. The lack of fuel made it impossible to simply roast everything like Europeans did, and forced Chinese

cooks to invent delicate and subtle methods, which remained undis-
covered in the West for a very long time.

Slowly the central hearth of medieval times gave way to wall
hearths with chimneys, where cooking was done in hanging pots
and frying pans. That situation lasted two hundred more years.
These hearths were huge, inefficient, and unpredictable, and their
eternal smoke a slow poison. Only in the early 1700s did new
designs based on the physics of heat change the shape of the chim-
ney. Draft improved and wood fires became much easier to handle.

Europe promptly finished deforesting itself.

A century later, wood fires gave way to coal fires, and Europe
began poisoning itself all over again.

Well into the 1800s, Americans still cooked the same way their
European ancestors did—one-pot meals over open fires, joints of
meat roasted on spits, root vegetables, and coarse grains simmered
for hours. People cooked like this in the cities as well as on farms.
(Swedish immigrants had brought iron stoves over the sea a long
time before, but other colonists didn't pay attention.) Almost 2,000
years after the Romans learned to oven-bake bread, many American
pioneers longed for a swing arm for the single cookpot hanging
over the fire.

Though wood is, in some ways, the best fuel for cooking, it
became increasingly expensive and hard to find. By the mid-1800s,
the United States was catching up to Europe's deforestation. Coal
seemed an improvement here, too—easier to store than wood,
often easier to get, and cleaner, because it left less ash. But coal fires
were at least as smoky as wood fires and, because they were more
toxic, had to be burned in enclosed boxes. Improvements in iron
and steel manufacturing had made such boxes somewhat practical.

Around the turn of the century, the new electrical and gas utilities entered the field. Electricity as a mass community endeavor would flourish only if people bought it *en masse;* that was the nature of a "utility," after all. People would buy electricity only if they thought they needed electricity—and they would need it only if their lives changed again, only if they felt their lives had to change. Electricity was worthless in a coal-and-wood society. It couldn't succeed as a product in and of itself until people felt they needed it, for and by itself.

Natural gas and later electricity were routinely "described as 'economy fuels' to disguise the fact that this was precisely what they were not," says Waverley Root. But the idea of economy wasn't enough. These wholly new things had to be sold as part of a wholly new world, imbued with the vague value of modernity. This was portrayed by the utilities as no more or less than *the future.* Electricity was "new," it was "safe" and "clean" and "modern," and it powered all kinds of new products that promised to be safe and clean and modern, too.

Root points out that the expense of gas and electricity eliminated one kind of waste and pollution. "Imagine the Joy of a kitchen free from all dirt, smoke, ashes or soot. Your curtains and furnishings will remain spotlessly white if you install OXO GAS HEATING EQUIPMENT throughout your home." But they created another, more subtle waste. Since gas and electricity were too expensive to use for long periods, the traditional stockpot on the back of the stove where leftovers used to go was gone, too. One thing leads to another, as Root notes—to the end of the ubiquitous pot-au-feu, the long-simmering daily soup of meat and vegetables that so efficiently fed the family. Stews had to be replaced by other foods, quick cooking, more expensive foods— packaged foods.

The steady source of heat from a woodstove had made the kitchen the traditional gathering place for a family and provided a reliable supply of hot water. This was gone, too. People had to buy furnaces and hot water heaters—more gas, more electricity. As for cooking, gas was more limiting in terms of heat range than wood, and electricity far more limiting still. Even in the 1950s, Westinghouse touted a new stove because it had a special "Economizer" burner, which had both high *and* low settings. (The same stove had a lighter, so midnight snacks could be "accompanied by a cigarette.")

A majority of people had electric lighting in their homes in the teens and twenties. Along with the lightbulb and electric ranges came toasters, electric kettles, curling irons, vacuum cleaners, sewing machines, and mixers, though most of these were expensive and undependable novelties for several years. These objects of the convenience-bent future—these "mechanical servants"—required plenty of work from both the housewife, who had to wrestle with them, and her husband, who suddenly had to earn the extra money to pay for them.

The age of the labor-saving lie was born. The shift from the hearth fire to the closed stove had immediate effects not only on house design but on family roles. Men stopped cutting firewood and tending fires as part of their outdoor chores; instead, women shoveled coal and tended stoves as part of their cooking chores. "Stoves were labor-saving devices," writes Ruth Schwartz Cowan, "but the labor that they saved was male." By the time electricity came to the kitchen, male labor was no longer part of the equation at all.

"In the General Electric Kitchen, one kilowatt hour of electricity will do an hour's work of 13 people . . . With a complete General Electric Kitchen in her home the modern woman need spend only minutes in the kitchen." This is from a pamphlet put out by GE in 1935, with photographs of women playing bridge, driving cars, admiring their spotless kitchens. None of these women is cooking, and the implication is that they no longer need to do so. "Magic electric servants work for her, giving her new joyous hours of freedom—hours she can spend in any way she chooses." A suggested dinner menu includes cream of corn soup, a "chartreuse" of meat and rice with tomato sauce, lima beans, salad in individual molds, caramel ice cream, and coffee, apparently prepared entirely by the stove and refrigerator themselves. (In fact, many of the ingredients in the accompanying recipes are canned, frozen, and dried—expensive but relatively quick. "Quick" and "modern" became almost synonymous.) Also not discussed is the elaborate cleaning required to keep the kitchen in its "spotless" state, which at the time involved taking large portions of the appliances apart and using different cleansers and cloths on each part.

In April 1957, an advertisement in *Sunset* asked, "How does your kitchen rate on the electrical living scale? Is your kitchen really up-to-date? There are so many wonderful new ways to put electricity to work in your kitchen today—electric servants that give you more time and energy for yourself and your family." At the top of the scale, with two dozen electrical appliances, stands the beaming housewife. "Your kitchen works instead of you. Now you're really living better electrically!"

By then, that housewife could buy all the appliances her mother had owned, plus an electric skillet, a deep-fat fryer, a dishwasher, and Corning Ware, which moved conveniently from the (electric) freezer to the (electric) oven. She could buy toaster ovens, juicers, Veg-O-Matics, fondue pots, and waffle irons.

She could buy a microwave oven. The microwave was first developed by Raytheon in the mid-1940s, when researchers were attempting to find peacetime uses for war technologies like radar. A company scientist, Percy Spencer, was standing in front of a magnetron tube when he discovered that the candy bar in his pocket had melted. So he did the obvious thing and put a kernel of popcorn in front of the tube. The kernel popped. So he tried a raw egg, which exploded. The company first sold the "Radarange," an appliance the size of a refrigerator, in 1947, for between two and three thousand dollars. The first attempt at a domestic market was in cooperation with Tappan, which made a smaller but less powerful oven in 1955 for a whopping $1,300. It wasn't until Raytheon contracted with Amana in 1967 that the real countertop microwave was born. It had 650 watts, a single power level, and a timer, and sold for a still-daunting $495. (The government had to assign a frequency to microwave ovens, just like they do with television and radio stations.) The technology was so strange the company sent a home economist along on deliveries to make sure people could use the ovens.

Now the daughters of the women who bought the first microwave ovens can buy coffee grinders and espresso makers, bread machines and ice cream freezers, Mr. Sandwich fryers and food processors and French-fry machines and convection ovens. But my favorite electric appliance is the one that acts as final summation to the long equation of change: the Crock-Pot, designed to duplicate the "homemade" taste of a stew simmering slowly over an open wood fire.

MY MOTHER GREW UP IN A FAMILY OF STRONG, long-lived women and ghostly, quiet men. Her father was a truck driver and her mother a housewife who'd had to drop out of college because of illness. From the privileged point of view I held as her oldest daughter, I came to see her life as a timid one. She was older than my friends' mothers, and I held that against her. She was always tired. She was always making me help her with chores. She didn't have wall-to-wall carpeting or matching furniture or centerpieces on her table like the pictures in the magazines. I have been startled, gratified, and a little embarrassed to discover some sense of who she really was, to discover what she fought against simply to learn, simply to work. Something breaks in me, again and again, when I realize what it all cost.

She matured at a time when the tide was shifting for women — shifting downward. The percentage of women attending college dropped to a third of all students in midcentury; a third of those women dropped out without graduating — a much lower percentage than their mothers' generation. Graduate and professional schools made it startlingly difficult for women sometimes — refusing loans and even admission, deliberately flunking female students out of required classes, often requiring those who stayed to sit in the back of the lecture hall in a segregated section. "For the first time in 100 years, the educational gap between young middle-class women and men increased," writes Stephanie Coontz. Instead of going to college, women got married. The median age of marriage for both men and women dropped in midcentury, too—the typical bride was not yet twenty-one. More than 70 percent of women between twenty and twenty-four were married, and they were having kids quickly. More than two-thirds of all married women were housewives in the fifties, and even among working women, only half worked full-time.

My mother broke all these conventions. She went to college and graduated, spurred on by her own mother, who forever regretted not being able to finish due to illness. My mother refused to get married until she finished her degree at age twenty-five. After getting married, she went to work. She stayed home for a few brief and miserable years when all three of her children were under school age, but otherwise she worked full-time outside her home until she had to retire from illness at fifty-six.

Since my mother's death several years ago, I've gathered a pile of hundreds of recipes from the derangement of papers every death leaves behind. I added a few hundred more when my grandmother—her mother-in-law—died a few years ago. This last cache of papers surprised me; I don't remember my grandmother ever cooking a meal for anyone. She lived next door to my mother and father for the last twenty years of her life, a perpetual guest in my mother's living room, subsisting mainly on cigarettes and beer and the hot dishes cooked by other women and brought to her like peace offerings.

Still, here they are: recipes, hundreds of recipes, cut out of newspapers and magazines, from the bottom of advertisements and off can labels and on index cards and notepaper. Some are in my grandmother's crabbed, backward writing, but most are in my mother's meticulous schoolteacher's penmanship. A few are in mysterious hands, gifts from long-gone friends and neighbors scribbled on the backs of envelopes, bits of stationery, handed on, copied again and again.

These aren't lost classics or great secrets. Most of them share a single quality — speed. Here is Vegetable A La Supreme, requiring cream of mushroom soup, frozen broccoli, Minute rice, and an entire bottle of Cheez Whiz. Here is Tomato Soup Salad, with canned soup, Knox gelatin, cottage cheese, mayonnaise, and stuffed olives. Here is Easy Deviled Ham 'n' Cheesewich, Saccharin Pickles, Chicken Spaghetti. There are a great many recipes using zucchini: zucchini with tomato juice, with fried onion rings, with cream cheese, with whipped cream, with cream of mushroom soup, with nuts and crushed pineapple. These dishes are based in convenience, the ingenuity of making do with a few odd cans and boxes, combining anything and everything you can put your hands on so as to avoid yet another trip to the store. Here are the endless reinventions of fusion cuisine, the creativity of limited ethnic poverty, the surprise of nouvelle, the patent simplicity of country people, all wrapped into a Jet Age suburban gift box. Weird and wonderful, this criminal's urge to avoid work, this wily feminine conspiracy of 3 X 5 cards. My mother worked a lot. At the end of the day, what my mother wanted wasn't food but *time* — time out of her labor, time to goof off in her armchair reading romances and drinking coffee, smoking while she watched Mike Douglas watch someone else cook something.

In this whole pile are only a few familiar items, like Porcupine Meatballs—hamburger and rice rolled into balls and baked in a sauce of canned tomato soup—and Pigs in Blankets. I don't know if I loved the name, evocative of luxury and comfort, or the doughy combination of Vienna sausages and Bisquick, but they were one of my favorite treats, rarely had. The fact is that she cooked the same few things over and over. After a few swings at Porcupine Meatballs or Scalloped-Potatoes-and-Spam you don't need a recipe. You don't even need a shopping list, and so you don't need to plan too much or think too far ahead. She kept a pantry stocked well enough for cataclysmic natural disasters, but the hundreds of boxes and cans were simply variations on a few basic things. (You can make Porcupine Meatballs with tomato soup, with mushroom soup, with cheese soup, and call it something different every time.)

So why did she keep a recipe for eggplant stuffed with lunch meat, something our entire family (and perhaps the whole human race) would have loathed? Why did she save how-to plans for time-consuming, multilayer tortes when she never baked? Why menus for party foods and coffee klatches written in the careful hand of a woman who rarely went to parties and never entertained? I wonder if my mother indulged in what Rosalind Coward, decades later, coined "food pornography." "All the women I have talked to about food have confessed to enjoying it," wrote Coward. "Few activities it seems rival relaxing in bed with a good recipe book. Some indulged in full colour pictures of gleaming bodies of Cold Mackerel Basquaise lying invitingly on a bed of peppers, or perfectly formed chocolate mousse topped with mounds of cream. The intellectuals expressed a preference for erotica, Elizabeth David's historical and literary titillation. All of us used the recipe books as aids to oral gratification, stimulants to imagine new combinations of food, ideas for producing a lovely meal."

I keep a thick folder of untried recipes, too, torn from the newspaper and various magazines, handed to me by friends or scribbled from conversations. There are elaborate desserts meant to be served on linen tablecloths by candlelight, and hearty family suppers for a family I no longer have to feed. I'm still caught, like her, between what I've imagined and what I've known, what's been given and what I've been able to take. I rarely use any of them. Like impulsively chosen lovers, a lot of recipes look less appetizing in the cold light of day.

One of my mother's old recipes is on a bit of stationery from a hotel in Reno. I don't remember her going to Reno, and when I found it, I was suddenly, unreasonably glad that she went there. I could see her, laughing, drinking a martini, playing slot machines, staying up late with other secretly dissident women, smoking cigarettes, and not missing their husbands. But I was struck as well by a sudden small grief that she spent even one minute there in Reno copying down a recipe. When I think of her, I never see her in the kitchen. I see her loafing around the living room with a cup of coffee, putting off supper for a few minutes more. I see her rising heavily, dutifully, to begin.

I asked my sister, Susan, what she remembered of the suppers of our childhood. She was quiet for a long moment and then said, in a very small voice, "What I remember is that she wasn't a very good cook." Susan said this as though she were speaking betrayal, and I know how she felt. Our mother was easily hurt, and she knew she wasn't a good cook, which to her somehow meant she wasn't entirely a good woman.

She did her needlework in the weary evening hours while my father slept stretched out loosely across the couch. Women's work is all details, a lot of small stitches put into life one at a time. Needles keep the hands busy while the heart stirs in its difficult sleep; they weave a hypnotic and deliberate calm. Women have always done these things, made scarves, gloves, headdresses, quivers, swaddling boards, vestments, moccasins, veils, christening gowns, beaded necklaces to rattle in the dance—inner turmoil brought to ground and herded into pattern. Women rein in their sorrows, their loneliness and denial, and make it into beautiful things bursting with erotic, joyful color, beautiful things not called art because they are useful. My weary, educated mother not only collected useless recipes but she bought craft kits and sequins and felt and fabric paint and Rit dye. She took up embroidery in middle age. I was disappointed in her when she did, of course. I was too restless for needles, too mad about the world. I wanted her to complain—not cook and clean, not sew.

I was a fool.

I believe now that my mother's life was one of wrenchingly difficult choices. Only the fearful need courage, and only the lazy need discipline. Her courage was to go on, day by day, in spite of hungers buried deep. The needlework she tried (and failed) to master may have been a last-ditch attempt to be what she was not, what she could not be but spent her whole life trying to become.

After dinner she cleared the table, put away food, washed the pots and pans, wiped the counter, and then closed the kitchen door against the sloshing roar of the dishwasher.

Such discipline—day in and day out, for many long years.

CLAUDE LÉVI-STRAUSS BELIEVED THAT TO study a myth correctly one has to study each variation of a myth, has to be willing to see that any given myth takes on different forms in different places and times. Mythic ideals must be interpreted widely in order to stay alive—in order to serve the varied purposes of myth. The writer and philosopher William Irwin Thompson adds a crucial point: "All the modern schools of thought are the equivalents of variations of a myth, and all must be taken into account." Thompson thinks that any discussion of a myth (including Lévi-Strauss's and his own thoughts about such discussions) is also a variant of the myth. He believes that our attempts to know and understand archetypes act as a kind of umbrella, a meta-myth, gently subsuming all our efforts to be objective, to be outside the myth we study. Instead of wrangling over which version of human history is true, we can see that the most dependable human truth is the endless variations of truth humans tell one another. We can't really distinguish a myth from how we feel about it, talk about it, explain it to ourselves, and so cannot always know what is myth and what is not.

One of the most fundamental and profound myths of modern life is that of family. The modern struggle over what constitutes "the family" is more than a sign of a heterogeneous and changing world. It's a sign of how continually changing what we call family is and always has been.

What we now call a nuclear family is sometimes called a conjugal family in historical contexts—legal units based in heterosexual union and the rearing of children. It is most important to keep in mind when statistics are used to describe families that only such units are legally recognized as marriage; that is not to say that they are the only marriages around. Such families constituted only about half of all families in 1970. More than a century earlier, in 1850, they also constituted about half of all families.

In 1850, the Census Office defined a family as people who live together. The number of families hasn't changed in 150 years partly because the definition of family did change. Census policy in 1850 was absurdly broad: "A widow living alone and separately providing for herself, or 200 individuals living together . . . should each be numbered as one family. The resident inmates of a hotel, jail, garrison, hospital, an asylum . . . should be reckoned as one family . . . All landlords, jailers, superintenders of poorhouses . . . [etc.] are to be considered as heads of their respective families." As late as 1940, the Census Bureau still included servants and lodgers in its count of private family members.

Several things happened with this definition, and they all served to feed the emerging myth that small nuclear families are normal and natural. Many individuals supporting themselves (like servants) disappear from sight because they are absorbed under the wing of another wage earner. But people who *don't* support themselves disappear, too. People being supported by the state, for whatever reason, are almost invisible, and so the amount of welfare provided is greatly diminished to view.

Another effect is that the status of both men and women is misconstrued. The social researcher Nancy Folbre compared local records of two Massachusetts towns in 1880, looking for evidence of where adults lived. In one town about 28 percent of the single adult women lived as boarders or servants. In a nearby town, about 34.5 percent of single women lived either alone, as above, or in households without a male head. In both towns the official local census subsumed most of these women into family groupings headed by men—their landlords and bosses. Men appeared to be supporting more people, and especially more women, than they really did, and women appeared not to support themselves much at all. In a society where independent women aren't counted, any visibly independent woman appears to be aberrant. (A third of the single women in an 1850 town self-supporting? How could this be? Our first reaction is to question the facts.)

In 1910, the U.S. Bureau of Labor officially used the term "women adrift" to refer to women who supported themselves. This term was applied even to separated married women who supported children. Fourteen percent of all women fit this category of deviance, which begs the question of deviance. By 1950, the census enumerators were instructed to count as the head of the household whosoever declared himself or herself to be so, with one exception—married women living with their husbands. In that case, according to the census takers' instructions, even if the woman said she was the head of household, "such families are edited to show the husband as the head." So an invalid man becomes a provider, and a self-supporting woman becomes a dependent. (In fact, until 1980, the husband was always considered the householder among couples.)

Laws and social policies, as well as the somewhat softer persuasions of advertising and the media, are designed with the defined norms in mind, whether the norms are true or not. This repeated invocation of *normal* as though it were a definable quality eventually works its will on conventional wisdom. The aberrant remain outside, objects of suspicion. Many or few, they will not be given room.

In the United States Census today, distinctions are made between "households" and "families," and the term "family" is now applied to a variety of groups. A "household" is simply the people who occupy a housing unit. A "family" is a group of two or more people related legally in some way—by marriage, adoption, or birth. About 70 percent of the households in the United States are "families," but only about a third of the "families" are married couples with children. The rest are childless couples, extended families, and single-parent families.

The other 30 percent of the population are people living alone or living in families not legally recognized as such, like homosexual couples and communal friendship groups. Of course, a lot of this latter category *are* families in every social sense of the word, but they fall outside most "family" statistics and therefore often are left out of any conversation about what families *are*, what they look like, how they work.

The census misinformation has been somewhat corrected in recent years by more accurate definitions, less fiddling behind the scenes. But the results still have been put to use in interesting ways. When it comes to the structure of the family, there seems to be no such thing as neutral information. That the past was not what we think it is, that the present is not as new as it seems, might be used to teach us how to read history accurately. But the opposite occurs. Census statistics are now frequently used as evidence of a radical change in our current social makeup, without reference to the definitions used, the endless meddling with the results.

The historian T. J. Jackson Lears sees the late nineteenth century as a time of psychological fragmentation, a time of change so rapid it was a kind of existential threat to identity. Lears notes how important it had been in the 1800s to cultivate a certain asceticism in the midst of plenty. The control of one's appetites in every way was considered an essential mark of civility. This changed in the latter part of that century, in part because mysticism gave way to a vague sense of individuation and self-sacrifice was traded for a concern with health. "The quest for health," writes Lears, "was becoming an entirely secular and self-referential project, rooted in peculiarly modern emotional needs—above all the need to renew a sense of selfhood that had grown fragmented, diffuse, and somehow 'unreal.'"

Lears calls this the "therapeutic ethos," a product of the unnatural marriage between advertising and mores. This ethos created a kind of moral pressure on the body—all bodies, individual and communal. Early advertising sold products, but quickly the focus shifted from the product to the product's user. Lears believes this philosophy was less conscious than not, as the copywriters themselves were at the mercy of large social forces. Either way, as deliberate manipulation or as a cultural side-effect, modern advertising helped to create an atmosphere of personalized hopes and fears connected directly to what one bought, used, and owned. Modern advertisers told the consumer quite bluntly that "social ostracism and shame were the prices for failure to use the product," in the words of another historian. Women in particular were responsible for what the family bought and therefore for their husbands' success, their children's social status, reflected in everything from laxatives and suits to breakfast cereal and drapes. In 1912, the *Good*

Housekeeping Seal of Approval appeared, a manifest sign of the benign, almost parental corporation. Every problem had a solution, and every solution was a product.

Advertising began also to speak to inarticulate longings and inner hungers. Consumption ceased to be a simple matter of survival or status, and gradually took on a meaning relevant to individual identity. That identity was, primarily, that of a consumer— a consumer among consumers, a member of a vast and growing community based on consuming, without end.

I read in current social criticism a bemoaning of the "new" emphasis on consumption as a source of self-esteem and identity. I read about the prevalence of violence, the breakdown of marriages, child abuse, the random assault of the media on our bodies, minds, and hopes. These forces and this criticism are not new. The turn of the century was a time of great uncertainty with high rates of domestic violence, separation, and divorce, as well as extensive poverty and random violent crime. Material consumption was both blamed as cause and (more often) turned to as antidote, just as now.

It was at the turn of the century that people began to complain about what we call information overload. They felt terrible pressure—too much work, too much to do, too many expectations and demands. People were overwhelmed by the continual buzz of possibility—this new product, that new trend. Social change was rapidly decreasing the physical contact people had with the raw stuff of their own lives, as well as with each other. Urban growth isolated people even as they crowded into noisier, smaller homes. Solitude was gone, to be replaced by loneliness. A new medical condition appeared—neurasthenia, a deep and apparently meaningless depression quite like the modern epidemic of sorrow we see today.

Nostalgia for a simpler, happier past filled magazines. *The Party Book*, published during the Depression, offers elaborately detailed instructions on how to put on a "Dude Ranch Rodeo"—"Put on your Levis—blue denim overalls will do, wear a plaid shirt and a bandanna neckerchief; and join the cowboys in this rootin', tootin' rodeo"—and how to host a "County Fair" at "Hickville Corners"— "Admission: Restricted to Country Bumpkins."

THE CENTRAL MODERN ARCHETYPE OF FAMILY is not only conjugal but nuclear—that is, reduced to the smallest number of components: male breadwinner, female homemaker, children cared for by mother. I think most of us accept this form of family as a historical truth, even if we don't, can't, live this way. Conservative Christian discussions of family utterly rely on this belief and go a step further, declaring the nuclear family to be the most "natural" human group. (The nuclear family can't be "under attack" or "endangered" if it never existed as more than a blip on humanity's radar screen; therefore, it must be a historical truth.) Whether we like it or not, whether we choose to live in such a struc- ture or not, we tend to assume that differences from this form are differences from tradition. However subconsciously, we look at other forms of family as variants—myth variants—and the nuclear structure as the core "truth" from which these forms vary.

In fact, the nuclear family is not only new but rare and strange. Far from natural, it is a radical departure from tradition and cer- tainly from the natural groupings human societies tend to form. Families have long been sprawling and evolving things, with both adults and children coming and going and returning, with shelter built and food raised by all, wages earned by none or many as the opportunity arose, household chores (including those involving food) divided among every member in complex, if ritual, ways. Though division of domestic chores by gender is quite old and surprisingly consistent in many distinct ways between cultures otherwise widely separated in space and time, domestic chores have always been shared. What is most peculiarly modern is the isolation and solitude of the homemaker, the separation of partners for most of their working hours, the separation of children from their parents, and the separation of adults from the results of their labor. That a man would leave the home for most of the daylight hours to work on something other than his immediate livelihood is unusual. That a woman would stay home for the same hours, alone, is unusual. Human history is one of working together. Formally separated economic spheres for men and women is a product of capitalism, an industrial idea, one of the most modern ideas of all.

Families, all kinds of families, began changing in the 1800s in ways as subtle, distant, intimate, and far-reaching as the ways the tin can and the refrigerated rail car changed the way we eat. As Americans became gradually more urban and drawn to jobs away from the homestead, their domestic roles changed. Instead of raising their own food and building their own homes, men were leaving to work—first in small shops and then in large factories, farther from home, requiring longer hours away. (One of the first casualties was the leisurely midday dinner.) Servants were harder to find and the cost of living was climbing, so fewer families could afford to hire help and others couldn't find any. Men's lives became regimented by clocks and workplace rules; women's by isolation and loneliness.

Men went elsewhere for work, and there (wherever there was) labored on an increasingly unseen product. Instead of growing or making something by hand, or simply working with raw material, men worked in mills and factories, processing the raw materials that other people grew or made (fewer and fewer people, as automation took over). These raw materials simply came from another, unseen elsewhere. More and more men learned paper trading—how to inventory and categorize the raw ingredients as symbols and numbers in a repeated set of clerical tasks. They created advertising, sold the ads and the products, and did it all at an increasing distance—importing and exporting invisible products made ever farther away in larger and larger quantities.

The nuclear family that gradually emerged in twentieth-century America is not, even today, the dominant family structure anywhere on the planet. It is an artificial construction, the result of narrowed options, social and economic pressures, rapid urbanization. (So is the growing number of people who live alone.) Like all artificial constructs, the nuclear family is probably doomed in time. But meanwhile, dominance by number doesn't matter so much as the perception of dominance. Another subconscious assumption is that the nuclear family is intrinsically European, northern, and white. More white people do live in simple nuclear families than do people of African, Hispanic, Asian, or aboriginal heritage, but more to the point, the mythic image itself is white. What such families are is *visible*. They are the dominant *myth* of family and as such are readily noticed and rewarded. From television commercials to tax deductions, the nuclear family is given an undue portion of what we might call sociopolitical weight. Such rewards increase the visibility of these families even more, further fueling their place in our unconscious as the only "true" kind of family. Everything from government policy to who cooks supper falls from that belief.

Along with information overload, people at the turn of the century began to express feelings of "unreality," and these feelings were immediately and powerfully reinforced by moral and intellectual leaders. Dissatisfaction had once had both philosophical and spiritual meaning—a matter of the spirit, the soul, a problem in one's relationship to the world as a cosmos and a place of mysterious and sometimes hidden meaning. The rise of advertising coupled with the disappearance of a local economic culture created a world based in well-being rather than being itself. But both metaphysical and social character as the mark of the well-lived life was doomed—to be "real" meant feeling good about oneself. (Today we call it self-esteem.) Dissatisfaction now has more material and economic meaning than spiritual, and to the extent that people experience malaise and depression, the cure has long been a material one. "If you sold your soul in the eighties," reads a new Volkswagen ad, "now's your chance to buy it back."

Advertising paid less and less attention to class differences, ignoring ethnicity, treating all women as one, all businessmen as one. Lears calls the world since the 1920s one of "other-directed anxieties." "The most comfortable people were also the most anxious." What we call the self now is largely a construct based in the opinions of others, in turn based on one's abilities to mingle, converse, and behave. The measure is external, shifting, and dependent on much we cannot see. It's no coincidence that as this developed, the idea that one should look younger than one's age suddenly marked not only advertising but all media. The worship of youth is by nature an impossible goal, an ever-vanishing hope, and thus a perfect foundation for a consumer economy. The corpulent belly of the successful businessman (once called a "corporation") gave way to slim hips and padded shoulders. The big-busted, bustled woman gave way to the flapper girl. "The body when sighted in its essence was now an articulated spine and a line of travel," writes Hillel Schwartz of the period. Hats were slicker, hair was sleeker, men shaved their faces and looked to the future while trying to look like their own past ideal selves.

Mass production of homes, tract housing, and the early version of suburbs began in the 1920s in earnest. Houses grew smaller and closer together, but the people in them grew more isolated from one another. The amount of duplication in each person's life multiplied. By the Depression, another reversal had taken place. Whereas only a few generations before, larger households were often wealthy households, by the 1930s, the fragmentation of families was so widespread that the more wealthy households had fewer people. This trend continues today, when almost a third of all households consist of a single person—many of them poor, to be sure, but many of them individuals leading lives marked by the conspicuous consumption of resources, space, and power. Such consumption is clearly marked off specifically for those with the wealth to appreciate it. In perfect contradiction, the large family is considered anachronistic, a bit slovenly, a sign of a lack of ambition.

By the 1950s, after my mother got married, the American family had turned into a strange organism, disconnected and reconnected in brand-new ways. The sphere in which she dwelled, what one sociologist called a "predictable, orderly, and settled" role, didn't translate into anything like happiness. I'm not sure it was supposed to do that. Reading her life, which is part of what I have to do in order to read my own, means reading her conflicts in a contra-dictory world, a place of grim cheer and empty promise.

In the late 1970s, after we kids were all grown, she won a short cruise to Mexico on a Princess ship in a supermarket contest. She reminisced about it for the rest of her life—the pampering, the attention, the small kindnesses of the crew who treated her better than I suspect anyone had treated her since she was a little girl. I like to imagine her now, widowed instead of widowing, lounging in a chaise on a beach conveniently near the outdoor café, with a pile of thrillers beside her in the sun. That's her heaven.

I hold my mother's life in one hand and my own in the other, and even now hers seems orderly and transparent in a way mine is not and never has been. My life instead is spacious and mobile, unpredictable, built on shifting sands. She was held in place, leashed down—I strain to throw out anchors in the shouting wind. We were so far apart, so much alike, becoming women and mothers in such different worlds, but I think with not such different pain in that becoming.

5

THE SHIFT FROM WHOLE GRAINS TO milled white flour seems a small thing at first, though it was certainly a stunning victory for the mills. But in such things are our lives made. The transition to white flour was a "crucial transition" for women, in Ruth Cowan's words. White flour couldn't be made into the kind of quick breads traditionally served at most meals. Wheat generally requires much more elaborate methods of preparation and far more time for rising, kneading, and baking. (Waverley Root mentions an "ordinary" cake recipe calling for twenty eggs "as part of the batter which the cook was instructed to beat vigorously for three hours.")

White flour doesn't rise as easily as whole wheat flour, so a little sugar has to be added to bread to encourage the rise. Sugar has the additional effect of increasing both the lightness and puffiness of bread. Commercial bakers began promoting their breads this way—lighter, airier, easier to digest than heavy homemade bread.

The marketing departments of the mills promoted whiteness and they also promoted fluffier cakes and lighter breads. Lightness, softness, whiteness—these were described as the sophisticated, civilized qualities, the modern way to eat, precisely because it was farther from the soil, from the labor of the poor, from the earth.

What had been a treat at Christmas quickly became a daily expectation. Fluffy, white breads and elaborate cakes quickly became a sign of middle-class status, a symbol of the movement away from the self-sufficient household of shared labor into the shining future of the lone housewife. One of the first Betty Crocker publications was a popular leaflet describing in detail what a perfect loaf of bread should look, taste, and feel like. It was thought that "housewives would welcome the chance to measure the product of their own ovens against an absolute standard."

Today, the chlorine used in bleaching flour improves the "baking performance" (in the words of General Mills) by making it easier for the grain to swell—that is, puff up. Some flour is also *matured* with products like ascorbic acid and potassium bromate to, as an industry source puts it, strengthen the "dough forming properties of the flour, thus improving gas retention of the gluten." What that means is finer, lighter, puffier loaves and "improved external characteristics"—precisely the selling points of white breads and cakes.

Until the late 1800s, the middle class typically baked its own white bread and looked down on bakery bread as being inferior. This transformed when the lightest, fluffiest, whitest bread became the fad. In the course of a few decades, poor people who had had to buy commercial bread because they had no ovens or kitchen utensils had to find a way to bake their own because bakery prices had climbed beyond their means. As prices rose, women who had taken pride in doing their own baking felt more pride in being able to afford an obviously ready-made loaf, a loaf that met an absolute standard.

Of Bisquick, James Gray wrote in 1954, "It is probably as difficult for the modern woman to conceive of the rudimentary demands that were made on the creativity of the cook twenty years ago, as it would be for modern man to conceive of what the problem of transportation would be if he had first to invent and construct the wheel." It has taken me to my own middle age to realize that the cake I hold in my dreams, the pretty layer cakes Mom was supposed to make and didn't, disappointing me, were a kind of corporate symbol. I pulled the image out of Betty Crocker, after all, delicately woven stock-in-trade for an international conglomerate intent on the hundred-ton weight.

PIERRE BOURDIEU, IN *DISTINCTION,* HIS RE-markable study of French class differences, makes a significant point about the value of women's work. Women's labor, says Bourdieu, is always considered more valuable to the higher classes. Upper-class women are better educated, more likely to bring in a real income or support their husbands' incomes. He contends this is one reason why the upper classes eat simpler food at home than the lower classes, and dine out frequently. The long-simmering pot is too much trouble for a woman who can earn more, be worth more, somewhere other than the kitchen. The upper-class woman saves demanding dishes for special meals—the events that prosperous women know how to orchestrate, events often designed to further the family's economic rather than domestic prospects. A slow-cooked meal isn't so costly to the poor, because the poor woman's labor isn't going anywhere. He adds, almost as an aside, "a woman entirely devoted to housework is called 'pot-au-feu.' "

In 1870, more than half of all employed women were in domestic service. Fifty years later, that number had dropped to one in five. Everything from the expanding frontier to war had changed the servant class. More and sometimes better-paying opportunities appeared, including the possibility of leaving the peculiarly bound class of domestic servants altogether. Servants were, more than most people in America, consigned to a "distinction" difficult or impossible to shed until the twentieth century, when the middle class appeared. And that middle was available only to those with both the wages and the status of a job in the market economy. Cookbooks started including recipes and entertainment advice for the presumably bewildered woman who found herself in charge of a "maidless home." In 1932, a cookbook was published called *The Worldly Modern Cook Book for the Busy Woman*.

The loss of servants was a boon to the manufacturers of household gadgets. They saw profit in women's dread of housework, and from its early days, the appliance industry promised to free harried women from their drudgery. Adrian Forty calls it an "absurd and impossible idea" that using labor-saving devices meant less labor, but it was an idea that was nevertheless widely believed. What labor-saving appliances really meant was *More Work for Mother*, the title of Ruth Schwartz Cowan's harrowing study of the housewife. Even wealthy women worked more in their own homes after appliances "replaced" domestic help.

So-called labor-saving devices replaced a small portion of the labor of men who had left the home to work elsewhere, and the labor of children freed from such chores in the name of education and self-realization. The remainder of that household labor was given to the woman who had previously shared and supervised it. Cowan concluded that in the early twentieth century, women in the same class as their mothers not only did the same amount of domestic work as their mothers had but they also did almost all the work now-absent servants had done to help their mothers.

There "emerged the idea of housework as 'different' work," wrote one historian, "labor that did not require any financial reward because of the returns of emotional fulfillment it brought." A social critic writes that "the nurturing of husbands and fathers only came to be recognized when expressed in a paycheck. At the same time, the labor of wives and mothers came not to be recognized at all. It was relabeled as love . . ." As more and more women became this new thing, this housewife, cleaning house and cooking meals began to take on the vague qualities of virtue. Housework was alternately described in advertising and women's magazines as self-fulfillment, the nourishment of others, a peculiarly female craft, even a profession—albeit one without visible compensation.

By the 1930s, the home was a "national asset," according to Adrian Forty in his history of home decoration. People weren't expected to like their jobs, and home was the refuge from a difficult world of work, a world often requiring shadowy and dubious behavior. It was up to women to create the refuge; this was their spiritual expression, their duty. "While for men the ideal American home is a haven from work, for women it is defined as a site for labor," writes Ellen Lupton, a historian of American home design.

That labor was good citizenship. A strong nation required harmony and morality at home, and this was a woman's responsibility.

The political sphere stood ready to identify problems, the scientific sphere stood ready to solve them, and the industrial sphere stood ready to make the products that would carry out the solutions. All women had to do was buy and use the products.

Advertising cheerfully noted that a woman's work was never done—and added as a subtext that it could never, should never, be done. Betty Crocker dedicated her first cookbook "to homemakers everywhere—to all of you who like to minister to your dear ones by serving them good food." To "minister" to those one loved was a work infinite in scope; you could never minister enough. "Let your head save your heels," counseled Betty Crocker. "Minutes saved can easily grow into the extra hour or two a day so many busy women want and need . . ." Hours they want and need in order to finish the unending tasks before them, the task of household ministry.

This belief sounds both quaint and cruel today—though we still act upon it, still believe it and suffer in response just as our mothers and grandmothers did. It seeped into a million images, a million words, until a lot of people believed it. In the 1960 volume *American Cooking*, part of the *Time-Life Foods of the World* series, Dale Brown wrote, "American women may have actually preferred to work unaided. They were motivated by love of their families, and they cooked and cleaned with a devotion no servant could ever have mastered."

I think my mother was haunted by this feeling all her life. She hated to clean house almost as much as she hated to cook. For several years when I was in elementary school, she tried hiring housekeepers to come in once a week. She could barely afford them, and I think they represented both a distant ideal of real leisure time and her own naughty predilection to do anything but housewifely duties. None of them stayed with us long. In her guilty desire, she was a dream employer. One housekeeper after the other stole from her purse and nipped at my father's whiskey. She never complained, only quietly let them go and picked up the vacuum again. Her mixture of pride at being able to afford help and her shame at needing it was like a traffic accident seen coming from a long way off, and in that she was a perfect product of her time.

Such brilliant doublespeak. The adman first assured the housewife that her work wasn't really work but something more mystical and emotive than that. Then he assured her that with the right products she would hardly have to work at all. Next, he added that while she was, naturally, budget-conscious, she wasn't in any way *poor*—not the way women without servants used to be. Besides, if she bought the proffered gadget, it would save her money in the end by saving her time. (Thus it turned out that a woman's time magically *was* money, as long as she remained in the domestic sphere.)

Most important was to disguise the truth about the products themselves. The continual use of words like *freedom* and *leisure* to sell appliances was part of this. The oven cooked the meals, the vacuum cleaners swept the floors, the washing machine did the laundry, the sewing machine made the clothes—while a smiling woman hovered nearby. Advertisements for appliances promising only "minutes of work" and the "freedom" to "do what you want to do" read today like a kind of magical thinking, rather naïve—except that they were shockingly successful and we all buy products today with the same kind of ritual hope.

One reason middle-class women began working harder than poorer women of previous generations had was that standards climbed in exact proportion to the number of promises of freedom from work. Just as the cast-iron stove rapidly led to a demand for more elaborate meals, new housecleaning tools simply meant higher standards of cleanliness—whiter sheets, tidier bathrooms, shinier floors, all "spotlessly clean" and free of germs. What had happened with bread and cake happened with clothing, cleaning, laundry, child care, sewing, and entertainment.

The cultural propaganda required to sell people on their rapidly changing lives and call it progress was almost religious in its emotion, its wordy, confounding claims. Early advertising worked in the realm where wishes are horses and beggars all ride. Ellen Lupton borrows the Marxist use of the word *fetish* to describe the selling of appliances: "The object becomes a fetish as its functional aspects give way to psychological incentives. The inanimate object speaks through advertising . . . each [object] can become the target of desire, invested with intense emotional significance." The object and the woman who wielded it gradually became one in the cultural mind, inseparable.

A HALLMARK OF MODERN LIFE IS THE SIG-nificant change in each person's fund of information—the skills, craft, knowledge, and experience adults slowly accumulate in the course of their daily lives. Not that long ago, most people learned over the course of their young years a great deal of practical information needed for basic physical survival simply by imitation and observation, and they mastered these skills by working side by side with their parents and neighbors.

As houses grew smaller, the functions of the house were separated into different rooms. As each family unit shrank and pulled away from other units, each individual in the family became more dependent on a faceless system—first local, then regional, then a nationwide web of production and transportation so large no person can manage or even understand it. For a century, most Americans have relied on corporate utilities, multinational farms, and international transportation networks for their welfare instead of their own experience and skill. Freed from the tyranny of child labor, granted years of formal education, we glean our view of the world from books and magazines and various screens at least as much as from interaction and observation. The fund of information most adults hold now is like none before—we know a lot about things inconsequential and distant, almost nothing of our surroundings. Very little of it is relevant to basic needs. I am not as surprised as I would like to be to discover that good friends of mine, professionals in their forties, do not know how to make a pot of rice. Most Americans, left alone, would not know how to survive even a few days on their own merits.

As social relations separated and the nuclear family became the norm, there was no longer anyone to ask for help when help was needed. The aunts, grandparents, older siblings, and friendly neighbors were lost to their own shrinking family units. Women no longer lived intimately near their own mothers and grandmothers after marriage. To make the home they were told to make, they had to rely on books, like *The Bride's Cook Book* from 1917, with its elaborate directions for cleaning, of which this is only a brief excerpt:

Do not put knife-handles in water. Water discolors and cracks ivory and bone handles, and may loosen wooden ones. After washing knives, scour them with bath brick. Do not wash bread-board

or rolling-pin at an iron sink. The iron will leave marks on them.
Wash them at the table. Be careful not to wet the cogs of a Dover
egg-beater. Wash the lower part, and wipe off the handles with a
damp cloth. Water washes the oil from the cogs, making the beater
hard to turn. Dry the seams of a double-boiler carefully. Do not
waste time polishing tins. It is sufficient to have them clean and
dry. Dip glasses into hot water, so that they will be wet inside and
outside at the same time. Silver and glass are brightest if wiped
directly from clean, hot suds, without being rinsed. A damp towel
makes dull spoons and glasses . . .

Advertising was the most important teacher, sometimes
instructing with only pictures — subversive and demanding images
of a home life and family sphere not quite possible but beckoning,
expectant — and somehow entirely a woman's responsibility. But
other experts appeared — experts in cooking, child rearing, nutrition, ethical education, efficiency — teaching in books, lectures,
and classes. Especially books, and especially cookbooks.

The Joy of Cooking, published in its large version for the first time
in 1943, succeeded because it took to heart this bewildering combination of needs. Irma Rombauer wrote a conversational and user-
friendly cookbook of considerable breadth. *Joy* promoted no
products and wasn't sponsored by a company — in fact, Rombauer
gently opposed the use of many convenience foods, such as cake
mixes, on the grounds that the results of scratch cooking were so
much better and cooking itself so much easier than people presumed. And all this was said without condescension in Rombauer's
light and pleasant voice, a voice that seems both casual and experienced — a voice I've heard whispering to me for as long as I've been

cooking on my own. Yet Rombauer also managed to convey to the reader that the authors once knew nothing about cooking and had had their share of kitchen disasters—which was quite true. A vital part of Irma Rombauer's breezy style came from her own rather breezy ways. She was of a generation of women who did not learn to cook at mother's knee, and those were the women to whom she wrote, embracing shortcuts, raiding church-supper and service-club recipe booklets, and freely asking for advice.

Some feminists attacked processed foods in the 1970s on the grounds that they eliminated the need to cook from scratch, thus degrading a vital female chain of knowledge and skill. The question flipped back and forth: Did processed foods help free women from the drudgery of cooking, allow them to enter the marketplace and the culture in a new way? Or did they denigrate one of the greatest provinces of female culture? And in both ways the question was a red herring, a distraction, because in both ways it presumed that women would continue to be the cooks of the world, one way or the other.

Dale Brown thought that a pioneer woman who had to work with her own raw ingredients was "less a cook than a processor of foodstuffs," tied to her pantry and the cow. He claimed that only the revolution in convenience foods and appliances could make women true masters of the art. "Behind this culinary revolution modestly stands the American woman. She helped launch it when she began to protest her domestic servitude a century ago, and her battle-ground became the kitchen. All the labor-saving devices (and labor-saving foods) she uses there today, all the fine cookbooks she owns, she more than deserves." Brown neatly tied together two seemingly incompatible beliefs about the housewife: that she is a modern woman who partakes of all that science can offer in order to do her job as efficiently as possible, and that she is a nurturing, maternal symbol of the hearth. After praising her "protest" of "domestic servitude," Brown adds: "Not one to rest on her laurels, she is busily applying much of the time and energy she has thus gained to improving her cooking . . ." I was three years old when Brown wrote that, and my mother was going slowly batty chasing three tiny children around a small house, longing to go back to her career.

The domestic sphere had come to represent more than it had before precisely because women began to leave it behind to work. The threat of women abandoning the hearth seemed quite real to many people in the early twentieth century, and within a few decades, two messages murmured ceaselessly in women's ears. One was the importance of her nurturing role. The other was the promise that she could "save her labor" with the right appliance, that she could do the housework, love her family, and still lead a life of bridge parties and craft projects.

As the roles of women in the home changed, the home itself changed—and which was cause, which effect, isn't always clear. At the turn of the century, the kitchen became a "brisk machine shop," a "spartan laboratory," writes Hillel Schwartz. A short time later, the clunky icebox became a shiny, white refrigerator, slumped into curves, sleek and smooth—"the physical embodiment of health and purity," in Adrian Forty's words. It was, of course, white—if you have ever cursed the whiteness of the refrigerator because it shows every stain and fingerprint, bear in mind that this is exactly *why* it is white.

"The modern kitchen," wrote Ellen Lupton in her design study called *The Bathroom, the Kitchen, and the Aesthetics of Waste: A Process of*

Elimination, "reflected the production ideal of the modern factory, whose linear sequence of work stations enabled an unbroken flow of activity. This norm, which we call the *continuous kitchen,*" was a product of a "flexible but rule-bound grammar" involving corporate utilities, suburban architecture, marketing, and food industrialization. This meant built-in, fixed appliances, unbroken and nonporous surfaces, lots of shine, and little additions like splashbacks and other soft seams designed to hide holes and cracks. "Today Kitchens Come Packaged: It's flexible and expandable . . . pre-wired, pre-plumbed, pre-lighted, and pre-ventilated. Appliances and cabinets blend to give the much-wanted 'built-in' look." The entire layout was supposed to eliminate extra steps, which meant recasting the experience of cooking entirely—into "maximum convenience in minimum space."

"This smart new General Electric Refrigerator-Freezer with its trim new 'Straight-Line' look was designed for beauty—and convenience. Not a hinge or handle protrudes to mar its smooth, straight lines. Sides, top, and back are all *flat and straight*. That's why you can set it flush against the wall in line with your other appliances . . ." *Streamlining* was a new word, taken from hydrodynamics. It is a word that rapidly came to have not only aesthetic but moral meaning, to imply in objects qualities previously reserved for human beings: courage, will, strength. Streamlining was supposed to promote speed, efficiency, and hygiene. "The modern concept of Frigidaire 'Sheer Look' design eliminates space-wasting bulges, meaningless curves and dust-trap gaps . . . straight, clean and square." "There's hardly a seam . . . hardly a place where dust can hide."

Lupton confronts the anal, controlling nature of this shift and the way large corporate points of view are contained in small, private spaces. Streamlining expressed, she writes, "the new ideal of the object as a continuous, organic body, its moving parts hidden behind a seamless shell, appearing to be molded out of a single piece of material." A new ideal, indeed. A friend of mine, Connie McDowell, wrote me a note when she learned I was writing this book: "You must mention the aspic and gelatin phenomenon. In the 50s, neither our molded salads nor our breasts could jiggle. Firmness in salads on our tables as well as firm body lines under tormenting undergarments ruled the day. No wonder the 60s happened."

By the 1950s, kitchens had evolved into extraordinary expressions of conformity, with millions of kitchens in new homes limited to a few designs dictated by industry. Their flat surfaces and open spaces, the fitted appliances and carefully seamless corners were fixed, as though in time. "While housewives had long been accustomed to the world as a rich, messy space of spontaneous eruptions, plentiful attachments and supervening bodies," says Hillel Schwartz of the early 1900s, "home economists urged a clean, lean, purposeful flow." The "messy space" was gone, wiped clean inside and out. Countertops were all one height, so the cook could no longer work sitting down. Corner cabinets appeared, difficult to use, so that food and tools had to be stored near the floor or out of reach. There was to be no "wasted" space even in the midst of flagrantly ambitious consumption. Wasted space took on the same moral quality as a wasted life.

Women worked harder than ever in the home as the century wore on, but produced less and less. The basic, local foods cooks had once used, the raw, living, unmilled and unchurned and uncut food, required something from almost every member of the family. But then mealmaking ceased to be cooperative, and women cooked alone. The meal itself gradually became ready-made, and the cook merely a package-opener, a heater, a server. In the world of the housewife, cooking meals is one of her only productive acts. Her true place in the economy is as a consumer. She sends her husband off to his work, drives to the store to buy canned food, heats up the contents with electricity from a distant source, and serves it to him when he comes home from his job at the cannery or power plant. She mediates and redirects, the switchboard of capitalism.

From the turn of this century, food and cooking took on an ever deeper metaphoric meaning. Eating is the final act of consumption in the consumer's life. But more than that, our consumption of the products involved is a kind of *eating up* of the economic web we're in. Partake of abundance or betray the culture of abundance. The housewife, more than anyone, is the one whose duty is to endlessly digest and replenish supplies, to be a mouth to the world of anonymous, endless production.

FOR ALL THE TIME MY MOTHER SPENT IN THE kitchen, I learned very little about cooking when I was a girl. Mom preferred to do it herself; I only realized after I had children that this was the only time in her day when she was alone. But there was very little to learn in the bountiful world of convenience. Still lots to do, but not much to learn—here was the can opener, there the freezer. I learned to make snickerdoodles for Christmas, toasted cheese sandwiches, how to frost the cake-mix cake with the frosting-mix frosting. I liked baking most of all, because the electric beater was usually involved and so it felt, somehow, like cooking.

What I learned and what I *thought* about cooking were different things. What I thought came from hours of perusing the first edition of *Betty Crocker's Picture Cook Book*.

In 1921, the Washburn Crosby Company, a milling concern that was to become the core of General Mills, ran a puzzle contest. To the marketing department's vast surprise, they received more than 30,000 responses, and among them, many hundreds of cooking questions. Here were more than 30,000 women who must have represented many thousands more women, and they were asking questions that made it plain they'd never learned basic cooking techniques. They lived away from their mothers and sisters and grandmothers and had no one but a faceless brand name to turn to for help. Here was a marketing possibility the likes of which businessmen had only dreamed of before.

In a conference between the marketing and advertising departments, it was felt that such questions must certainly be answered, and if possible, the answers should come from a woman. Not a real woman, mind you—just another image of woman. Thus was born Betty Crocker, "a high priestess who presides over a cult of excellence," as James Gray described her, "the eternal and supreme housewife."

Betty Crocker was an instant success, quickly developing a literary style and manner, "a Betty Crocker set of values," wrote Gray. "Everyone who used her name was indoctrinated in the Betty Crocker philosophic system, simpler and narrower in range, to be sure, than that of Kant or Kierkegaard, but quite as carefully formulated." The "enclosing philosophy" of Betty Crocker was "that a woman is at her best when she is consciously proud of being a woman, when she realizes that her job has the deepest kind of significance, when she respects her own dependence on a man, knowing that only the magic of her femininity can release her husband's gift of leadership."

Letters, the marketing department eventually decided, weren't enough. They would go to the airwaves. The "Betty Crocker Cooking School of the Air" began in 1924 and lasted for twenty-four years, wildly popular. And that wasn't enough, either. Betty Crocker needed to test the recipes she shared, needed to develop products to meet the needs of the women who wrote and called.

The rationale for the Betty Crocker test kitchens was that the kitchens could "accomplish what it would take generation upon generation of housewives to learn in the old trial-and-error way." (That these might be happy and intimate days with one's older relatives and companions wasn't the point. Americans no longer lived in that kind of world.) Betty Crocker especially offered, without the pressure of appearing to advertise, recipes. She shifted emphasis on ingredients deftly from times of prosperity through the Depression and into the war. She invented the "one-bowl" cake in 1943. By then she had her name on products like presifted flour, she used General Mills products like Bisquick, and she was about to launch her phenomenally successful line of instant cake mixes. Starting in 1954, everything Betty Crocker approved was marked with the red spoon symbol of her approval and confidence. When the war was finally over and the ration books put away, the meat-loving soldiers came home and she finished the cookbook that put all her arts together into one.

The Betty Crocker cookbook became (and in later editions,

remains) one of the best-selling cookbooks of all time. Its recipes are simple and reliable, always carefully tested and worded with encouragement. The book provides instruction in both fundamental cooking techniques and sophisticated refinements. To meet divergent needs, Betty Crocker explained such things as how to crack an egg and peel a potato. She gave some extraordinarily basic directions—"*If you are a Good Mathematician* You May Safely REDUCE RECIPES ('To make half a recipe: Use exactly *one-half the amount of each ingredient*')"—but also described how to put on a formal twelve-course meal, with several pages of advice on silverware and centerpieces.

When I was young, I especially liked the step-by-step instructions, the design of a structured and predictable world. All through the book are queer line drawings of a young woman. She is always stirring and grating and icing; she is always smiling. She wears a dress with a Peter Pan collar and a ruffled apron, and her waist is nipped in tightly like Blondie Bumstead. She is fitted, unfussy, seamless—streamlined. Words hover around her head in cheery typeface as she stirs: "Cook over low heat" and "Boil 1 minute" buzz about her like flies. Page after page has black-and-white photographs of two female hands on a bowl and pan, or knife and spoon, showing how to melt chocolate, dissolve gelatin, make custard, mince an onion, spoon melon balls. How to be happy—how to be sophisticated—so I learned. How to be a woman. How to be.

The big color spreads show platters of cookies and cakes, dripping roasts and salads and formal place settings. These fading color photographs were my first introduction to food styling, to the idea of food as a show, an experience, as *presentation*. They were images of food that had very little to do with what I knew of food, and yet looked strangely familiar—like an old slovenly relative after a glamor makeover.

This, part of me still believes when I read these old books and magazines, look at these fantasy images, *this* is what a kitchen should be, *this* is how a mother should behave; children should smile like *that* as they sit happily down to a dinner table set just that way. I keep this old book out in my kitchen sometimes, and visitors never fail to notice it. "Oh," people say in almost the same words every time, "my mother had that cookbook, too." If I pull it off the shelf and open to a photograph of roasts, cookies, the picnic table, people sigh, first with the pleasure of memory and then with the slight embarrassment of being caught longing for such common things.

Betty Crocker was real to me—is still quite real to a lot of people. But she is a trademark designed with a crafty awareness of where the profits lay and the careful masking of the General Mills juggernaut from which she was born. This most domestic of all American women, this agent of femininity, eventually needed a face, and when she got one it had "features that might be claimed contentedly by various European groups." Betty Crocker was—is—evolving eternally but never really aging, changing with the changing times in the fits and starts of the twentieth century. The original, rather prim, Depression-era portrait of 1936 seemed good enough for nineteen years. But the 1965 painting lasted only three years, and the one after that only a few years more.

The book changed, too, though the people who work at the test kitchens refer to them all as "Big Red." In the second edition of the cookbook, in 1956, the suburban transition has begun, and there is more emphasis on convenience foods, new appliances, and pseudo-ethnic foods like lasagna. The third edition, in 1961, features a cherry pie, a pink cake, cookies, a turkey, and a tiny box of frozen vegetables on the cover. (This is also the only one that isn't red.) By 1969, convenience was key, especially in the use of frozen foods. Betty Crocker acknowledged that many women had entered the workforce, after all (and that was nothing to be ashamed of), and needed to save time at home wherever possible. Presentation, entertainment, formality are set aside. Only the barbecue grill remained for special occasions.

Of course, the central irony is that Betty Crocker was the product of professional women in a powerfully male-dominated world. Her signature, her portrait, her voice on the radio all were provided by working women, women who were emphatically not the women to whom Betty Crocker spoke. Two of her puppeteers—Janette Kelley and especially Marjorie Child Husted—ended up spending most of their successful business careers posing as a mythical housewife. They were the true authors of *Betty Crocker's Picture Cook Book* of 1950. Husted's and Kelley's professional talents were used to convince other women (as many women as possible, in fact) that being a housewife is a career as vital as, and more spiritually significant and personally satisfying than, their own nearly invisible careers in the corporate world could ever hope to be. Husted was reportedly given the company's official blessing to state in public that she *was*, in fact, Betty Crocker, and she did this for twenty years.

Back in the 1950s, the male executives of General Mills were not thrilled with the increasing divergence between Betty Crocker's image and the reality of her creators. The company eventually decided no real woman could possibly embody all the perfections of Betty Crocker—most especially a professional woman. Husted retired in the 1950s, shortly after the cookbook made its successful debut, and Kelley died a few years later. Only historians seem to remember them now. The publicity material routinely sent out in response to requests about Betty Crocker doesn't mention either of them, nor did the big press packet made up in 1996 to celebrate the seventy-fifth anniversary of Betty Crocker's "existence."

I'VE BEEN CONSIDERING MY MOTHER'S AND grandmothers' lives, reading the history of their time, and I still write of it with a sense of dislocation. The radical cultural explanations for the nineteenth-century drama of change is still a surprise. So is the power with which that message was delivered and the willingness with which it was received. Messages about family, gender, cooking, and the house were pronounced with the marching-band rhythm of unquestionable authority. Women who protested or went against the grain were punished in ways similar to the ways women are still punished today if they complain about sexist jokes and offensive stereotypes. Sometimes I read the advertisements and the magazines of the first half of this century and shake my head—it is all so strange to me, so far from my life. Then I am suddenly upside-down, because none of this is far from my life. It marks my life, marks me.

The speed with which people's lives have changed is difficult to fathom. But there was a fairly linear motion at work, a move toward mobility and an expansion at least in what people could see of others' choices, other ways. Then, a halt. The 1950s saw a sharp reverse: Though the number of households made up by families is about the same now as it was 150 years ago, for a brief spurt during the 1950s, that number went way up, until 90 percent of the households in this country looked like families on television. Stephanie Coontz, a long-time student of social mores, calls the sudden emergence of the pure nuclear family a kind of "*experimentation* with the possibilities of a new kind of family," a family with "much more predictable, orderly, and settled" roles in the 1950s than had ever been seen before.

It was an experiment one can easily imagine was rooted in retreat—from too much change, from war, and from a frightening postwar world mocked up as the future everyone desired and no one understood. In 1946, almost a third of all marriages ended in divorce—the war meant a lot of things came unglued. But in the 1950s, the divorce rate plummeted. People started marrying younger, having children younger and closer together. Fewer women attended or finished college. People came to live by the millions in new communities, developments and suburbs and subdivisions without any familiar roots.

In their book on midcentury epicurism, *American Gourmet*, Jane and Michael Stern call the years 1946 to 1971 a time when cookbooks were "brimful of idealism" and gastronomy was a discipline of "excitement, mystique and sheer sensual delight." According to a number of cookbooks, innovation was the rule of the day—new combinations, new conventions, new choices. The war was over, the future was now; according to the Sterns, the "horizon was infinite." Craig Claiborne famously pegs June of 1947 as the beginning of modern cuisine, because that's when Pan Am started round-the-world flights. But the Sterns claim the 1950s were also a time of philosophically broad and psychologically wide horizons.

The Sterns are fond of sweeping generalizations convenient to their theme. The fact is that this time of undeniable expansion and exposure was also—and not coincidentally—a time of extraordinary contraction and retreat as well. One *could* do anything at all, as long as it fell inside the carefully delineated boundaries of social propriety based in the primacy of a particular "American" way of life. These boundaries were beyond question, and transgression was punished harshly. From here, the middle of the century looks like a world of addled tyranny. Thousands of people were flying to Paris and hunting out neighborhood bistros, then coming home to try their hand at brioche mousseline. But millions of people were retreating into ranch houses and shopping malls, and eating from a slim buffet flavored with canned white sauce.

Back from the war, many men wanted food just like Uncle Sam used to make. "Frozen peas, leg of lamb, flank steak, potatoes," says one woman who cooked every day during that time. "A meal consisted of meat, potatoes, vegetables, bread," says another. "Peanut butter on everything—peanut butter on celery, peanut butter on crackers, peanut butter sandwiches." What the Sterns really mean by "infinite" is hamburger stroganoff. Green beans with cream of mushroom soup and Durkee's onion rings. Green Jell-O with cream cheese. Pigs in blankets dipped in cocktail sauce mixed with grape jelly. Women alone, working in isolation. Men just working and working. The postwar cycle of increased economic opportunity meant ever more new products and more pressure to buy them—which meant one needed to work more to get the money to buy them, which increased the need for processed and convenience foods, which were more expensive—and so on in a cycle of men and women working at playing with that all-important "leisure" time in their new free world.

Our lives are not like that, are they? Oh, yes—Ruth Cowan

believes that younger women now have "discovered that they were working even longer hours than *their* mothers had worked, because of the double burden of housework and outside employment." Women in the educated middle class today not only work harder than poorer women of the 1800s, they do some of the work many of those women considered below them—laundry, washing floors, mending, and so on. Unfortunately, those who remain poor today are not saved by the exhaustion and despair of the materially wealthy next door, but there are strange alliances beneath the surface of our divergent lives. These days, only the very wealthiest and the very poorest women can stay home all day—are *homemakers*. Few forced to stay home want to do so; some who must leave would much rather stay. Most women with chidren work double shifts between home and work, caught in a dilemma Stephanie Coontz neatly labels "role strain."

I quit writing this chapter a few hours ago, to cook dinner for my family. I really didn't want to stop writing, but I had said I would cook tonight, and hardly anyone else in my household ever does. Mainly, I cook when I want to cook, but once committed, I also resent the expectation. Part of the strain. After dinner, I left two teenagers in the dirty kitchen and I walked away, but not with an entirely clear mind. Part of me resides there and always will, wanting to be more and less at once—wanting to be what a primitive part of me believes I should be, wanting never to want that again. The difference between my mother and me, perhaps the biggest difference of all, is that I did leave. I have always left—her house and my house, as well as my kitchen, walking, driving, flying away. I don't go without a care, but I go, and she did not.

From my admittedly comfortable vantage point, the housewife

looks like the strangest collision of our century: the inhuman savior
of technology bound painfully to the warm bosom of women, the
central character in a macabre fantasia narrated by the fictional
Betty Crocker. She cooked a kind of nuclear cuisine, this dream cuisine, which "takes only minutes" and "fulfills all your wishes," a "joyous" and "nourishing" cuisine possible only in a carefully constructed
and unreal world.

The differences between that woman and myself look smaller
than they once did to me. I feel that I know her, know her tension—
a tension that is unresolvable, a mix of oil and water. She is keeper
of hearth and home, but the home is prefabricated and the hearth is
automatic. The *housewife* is relationship personified, defined solely
by how she affects objects and other people. But she spends her days
alone. My mother was one of that lucky generation, the first of this
completely modern breed of homemaker, and like the rest she was
expected to embrace both the consumer experience and the nurturing role. Like the women on the new, grainy television shows,
this meant nurturing without effort, but also without end.

While I read Betty Crocker, Mom flipped through *The I Hate to
Cook Book*, first published in 1960. She had small crimes, little rebel-
lions; Peg Bracken was one of them.

"This book is for those of us who want to fold our big dish-
water hands around a dry Martini instead of a wet flounder, come
the end of a long day," writes Bracken at the beginning. She is subversive, acerbic, all chummy with her "girls" this and "girls" that,
"each girl" and "every girl" and no boys allowed because—well,
because that's the way life is. "The average man doesn't care much
for the frozen-food department, nor for the pizza man, nor for the
chicken-pie lady," she writes. "He wants to see you knead that bread

and tote that bale, before you go down cellar to make the soap. This is known as Woman's Burden."

What Bracken offered—what she claimed came to her through bitter experience and the willingness to spend more time avoiding work than working would take—are fast, simple, do-ahead recipes, which might pass for more than they were. ("Sometimes, it is comforting to reflect that you didn't spend a bit more time making it than it took the family to dispose of it.") She calls for gallons of cream of mushroom soup, Parmesan in a can, lots of parsley, dried onion soup mix, cream cheese, and refrigerated biscuit dough. She sprinkles her recipes with the kind of advice every harried cook needs to hear sometimes: "If you don't like this, leave it out," and "Put this in if you have any," and "Serve it on practically anything." She tells her readers that from now on they have permission to "throw leftovers away." This is what my mother liked to read in the kitchen.

Some of these concoctions must be truly awful. They have names like Hurry Curry and Eiffel Trifle (which involves leftover roast beef) and The Solution to Canned Peas and Something Else to Do with New Potatoes Besides Boiling Them and Rolling Them in Melted Butter and Parsley. Her super-fast, last-minute suppers sound like the code words used by addicts: Let 'Er Buck and Speed Balls and Muffinburgers. The book was immensely popular; Connie's husband still asks for Spam Soufflé. It is a funny, sly book, and transparently sad in its description of a world of profound meaninglessness.

More than twenty years later, Bracken wrote in a memoir of her "disillusionment with domesticity . . . I believed when I was first married that the spirit-warming, life-sustaining properties of home-baked cookies and flowers in a blue bowl and fresh curtains blowing in a lilac-scented breeze would all add up to live-happily-ever-after, and then I discovered that somehow they didn't. As millions of women have done before me, I pulled domesticity over my head like a blanket and found I was still cold."

The isolation that is essential to the modern domestic life is sometimes quite terrible. "I was so lonely," my friend Connie tells me after laughing over her recipes. "I had the most immaculate house and I started taking long afternoon naps." Our friend Peggy, who lived as a young doctor's wife on a reservation in Montana in the early 1960s, says, "I was so isolated I bought a floor buffer to have something to do. I read Betty Friedan and thought, 'Oh, God, this is me.' "

I testify to this loneliness, decades later. I've never been a housewife, just a woman with children and a variety of jobs and desires, caged by my own choices as well as the world around me. But I know this. Most American women know, American women have known this now for generations, what it is to spend day after day, week after week—year after year— separated from one another by fences, city blocks, prairie miles. The housewife has only passing relationships with other adults, most of them women in the same situation, marbled with the slim interface of male shopkeepers, the glancing touch of the mailman or the bank clerk. Almost all her social moments are centered around food—gender-split schedules of coffees and luncheons, teas and church suppers, in between the shopping, cooking, and cleaning required for the meals at home.

Recipe pamphlets and service-club newsletters often are so cheerful as to be close to hysteria. There is something frenetic in many of them, a bared-teeth hunger in the murmuring confidences of all the fun and excitement awaiting the lucky woman who can "stay home," who does not "need" to work, who is the Princess, the Queen, of her own happy home. "Harbor pleasant thoughts while working," said Betty Crocker. "It will make every task lighter and pleasanter."

We joke about it now, of course; the imaginary housewife is the stuff of kitsch catalogs and cable channels now. But there was nothing funny about the real lives lived, about the unending days of the Mrs. Bridges and her less prosperous sisters. I haven't needed to live this life in order to be touched by its cool, spreading shadow. The housewife—part *house*, part *wife*—is not supposed to sweat, get sick, get tired, or feel depressed, just as she's not supposed to be too short or too tall or too fat or too thin. She is supposed to fit her house just as the house fits around her.

Her imaginary streamlined behavior has nothing to do with her real life of sticky toddlers and door-to-door salesmen. To be streamlined is to be aerodynamic in the broadest sense of the word; it is to be effortless, to allow the fast-moving world to flow around one. The excellent housewife is herself that "continuous, organic body," her "moving parts hidden behind a seamless shell." Her job is to fuel the body machine.

And so, every day, a lot of women struggle to do as much of the fantasy housewife's duties as they can, gasping for breath between chores. The housewife makes breakfast and lunch and dinner. Several times a week, she buys groceries. Every evening, she does dishes. In between these repeated tasks, she cleans toilets, floors, counters, children's faces, her own smoothly shaved armpits. Day after day after day. Night after night—it goes on and on, new and not so new. In 1900, a home economist, lamenting the sense of "reward" social and industrial changes had taken from the home-maker, wrote, "What is cooked one hour is eaten the next; the clean-ing of one day must be repeated the next, and the hopelessness of it all has sunk into women's souls."

MARTHA STEWART, COOKING ON TELEVISION WITH Julia Child, couldn't stop correcting Julia's work. She quietly picked, picked, picked away at this and that, and Julia Child, in her inimitable, breezy way, just let the criticisms float by.

Julia Child, for all the years of complaints about her technique, has never failed to express her firm belief that good food is part of a well-lived life with rough edges and a few untidy corners. She is a woman of appetite and undenied pleasure. Martha Stewart's vision of a well-lived life has no untidy corners; tidy corners may be her version of heaven. Control, not comfort, is her joy. Julia Child once told a friend she didn't think Martha Stewart would ever be happy.

Stewart has long made the point that everyone can benefit from her advice, be they rich or poor. But improvement is a relative term. Stewart appears to be all flat, reflective surface, but you can read her equally as being all subtext: The medium *is* the message, because the medium is *your life* and the message is appearance. She is pre-sentation as experience, substance as surface, surface *as* substance.

Margaret Talbot, in a trenchant *New Republic* essay a few years ago, points out that Stewart's repeated concern with "quality"—quality of life, table setting, craft project—is precisely and exactly concern with the appearance of those things. For most of us, to talk about the quality of our lives is to speak directly to what lies below the often-flawed exterior. Stewart sees things differently; she seems to believe that if you can just get the surface right, you don't need to worry about what's below.

Her beloved hearth is sanctuary from a cold, hard world, just as the Victorian hearth was meant to be. For this famously difficult and unsympathetic woman, *home* is a word with immense iconic power. Hers is a fantasy hearth from a fantasy yesterday, without any of the concomitant real discomforts of a real yesterday. It's an extremely complicated simplicity and has more in common than a lot of women would like to admit with the half-forgotten Betty Crocker–era housewife who strives to combine the modern and the traditional. (She's calculatedly inclusive of various ethnic and religious traditions—at least in their superficial manifestations. Her holiday instructions regularly intersperse menorahs and Christmas trees, both of which are excellent decorations. But I simply can't imagine Martha Stewart in prayer.)

Savvy tycoon that she is, Martha loves online shopping. (That way, you can stay near the hearth.) We're back to (and perhaps never left) the world where women are most competent in the home because home is where the elusive quality of womanliness most readily shines. A woman's home, at its best, is a small, precious place free of chaos, visible effort, and existential suffering.

Stewart says she wants only to share "the vast amount of experience" she has in hosting and homemaking. (She has more than once complained in interviews about how lazy most people are. Laziness offends her, with its slightly unkempt look of relaxation, that whiff of postcoital satisfaction ignoring the mess the sheets are in.) The very fragility of her brittle smile may be part of her popularity. Women know she's not what she claims to be, that the life

she promulgates is a lie—that, in Talbot's words, she's "not remotely interested in the messy contingencies of family life." So they
can read her as fantasy, as soap opera, as daydream. They appreciate
her laughing all the way to the bank because it implies they might
be able to get away with the same kind of counterstroke. Martha is
the perfect housewife because she's in command of every situation;
her only weakness is that her icy heart sometimes peeks through.

Cooking is all skill, no art, in Martha Stewart's world. Even
describing mashed potatoes, she talks only about their pleasant
aroma, their silky color. Taste isn't the issue. *Food* isn't the issue.
"Martha is a Puritan who prepares 'sinful' foods," wrote Talbot, "that
are redeemed by the prodigious labors" they require to make.
Anyone who has the willpower, time, and dedication to make a
perfect-looking torte certainly has the willpower to skip having a
piece. If we are afraid of following her rich recipes because we might
overindulge, we're already out of her league; Martha herself never
worries about it. She may not know what it's like to worry about
such things, because Martha Stewart will never eat too much or skip
a workout. For her, disheveled indulgence and spontaneous delights
seem as painful and unnatural as constant dieting and exercise are
to others. She surrounds herself not with the satisfying of appetites
as much as the dream of being satisfied.

"We describe her as aspirational," said Marcia Copeland of the
Betty Crocker Kitchens, when I asked her what she thought of
Stewart's universe. "She's for those people who want it all. They
want to have a fantastic home, the great food, the career, they want
everything to be extravagant.

"I have tried to cook from some of her recipes and sometimes they work and sometimes they don't. They sure take more time and energy than most people are willing to put into it." Lazy sods.

COOKING HAS TRADITIONALLY BEEN HELD IN higher acclaim than cleaning. But a chef's work holds far greater acclaim than a cook's. The social distinction between cook and chef is relatively new, dating from the late 1700s. The difference is not so much one of degree but of conception. Chefs are professionally allied to the preparation of food for others, but their role is one of imagination: They plan and create dishes and whole meals, and their skill is characterized by the degree of both daring and consistency with which they do this. Chefs have assistants who learn from them by observation and repetition; the assistants learn this as they shop, chop, and clean up after. Cooks also plan and create dishes and meals—and they shop and chop and clean up after, too. This last necessity undercuts the former skill; cooks do everything by themselves, so are valued less.

Women cook *for* men and *with* each other. In 1950, Betty Crocker called a section of her cookie recipes Beau-Catchers and Husband-Keepers. (The 1999 television campaign for Betty Crocker brand mixes uses seductive, brassy music and the slogan "Betty Knows . . . What Men Want.") The ritual of women cooking for men is deeply embedded. Women cook for men to please them, placate them, nourish them, honor them, seduce them, to earn their protection. In turn, women cooking for men are often bruised—by their inattention, their criticism of food, their dispassion toward food.

Hoping to please my father, with whom I have a difficult and tense relationship, I made him corned beef. Since my mother's death, he has cooked for himself (mostly defrosting and heating up), fussy and particular in the kitchen and chafing at female care. But some of this chafing is his wish to be cared for, and corned beef is his favorite food. I don't eat much beef and had never made corned beef, one of his favorite dishes. So I started from scratch, studied recipes, bought the best cut, devoted the day to it. He sat down to the table, florid, breathless, before taking a bite, and said, "What makes you think you know how to cook corned beef?"

Many years ago, a man I was falling in love with cooked for me; it was the first time this happened and I will never forget it. He made me sit at a table already set with linen and china and candles. He disappeared into the kitchen and emerged a few moments later, smiling, bearing a whole fish displayed neatly on a platter like the hunter home from the hills—but also, the way a mother might give food to her child. Then he brought out potatoes and asparagus and some sweet, syrupy dessert. The details of the food fade into the details of his eyes, the murmuring conversation, the certainty of mutual seduction in all its heart-racing, hurried thrill. I was already his to have, if he wanted, but that he cooked for me—served me, *fed* me—sealed and defined all that followed into a whole and wholesome love affair and, later, an intimate friendship we still hold dear. We nourished each other then, and do so still.

Men cooking in the domestic sphere are praised; it is so rare a thing. Men don't arrive at dinner parties and walk straight into the kitchen saying, "What can I do to help?" Women do. I find it difficult to just watch another woman cook; my hands want to be busy, involved. Women cooking for women cook dessert—in friendship, as seduction, love, romance. Women feed one another, taking turns—bite by bite, mouth to mouth. They are sharing the cooking itself, the making and creating, even more than the food. Cooking can be a terrible task, a solitary pleasure, and sometimes a communion. When someone is cooking near me, I am pulled toward it, I want to be involved.

I have friends over for dinner now and then and cook something special. But I find most of the women I know have the task deep in their veins. They inevitably ask, "What can I bring?" and are a little dismayed if I tell them to bring nothing. I asked a close friend about this, about why she didn't like me to refuse her offer. "It's because women *know*," she said. I don't have to ask her, "Know what?" I know, too.

Sally Cline, a feminist writer, thinks it all begins with breast-feeding. Something innate. I don't know. But whether we feed a man, a woman, a lover, a friend, a child, we feed them our bodies; we say, I'm yours, I am undefended, I am open to you. "When we give food to other people," writes Cline, "we give up a part of ourselves, open ourselves up, lay ourselves on the line." Words with shared roots: *carnal* and *carnivore, consume* and *consummate*. You are my honey, my cherry, my dish, my sweet. We will eat each other up. We want to control our appetites lest they control us—mustn't "let ourselves *go*" lest we be found wanting—*wanting*, wanton, abandoned to desire. So many ways to let go. To give up.

I have dinner with a woman I do not know well, in a noisy café at a small table by the door. It is drafty and too bright. There are strangers near. We spread feta cheese soaked in olive oil on bits of bread, and talk of work. We spoon out minced Kalamata olives and roasted red peppers, and talk of art. We share tiny bites of sharp capers. Oh, she says, breathless—oh, this is the best thing I've ever tasted!

Where does the bread end and she begin? Who is eating, who is consumed? We hold our creations up for the other to taste. The noise, the crowd, fades away into distance; her face fills the world. Open wide, she says. Enjoy.

I WENT TO MY MOTHER-IN-LAW'S HOUSE FOR Thanksgiving, several thousand miles from my own cookbooks. She asked me to make a pie. I found in her cupboard a familiar red-and-white book, and made one of Betty's pies. We worked all day, my mother-in-law and two sisters-in-law and me, and toward the end of the day, the aunts and female cousins and cousins' wives joined us in the kitchen as soon as each arrived, bearing dishes. We fed about twenty-five people, spread between two rooms because no table was big enough.

After dinner, a lot of people went off to watch the football game, and I followed. After a while my mother-in-law peeked in and saw me. When she caught my eye, I suddenly realized I was the only woman in the room. "What are you doing in here with the men?" she asked in a tone thick with disapproval. "There's dishes to be done."

"WHEN YOU HATE TO COOK, A SUPERMARKET is an appalling place," wrote Peg Bracken. I have the luxury of controlling my work schedule, so I often do my grocery shopping in the middle of a weekday, when only old people and the unemployed are in the store. Sometimes I zip in and out as fast as possible. Sometimes I linger, wandering up and down each aisle, snooping in other people's baskets, wondering about the stooped old man in a polyester golf shirt who's buying three jars of maraschino cherries. I have gone to the same locally owned supermarket for fourteen years; I know the clerks and they know me. It's not perfect, and I frequently make extra trips elsewhere for better produce and less common ingredients, but it mostly works. I forget what a luxury this is.

Not long ago, I was in a strange part of town on an errand with my daughter, and she asked if we could bake cookies in the evening. I knew we'd need a few things. So I stopped at 5:30 in the afternoon at a chain store, one of the ugly retail warehouse stores America is growing now, where you can buy rubber cement, bagels, shampoo, plumbing fixtures, sanitary pads, bananas, fireworks, and a lot more. In this block-square box, with its video store, coffee bar, bank, and beauty salon attached to the corners like polyps, its echoing high ceilings and distant fluorescent lights, the rows march up and down in vanishing lines of too much, so much, too much. We walked, hungry, up and down and back and forth in the sickly light, in a crowd of people who seemed just as lost, and in the harsh glare everything I saw looked awful. I saw a chasm of despair open up and myself sliding down into an acute sense of failure, of having made the wrong turn for years. I felt a terrible loss taking place, holding a frozen pizza in my hand, blinking back tears. It *was* appalling, appalling to an existential degree, an appalling moment at an appalling time in a long human history of excess and hunger and need. It is the future we have been careening toward, slouching toward, buying for ourselves, this world of too much and not good enough, this future both foisted upon us and paid for dearly.

The day passed. I return to my small, ordinary neighborhood store, which has just been sold to a speculating national chain of cut-rate warehouse pharmacies. It will close in a few weeks and become something else, less familiar. I go and try to untangle fact from wish. I have a compelling memory of long-ago Saturday mornings when my mother and I went grocery shopping. I close my eyes and those mornings are right in front of me. My mother and I are alone, intimate. I help her ferry the bags into the kitchen, and the bags are magically emptied and the cupboards and refrigerator once again filled with the commonplace luxury of the American menu. We take our candy bars and new library books into the living room, happy as pigs in blankets.

6

MEALTIME IS A SOCIAL EXPERI-
ence, shared with family, friends, co-workers.
Many thousands of years impel this drive in us
to eat together; almost every human group does so, has always done
so. Meals are intimacies, reminders of commitment, ceremonies of
power, complex dances of rank and deference. The business lunch
and the state dinner; the holiday meal when every unspoken agenda
of several generations is enacted as though on stage; the seductive
tête-à-tête, when each mouthful is a promise—all are versions of
an ancient rite.

The rules for how, when, and what we eat, where and with
whom, are so embedded as to be almost invisible. Many people feel
the way they learned to eat when they were young is the only right
way to eat, as certain as mathematical equations or physical laws.
We learn these rules as we learn language, by observation, rejection
and humiliation, encouragement and praise, until they no longer

require thought. The child is made normative—normal—by being brought into the fold of the meal. He is punished by being put aside from the table, sent to bed without supper.

Says Margaret Visser in *The Rituals of Dinner*, her history of table manners, that the way we eat is inevitably "guarded, enculturated, ritualized, and even taboo-laden." Visser was able to write an entire book on table manners because each element of manners has been discussed and dissected at great length for centuries; it is a source of fascination and microscopic analysis. Centuries' worth of diaries, guidebooks, poems, histories, cookbooks, and scholarly treatises cover everything from how people sit at the table, what utensils they use for which food, who is served in what order, and the symbolic meaning of each small procedure involved. Visser herself believes that the necessity of food is exactly what makes it an object of complex prescription. Only food, sleep, and the toilet offer such a potent combination of necessity and repetition in our lives. We simply need to do this every day, from birth until death, with no guarantee of success from one hour to the next. Relatively few Americans, as global history goes, know what it is to be truly hungry, but even in its first pangs hunger is fearsome, a test of greed and kindness. Eating is a moral slide rule. Through all the world there is no more common way to accept a stranger or be accepted by him than to share food. (No surer way to give offense than to do this wrong.) Our hunger requires so much work, its prohibition is so painful and its satisfaction so grand—nothing else in our days can have such repeated and threatening force. Our hungers are literally insatiable. Eating can't be *done*, ever.

Just about everywhere, just about all the time—everywhere but here and now, that is—the table setting itself counts almost as much as what is on the table. It matters who is to the left of the host and to the right, how men and women are distributed, who is physically higher or lower, standing or sitting or prone, who is speaking and who silent. Unwritten degrees of status are always denoted at the table, and we don't like to talk about it. Americans are uncomfortable with the concept of seating arrangements; such plans make manifest secrets of class and power we don't like to admit. (One of our new rules is to pretend class does not exist even as we assert our own.) Place cards make us insecure because they cause us to question our *place*. That's their point.

Americans are famously, peculiarly, casual, but that doesn't mean we're not concerned with being correct. The trick is that *correct* in America often means "unremarkable." In a society based at least philosophically on equality, most people feel best when they are average. Medium is always preferable to large or small. Manners that are too strict are as uncomfortable as manners that are too loose—though the definitions of *strict* and *loose* keep changing.

"Modern manners increasingly force us to be casual," writes Visser. "It has actually become rather rude to be formal." Notice the word *force*. The carefully delineated differences in status and power manifest in table rituals of the nineteenth century may be buried under what seems like anarchy, but they haven't disappeared. Every person who's been to a pointedly informal lunch with his or her boss knows exactly how present these traditional delineations still are at a meal. Part of our modern propriety is that it is now considered improper to note them.

Margaret Visser, like several social critics, considers all this apparent reduction in formality and competition to be a flattening out of complexity in relationships—a revolt against modern chaos and society-wide isolation. But the joke is on us; extreme casualness adds a new and frustratingly impenetrable layer of complexity. Just as many people now have no idea how to sign a letter to a new acquaintance—"Yours truly" is too formal, "Sincerely" seems old-fashioned—more and more often a meal with people one doesn't know is a dance in which no one really knows the steps. Giving and taking offense is even easier than it was when we all knew the rules. Another new aspect of propriety is that it's considered rude to take offense, to mention rudeness.

As an American, I am free to express how my own hunger feels, and I'm also bound by how that freedom dilutes what I can express. We have few overt rituals, and when anything goes, when "Suit yourself" is the rule, there is little to share. With breadth comes shallowness. Feeding our American hunger is a rite stripped of its potency, pallid and dull, a thin inheritance.

Margaret Visser describes a feast: "Arabs will create morsels of rice enclosing different fillings, chosen and juxtaposed at the will of the eater: a bit of meat, for instance, a date, a nut, and some rice. The whole is dexterously moulded into a self-sufficient 'bite-sized' riceball, which may be different from all the other 'creations' put together by the diner in the course of the meal. All this is done with one hand . . . and diners are conscious of enjoying the feel and temperature of the food before it goes into their mouths. In the creation of such a morsel (the Arabic word for it is a *logmah*) one must select, pinch, fold, and compress in the hand . . . It is often the done thing to flick the finished ball into the mouth with the thumb." I open my mouth and the words appear, a perfect imitation of my mother's voice: "Don't play with your food. Don't eat with your hands. Use your spoon."

How delightful the vision of the Arab meal—and how deprived I can feel, knowing that instead I am haunted by the voice whispering, "Don't touch." I know the pleasure of clams eaten by hand, with the help of tiny forks for digging into the rough gray shells, gripping the tidbit between pearly body and black ruffle, to dip in aromatic broth. And artichokes, peeled off leaf by spiny leaf, scraped clean, piled up, a slow, flirtatious ritual. The dribbling juice of corn on the cob, dough from the loaf, batter from the bowl, familiar—familial. My daughter still absentmindedly eats pasta one piece at a time, delicately, with the tips of her fingers. But day after day with the knife and fork and spoon have marked me, and her; the strictures are learned. Small variations are enjoyable, large ones make us all a little nervous. (Knives are banned at some tables because they can be turned to weapons. Those rules didn't stop my father's temper, and when I remember him at the table, I often remember him angry and pointing at me with a knife—a carving knife, pointing out my mistakes.)

Breaking such conventions is always either very rude or very intimate. Barbecues are deliberately primitive events among friends; they work because they are planned, agreed-upon enactments and they don't stray too far from the middle. To pick food off another's plate, to let someone feed you with their fingers, to feed another, does go too far—these are signals of an entirely new set of rules coming into play.

Whenever we speak of "revolution" in food and cooking, part of what we mean is this breaking and remaking of small, quotidian rules—all kinds of rules, human and environmental. The talent required to break out of conventions and create something new without going too far is what makes an artist's career, after all.

Anything can qualify as revolution: what we are allowed to eat in the first place, how food should be cooked and by whom and with which tool, when it should (and should not) be eaten, how one dresses and speaks, how we use our hands and mouths, even whether meals are dimly or brightly lit.

At medieval banquets, food was piled in the middle of the table in layers, surrounded by sauces, and diners took apart the pyramids as their appetites led them. People ate straight from the serving bowls, mostly by hand, sometimes helping themselves with personal knives or the occasional spoon. Some diners used trenchers, hollowed-out pieces of bread, and later, pieces of wood. Flat plates weren't used at all until the early 1500s, and they weren't common for some time after that. Even then people often shared a plate, using forks only for snaring bits of food from the common platters.

One helped oneself to what was near, passed special treats to others out of courtesy, occasionally asked for something to be passed. "All the dishes were put on the table simultaneously, and it is evident that no one was necessarily supposed to partake of *everything* laid out for the guests," wrote Jean-François Revel. "Consumption was limited by the place at which he found himself at table and by how far away the various dishes were."

What we call "doggy bags" are common all over the world, common throughout history. We claim them for the dog because we're a little embarrassed to claim leftover food for ourselves. It's never done at the "best" tables—the tables where the most exquisite food is supposed to be served. Such control is part of the presentation, part of the food. Women, especially, have long been counseled to leave something on their plate lest they appear to have appetites in the first place. Women are not supposed to be *hungry*, and no one, male or female, is supposed to be controlled by hunger. This is really why it's considered important to have more than enough food when serving guests—not so that they're satisfied but so that all the diners can cooperatively exhibit their control, their ability to leave something behind. Leaving good food untouched is the hardest thing for an animal to do.

Any new point of etiquette threatens a stable order and generally filters into daily use rather slowly. The fork was introduced to Europe roughly around the eleventh century, but it wasn't widely used for almost 800 years. By the 1700s, as the pace of change increased, serving patterns had shifted far from medieval form. Many meals were still enormous, time-consuming affairs requiring dozens of animals and birds served by entire staffs, but a certain kind of decorum had taken over. By the early 1800s, European society was widely enamored of service à la française, where one or two courses are brought to the table at a time, cut there, and shared out to all, either by the diners themselves or by servants. This sounds rather homey, but French service was far more rule-bound than the familiarity of the medieval table. Each of its parts was carefully defined by what one could and could not do, say, or ask. The successor to service à la française was service à la Russe. Russian service was common in the United States into this century and still is used at very formal meals. Each course in succession is displayed to the table whole, then either taken to the sideboard or kitchen to be cut into even portions and passed in succession to each diner, or divided onto plates out of sight.

These shifts express much more than the nuances of entree and dessert. Since the food was handled elsewhere, tables grew more crowded with the display of hostly luxury, more decorated by the inedible, more *served*. The succession of courses meant a simpler menu was required, else meals might last forever. The invisible servant was at least as important as the charming host. The sideboard became essential, and people began to follow precise rules for table setting.

The move away from common platters was more than a change in eating patterns. It was a global change, a fundamental transition in social patterns. The age of specialization had begun; daily life was dividing into compartments never seen before. People were literally living different kinds of lives, in different kinds of houses, in different kinds of families from those of their recent ancestors. A new obsession with cleanliness and sanitation had begun (though its crudeness may make us cringe now), and the new desire for physical integrity was expressed in clothing, sexual behavior, and social etiquette. The day of the utensil had truly arrived. "The move towards the diversification of implements was already under way," writes Visser. "It coincided with the specialization of the rooms in the European house, and with the proliferation of furniture with specific uses: different tables for dining, writing, kitchen, drawing room, cards." Utensils coincided with the growing separation of the members of each family throughout their daily lives. The many kinds of cutlery that appeared, like social roles, were specific and specialized and not to be interchanged.

At the table, people no longer touched one another or ate from the same platter. They didn't pass food to one another or share food from their plates. New, strict rules developed about who spoke to whom at the table, even about the topics of conversation on which they conversed. Shifts in conversation were sometimes controlled by the host from course to course. A man might be directed to speak first to the woman on his left and later to the woman on his right. Every moment was choreographed.

A common standard of formality died slowly in the American middle class, a class forever uncertain about its own membership, forever wondering if it had been let in the door by accident. By the twentieth century, the rules of propriety could take extreme shape in the name of simply knowing how to behave. "Modern day impatience with formula and rite is nowhere more eloquently expressed than in the growing custom of using different patterns for different courses, all related by the thread of harmony," wrote Prudence Penny in her 1939 cookbook. "The hostess of today considers sameness identical with boredom. If she uses a cobalt and gold service plate, she may elect to use a simple gold-banded entree plate. The fish plate perhaps may have yellow bands to match the flowers in the center. . . . Obviously, all dishes used in one course should match." Penny allowed for a little "modern day impatience," but just a little. She strongly recommended six kinds of plates, a dozen kinds of glasses and bowls, a variety of cutlery, all measured to a fare-thee-well. Tablecloths must have a hem "three-eighths of an inch to one-half an inch wide," and napkins a hem "from one-eighth of an inch to one-quarter of an inch wide." Monograms must be no larger than "two and one-half to five inches" on the tablecloth and must be precisely placed in a particular corner. The cloth must be "perfectly laundered" and have a single central crease, and "this fold is placed *exactly* in the center of the table." Setting the plates themselves must be done with equal care, so that each setting is the same: "Allow, if possible, the standard space of twenty-four inches, this space being measured from the center of one plate to the center of the next one . . . The edge of the service plate, the tips of the handles of the silver utensils, and the lower edge of the napkin should be placed in exact alignment, usually one inch from the edge of the table. Some hostesses prefer that the silver be placed two inches from the edge of the table . . ." Such exquisitely rigid distinctions are a kind of magical thinking about equality. In making each of us identical at the table, our real differences are placed in the brightest of lights. One of the most pressing differences, of course, is who knew how to behave at the carefully defined table and all that behavior said about their lives.

The Prudence Penny Cook Book from which I quote was my grandmother's. I cannot imagine that petite, argumentative woman applying a measuring tape to any part of her table—but I can easily imagine her applying it to someone else's. She had plastic runners on her carpet and plastic covers on the sofa, and mounds of carefully folded linens and towels, mounds of rules for children to follow. But she couldn't really be bothered to put on a formal meal. Being taken out to a restaurant was far preferable, because above all, she liked to be served, felt she deserved serving. Like other women of her class—small-town, upwardly mobile professionals, the children and grandchildren of pioneers who had scraped dirt from beneath their fingernails a few years before—she had the china, linen, and silver required upon marriage, and she couldn't afford servants, after all. The china and silver were long dusty and discolored by the 1960s, when I started bothering her neat household routine. The dishes were relegated to a china cupboard, and Prudence Penny was lost in a drawer. Enough was enough. She ate TV dinners.

Twelve years and a world war after Prudence Penny, Betty Crocker wrote that there were "a number of approved methods for placing and removing dishes." Much had changed, there was room to breathe, but the fact that one's "tiny after-dinner coffee spoon is *always* placed on saucer" had not. There is, finally, no difference between style and substance here. The vital differences between table settings for a tea and a buffet, between a formal dinner and simple family suppers still counted in Betty Crocker's day because presentation *was* the meal, one with the food. Presentation was identity, self, place, status, and security all at once.

Rules always amount to more than what we're supposed to do. The immensely detailed structure of such rules functions like a belief system, a little like formal religion. It is a bit sacred. We learn not to question divine pronouncements even if we don't choose to live by them — it's enough to know they have been made. It wouldn't do to say out loud that these unquestioned laws are in fact nothing special. Even when my grandmother ignored her china as well as her duty, she wouldn't have agreed with me that her duty was a dream — that someone *just made it up*.

Western social history is a broken but fairly straight line, one of increasingly large populations of people living ever closer to one another and being driven to reduce contact with one another whenever possible. That is to say, as we became what we call modern, as we came to live irrevocably in ever larger and denser cities, with less open space among us, we have deliberately created forms of psychic space instead. In that transition we've come to see ourselves as far more relaxed than our ancestors, even as the intimacy between us steadily recedes.

Few of us ever experience Russian or French service; they are strictly state dinner and country estate now, and breathe a rare air. Most Americans are born and die in a world of "plate service." With plate service, each person has a separate, identical set of crockery and is given individual servings of each food from a central platter or a closed kitchen. Within families, where hierarchy still rules, complaints about the relative size of the slice of meat, the number of peas doled out to each diner, are dealt with as questions of preference and rank by the highest authority in the room, as they always have been.

When Pierre Bourdieu looked at class distinctions in France, a country far more comfortable with the enjoyment of food than the United States, he saw an inverse relation at the table. The working classes—people with the fewest choices—served the most casual and relaxed meals, meals meant for pleasure above all. The upper classes, by contrast far more mobile and self-directed, served rigidly contrived and formal meals, meals intended for advancement and power. He called the working person's way of eating an "ethic of convivial indulgence," the one ordinary part of life where restraints and rules can soften and even disappear.

Americans express their class clearly in restaurants: how often they go, which restaurant they choose and which table they receive there, what they order. But once seated, Americans usually pretend hierarchy disappears. At the restaurant table, servings of the same food are supposed to be exactly the same size. That's what we count on. Plate service is the ultimate flattening out of difference, so that no more flattening can be possible at a shared table. It is the ultimate displacement of communal appetite. Each person has a plate and a meal for his or her *private consumption*, each person has an equal share and keeps it private. Sharing between plates is either frowned upon or a sign of special approval.

Thus we came, step by step, to the culinary version of the strat-ification Americans call democracy. Everyone was served the same food in the same amount as everyone else, without having to com-pete hand over hand. Sometimes one could even choose exactly which portion he or she wanted from a platter of equal portions. Such externalized regulation means many of the occasions for help-ing one another at the table are eliminated. We are no longer respon-sible for one another's hunger, a vital change in the linkages of intimacy among us—a vital reduction in dependence, in giving and receiving, in trust. Meals, especially in public places, are not exactly shared now. With a few discreetly chosen exceptions, most restau-rant meals are pointedly about individual choice, individual plates, self-contained hunger.

Part of what is lost is any sense of play in satisfying the appetite. This play is what we long for, what we miss the most, I think, if not the corrupt forms it sometimes has taken. Play as a com-munal pleasure, as an open acknowledgment of shared desire and shared satisfaction, play as a form of love—love of food, love of one another.

"THE SOCIAL LIFE OF A HOUSEHOLD, WHETHER the household is a simple one or an elaborate one, centers about its dining-table," writes Prudence Penny at the end of the Depression. The dining table "represents, as no other piece of furniture can, the family as a whole," writes Margaret Visser. My family was a big white Formica table stuck between the kitchen, the couch, and the front door, in a space that was slightly more than a foyer and certainly less than a dining room. If the dining table represents the family, our dining table represented a set of conflicting fragments, the reluctance with which we sat down together like that of strangers who found themselves stranded on a deserted island with no place else to go.

As kitchens were growing rule-bound and conformist, dining rooms were disappearing. Architects and builders replaced dining rooms with the kind of space euphemistically called a "dining area" (designed partly for television viewing), or with dens and "family" rooms. The dining room was eliminated completely (along with the porch, another casualty of modern life) in the tiny houses of Levittown. Dining rooms weren't needed and would never be needed again in a world where people ate meals in restaurants, in their cars, in front of televisions, on the move, in hordes, alone.

"There was a time, long before the days of fast-forward lifestyles, when families sat down together at the dinner table. One generation nurtured the next on a diet of comfort and support as well as tasty victuals." So says a recent issue of *Better Homes and Gardens*. Everything from juvenile delinquency to drug addiction gets blamed on families not sitting down for dinner together. (In fact, the industrial age was the beginning of the end of family suppers, the second loss after commuting had destroyed the midday dinner itself. But the myth that this change also is new lives on.)

Still, my family sat down together for dinner every night. My mother made us do it. The dining table was forever covered with mail and schoolwork and the stuff of forgotten chores, but she insisted I set the table every night. I know one reason I was drawn to the idea of a truly formal table, to Betty Crocker's inviting photographs, was because we never had one; tables like that seemed sophisticated and rarefied. We had good china, the fine bone china with a silver filigree design Mom got when she married, but she would use it only at Thanksgiving and Christmas. The rest of the time she displayed it behind glass doors in the sideboard, half hidden behind the piles of mail and schoolwork and magazines that had spilled over from the table.

When I set the table, I began by clearing the mess away. Then I laid out blue woven placemats on top of the white Formica, white Corelle plates and blue plastic bowls, worn hot pads, and two salt-shakers, one for each end. We drank our breakfast orange juice (frozen concentrate) from old hourglass shrimp-cocktail jars, and at supper we drank our milk (powdered instant) from plastic tumblers. Our napkins were paper, bought by the thousand, and stacked in a leaning tower on the rickety cart by the kitchen door.

Stripped, but ritual nonetheless: We ate together and we always ate the proper foods at proper times. One didn't eat sandwiches for breakfast or scrambled eggs for lunch. One didn't eat cold leftovers or dessert first. We ate meat, meat at every meal—bologna, bacon, roast beef, hamburger, hash, chops, sausage, salami, steak, ham. The dinner table was a palette of earth tones—brown meat, creamy starches, pale-green and rust-red vegetables. Now and then my mother would make a big deal out of having "breakfast for dinner"—scrambled eggs, bacon, toast, and so on. That we rarely ate like this for breakfast was irrelevant; she would never have served Sugar Smacks for dinner.

We sat down together, night after night, but it didn't do me much good—I turned out to be a bit of a delinquent after all. We were statistically balanced, doing what we were supposed to do, but dinners were cold and awkward hours, dread hours, for all of us. My mother sat at the end of the table near the kitchen through tense and silent meals, crying quietly when fights erupted over the television news, clearing the plates away afterward, doing the dishes alone in the kitchen every night.

The routine varied only when my father was gone. He was a brooding, sharp-tongued man, not without a sense of humor, but as tight as a spring and always ready to be sprung. He was also a schoolteacher, a volunteer fireman, and a drinker, and not always in that order. Occasionally he ate early to go run the scoreboard for a high school football team. Sometimes, the fire whistle would blow before my mother started cooking dinner. He would wake up from his stuporous afternoon naps on the couch and stomp heavily out of the house, leaning perilously sideways, and jump into his pickup truck to race to the fire station. And the rest of us, giddy with freedom, hopped in the car and drove to A&W.

Writing this on a hot September afternoon at the end of the century, I feel a vast longing for those nights, that small ritual of burgers and floats in the backseat of the car under a dusky summer sky. I am as hungry for these shallow roots as I am for food sometimes, because there sometimes seems to be so few I should hold to each one I can find.

The A&W drive-in was a long, low building near the fairgrounds, across the street from the feed store. Mom parked the chocolate-brown Chevrolet Impala under the low roof, and a tall, pretty high school girl came out to take our order. The menu never changed—Papa Burgers, Mama Burgers, Teen Burgers, and Baby Burgers, floats and sodas and fries. We ordered the same food every time—for me, a Mama Burger, large fries, and an Orange Crush float, a soft mound of vanilla ice cream floating in soda, melting into pale peach-colored foam.

The A&W was a place where everything was always the same, a sameness that was far more comfort than stricture. California blended into Nebraska there, Nebraska blended into New Jersey, the whole country parked under a low roof on a summer evening with the windows down and the crickets beginning to sing in the warm, dry air, fragrant with the scent of frying meat. Susan and Bruce and I in our shorts and T-shirts blended into the crew-cut quarterback and his blond girlfriend in the Ford pickup beside us. You blended into me, and me into you, without ever having to touch at all. It was a homegrown joint, like the drugstore soda fountain and the pizza parlor on the edge of town, a place where everyone in town could go and be treated the same way. Only years later did I realize it was a chain, that there were A&Ws all over the country just the same, and when I found out, I felt a peculiar sorrow mixed with relief. Like most places I knew, A&W simply seemed ordinary, a little shabby in a homey, broken-in way. It was nothing like the Shamrock, the "nice" dinner restaurant where my parents went once or twice a year without us, a place I imagined to be lit in elegantly dim tones of red and gold with tablecloths and candles and waiters and maybe even music—a special place where, my mother told me, children weren't allowed.

The next day, I would set the table again.

IT WAS ONLY LAST YEAR THAT I PUT AWAY the plastic plates with children's drawings we'd used for a decade. The intimidating desire for elegance I felt as a small-town girl is gone now, partly because I know that it wasn't elegance I really wanted — just a container that seemed more interesting than the container I was in. I wanted a shared, warm circle like the pictures in the magazines.

When I was four years old, I found a golf ball. My mother had guests for dinner, a rare event, and I was most interested to see what would happen if I put my golf ball in the oven with her roast beef. I remember only the flagrant excitement of loud voices, black smoke, and embarrassed adults in the living room, wondering what to do next, and no dinner parties for a long time after that. The kitchen, wrote Roland Barthes, is where food "transmits a situation; it constitutes an information; it signifies."

After that, "entertaining" usually meant Grandma, Aunt Lucille and Uncle Fergy, Aunt Lois and her son Tom, the dour second cousin my father's age who drank whiskey on the rocks and often went an entire evening without saying a word. Mostly these were potluck to one degree or another. Prudence Penny called potlucks "hilarious" parties, and others of her time called them "Dutch treat parties." Penny had strict rules for such get-togethers, from invitations and decorations to proper attire. But in the mobile, casual West of the 1960s, we didn't even call them potlucks. You just brought food when you went over to Aunt Lucille's for dinner.

Entertaining in the summer meant hot dogs and potato salad, baked beans no one seemed to eat, and the children taking turns on the hand-cranked ice cream maker. On winter holidays we used the rarely seen tablecloth still faintly stained from the gravy spills of past years, ate pearl onions in white sauce, yams with tiny marsh-mallows, canned pumpkin pie, and quivering mounds of Jell-O with chunks of canned peaches and mandarin oranges hung like

Christmas ornaments in the bright red ether, with the same aunts, the same silent cousin.

On New Year's Eve, Mom sometimes gave a cocktail party, suffering in advance for the likely disasters ahead. She put out platters of crackers with little rubbery dollops of Cheez Whiz, triangular deviled ham sandwiches, shrimp cocktails with ketchup and Worcestershire sauce, and pigs in blankets, sweetmeats for the new age. Dad wore a tie, and Mom put on her fake pearls. The children were banished upstairs with bags of potato chips, where my father had filled the bathtub with gallons of clean ice cubes and bottles of soda. We played Monopoly with our friends Carol and Craig and Steve, or our cousins Cindy and Mitch and Geoff, listening to 45s on the pink record player and making terribly risqué jokes. If I sat on the stairs I could hear party sounds, the most elegant and exciting sounds in the world, the tinkly sounds of adults milling about the living room swirling ice in their glasses, laughing over the faint sound of the Percy Faith Orchestra. The murmuring conversation faded and rose when the doors opened and closed. When I remember those evenings now, I imagine Peg Bracken there, tall and slender in a blue silk sheath and pearls, holding a dry martini in one hand and a cigarette in the other while she flirts disconsolately with a neighbor's husband. I imagine her sampling the canapés, enjoying the chance to eat something another woman has cooked—my mother, ever a bit shy and uncertain, hovering near the kitchen door.

The transition from medieval feasts and peasant pots of barley gruel to the gradually emerging tables marked by French and Russian service took centuries. From there to how we eat now was a much quicker change, because from then to now families themselves changed so fast. The dining table represents the family, I read, and if so, plate service is the nuclear core, our shrinking withdrawal from one another.

Many people live alone now—about one-fourth of all American households consist of a single person. Many of us participate in attenuated friendships and frustrating romantic entanglements no one expects will last. We do much of our socializing over restaurant meals, two or three people, each of whom lives in separate quarters scattered across miles of urban landscape. We meet our dearest friends briefly in rooms crowded with the noise of other earnestly convivial strangers, and we order complete meals to be made by nameless strangers and put separately before us. We are proud of our self-reliance, crowded in mutual isolation. Pierre Bourdieu noted that in working-class French families, an undesired guest may be given an individual plate, while the family—the unit of intimacy—eats off a communal platter.

American mobility chips away at the deeply embedded, even organic, desire to manage and plan our meals. We are hungry animals, once again unsure of where the next meal will come from, all our carefully ordered history of ritual eating patterns fallen apart into a twenty-four-hour snacking day. With our unnaturally frantic schedules, with our cars and commutes beyond human-sized limits, with our absurdly fast food and delivery of everything, one strange new fact is that we can eat anywhere, anytime, and so have forgotten what it means simply to eat.

Americans can have whatever they want—all-you-can-eat buffets of mashed potatoes puddled with gravy and mounds of slowly cooling slices of meat; soggy, individual-sized, vending machine tuna-salad-on-rye sandwiches; expensive, carefully tended five-course dinners; drive-through archways, billions served. We have Happy Hour snacks and a breakfast burrito for the morning commute, protein bars for the daily visit to the gym, and takeout for after work. Here, everything goes, barriers fall away—and are replaced by new barriers, new walls. We don't know *where* our next meal will come from, but we certainly know it *will* come. No people have ever had this opportunity before, and we are so used to the fact that we get upset if any sudden appetite can't be gratified. We complain if the next exit doesn't have a drive-up window, if the gas station minimart is closed or the all-night grocery runs out of chocolate-chip ice cream. (We feel *deprived*.)

Slowly but surely, the world follows this descent. The intimacy of small morsels and common platters, the delicacy of chopsticks and fingers, slips away into plastic microwave tubs and Styrofoam coffee cups. We often eat and snack alone. The pot-au-feu has become the throwaway, microwavable plate, the shared bowl a bite on the bus on the way to work.

We are very far now from the feudal village feast, from the extended family of more recent centuries. With plate service, the growing walls between neighbors, families, relatives, and friends have finally extended to the last and oldest communal event. We have achieved the culinary nuclear family, each unit fully equipped and independent of all the others, duplicated, equal, and closed. Casual as we are, we touch one another much less than most other cultures, afraid to hold our best friends' hands, to walk arm in arm with our own mothers. The world devolves ever more into its peculiar, crowded loneliness, and Americans embrace a stage show of what's left behind: potlucks and dinner parties and all the world's traditional cuisines, the kind of meals with big platters brought to the center of the table "family" style, the kind of meals full of messy finger foods that we can sop up and dole out piecemeal to be dipped in the sauces we pass around to share.

I HAVE A FAMILY, BUT I LONG FOR FAMILY AT times, long for a dream—for a heresy, unconscious, unbidden. The family I want is the one none of us had but so many of us believe we were taken from—little match girls longing for a bit of Christmas supper. Sometimes I make a cake or a pie or bread because cake and pie and bread are dream-catchers for me. German chocolate and Lady Baltimore are black-market drugs so rich with inaccurate sensations of maternal comfort and infantile security they take my breath away.

Then I dream, and I am far from my own remodeled kitchen, in a world where families not only eat together, they work and play and thrive together in every possible combination. There are parties and spontaneous get-togethers, weddings and funerals and holidays—big romping occasions filled with odd cousins and risqué aunts and tottery great-grandmothers in the kitchen initiating the wide-eyed children into the mysteries of risotto and meringue.

I go to my father's house for Thanksgiving. My mother is ten years dead, and my sister, Susan, cooks. We eat a Foster Farms turkey with cornbread stuffing and gravy; mashed potatoes; sweet potatoes with brown sugar; green bean casserole with a little sherry, onions, and cream of mushroom soup; canned baby onions with canned white sauce; cranberry-orange relish; apple pudding; and a "salad" involving vanilla pudding, crushed pineapple, marshmallows, and a tub of Cool Whip. Then there's dessert: store-bought pumpkin pie and spray-on whipped cream. My dad lies in a heap on the couch afterward, bemused and silent, while Bruce and Susan and I play Clue with the kids. There are so many walls around and between us, so many complex passwords required here, among those who ought to be so intimate. All the words we can't say, bruises we are careful not to touch, subjects we are careful not to broach—so many old wounds near to opening again at a certain word, a tone of voice, I wonder we can speak at all.

We all, I think, are abandoned children—every one of us in this world. Childhood itself abandons us, throws us out on our ear long before we're ready. Here at Dad's old Formica dining table, a billowing phantasm arises. I want the fairy tale, and instead I feel as though I've been stolen away, a princess orphaned when June Cleaver was killed by Jane Jetson.

"Colonel Mustard in the library, with the knife." We throw the dice. My father watches, vaguely, listening to a distant music in his head. "Miss Peacock in the kitchen, with the lead pipe." I pick up the can of fake whipped cream and spray a gross dollop into my mouth, trying to disgust everyone. We laugh, and someone grabs it from my hand. "Professor Plum, in the ballroom, with the rope"—and then we're spraying one another with the sticky white goop, splattering Mr. Green and Miss Scarlett through clouds of white foam. And it seems briefly possible. For a few minutes, rubbing handfuls of bubbly cream into my niece's hair, I think it could be true. It is more fun than we've had together in a long time, than we will have together again for a long time to come.

7

THE OVERARCHING TREND IN AMERI-
can culture for centuries has been toward a strange aesthetic—an aesthetic of the ascetic. And a uniquely luxurious ascetic at that, often quite expensive and uncommon. We deprive ourselves through a stumbling repetition of
excess. We buy opulent, thickly upholstered furniture one year and
fine, bone-thin furniture the next. We wear rich, thick clothing, all
velvet and cashmere one year, and trade it all in for stylish khakis
and cotton shirts the next. We eat excessively and diet excessively.
Either way, excess is the key.

This is a major cycle in the history of cuisine: entire social classes
swinging between gluttony and self-denial, between large quantities of rich food and small quantities of light food, and back again.
Medieval banquets, with their huge portions of meat, incongruous
spices, and love of ostentation, have been repeated many times in
only slightly more restrained form, and are still with us today. Crash

diets, vegan asceticism, and evangelical nutrition have been around awhile, too. Sometimes the driving forces meet in small portions of expensive, rarely prepared food. The tiny servings of barely cooked root vegetables and carefully doled out "condiments" one might find at an expensive spa today is one of these collisions. The fat-free frugality people are willing to pay serious money for now represents the meeting point of two long waves.

This cycle has recurred a number of times just this century. The banquets and groaning boards common at the turn of the century gave way in the face of a new urban anxiety, a newly cosmopolitan insecurity, to simpler, blander foods. World War I, the glamorously youthful twenties, and the Depression each brought a fashion for simpler food and an obsession with individual health. But each hard time left the public clamoring for abundance as soon as possible— more food, more convenience, more choice. Rationing and years of insecurity in World War II left Americans longing not only for abundance but for familiar abundance, for nearly two decades of explosive materialism and comfortable, unchallenging meals. All that has followed, from the natural-foods revolution to gourmet extravagance to the tyranny of the lean, mean millennium, are swings in this cycle. It is not easy to live simply these days. Daily life is hectic, disheveled, cluttered for most of us. It is only the wealthy who can afford the empty space and silence and time required for simplicity.

In medieval Europe, what one ate "hinged on the at once clear and ambiguous idea of *quality*," writes the historian Massimo Montanari. "Expensive, elaborate and refined foods (those which only wealth and power could procure on a daily basis) were intended for noble stomachs, while coarse and common foods went into the stomachs of peasants." The observation that fine foods were meant for the rich gradually transformed itself into the belief that the rich could tolerate nothing else. Their stomachs were attuned *only* to fine and delicate foods, and the peasantry's only to thick, heavy ones. To eat outside one's rank was to go against one's nature — against what Montanari calls "a basic and ontological postulate" about humanity. Food became (not for the first or last time) a deep metaphor — the rich ate high, flying, light food, like birds. The poor ate low, thick, heavy food, earthy food, like root vegetables and dark grains.

Medieval feasts, wrote Jean-François Revel, share "all the most disturbing features of that period." Such feasts were a bit like gargantuan, disheveled Thanksgivings, an exaggeration of bounty and abundance in scarily uncertain times, feasts of decadent intensity. Medieval celebrants loved clever surprises. They liked fountains shooting wine, clowns and acrobats, mock battles and cross-dressing theatrical performances. They put wings on children and suspended them like angels from the ceiling. They invented the crackerjack prize: live birds hidden in linen napkins, in flower arrangements, inside casks, inside piecrusts. Sometimes the jesters and musicians themselves emerged from giant piecrusts. Elephants were always popular. At a wedding in Bruges in 1468, guests were treated, according to Margaret Visser, to "a dwarf riding into the banqueting hall on a gilded lion, a pedlar [*sic*] pretending to sleep while monkeys stole his wares and gave out purses, brooches, lace, and breads to the company, and a dromedary ridden in by a wild man who threw coloured balls among the guests." One fad involved a jester leaping without warning into a huge dish of custard in the middle of the table so that all the guests were sprayed with pudding.

In something of an understatement, Fernand Braudel wrote that "there was no sophisticated cooking in Europe before the fifteenth century." There were centuries of collapse and reversal between the ancient civilization and the Middle Ages; cooking was only one of many bodies of knowledge almost lost. The meat, fish, and fowl were accompanied by all manner of stews, sticky sweetmeats, coyly presented fruit, pastries perfumed with musk and ambergris, and wine, often flavored with spice and sometimes perfume. But "salt and smoke were the predominant flavors," write Reay Tannahill. The medieval rich man's table was an abundant but crude place.

A central hallmark was the very quantity of meat involved, a Brobdingnagian river of corrupted flesh. "Deer and ostrich surrounded by various pastelli, veal's head, boiled capons, veal breast and loin, goat, sausage and partridge" was a typical first course. Cooking meat and fowl in strong mixes of spice was both a mark of incoherent experimentation and a practical attempt to disguise the saltiness of preserved foods and the smell of decomposing whole animals. The effect was so nauseating at times that incense was burned to mask the odor of the meal itself. Many whole animals and birds were wrapped in their own decaying skin for the table. Jean-François Revel describes "a ram with four horns, poached in water and put back in its skin, standing in a golden basin looking as though it were alive." One report describes a goose cooked alive so carelessly that it cried out when carved at the table.

Some feasts took place on public stages, the diners surrounded by the watching poor, and ended with the leftovers being thrown to (and at) the crowd. There was always far more food at such banquets than people could eat. "The wealthy table came increasingly to be characterized by ostentation," writes Montanari. "Not that this quality had ever been lacking, but it became the principal underlying motivation."

This ostentation has been with us since ancient times. Royalty and the extremely rich have amused themselves for thousands of years by trying to redo and outdo gourmet extravaganzas of the even more ancient past—a kind of layer-upon-layer venality reaching far into the distance, endlessly into the future. There are almost as many examples of gargantuan feasts in this young country, some of them deliberately evocative of our romance with Europe's imagined past. One opulent meal at Delmonico's in 1873 purportedly included such medieval touches as swans swimming in a lake in the middle of the table.

But this *is* a cycle—each period of excess is followed by a period of asceticism. In this case, the resurgence of the banquet in places like Delmonico's was undermined by even larger economic and social cycles tending toward retreat. Feasts had to wait awhile.

PEOPLE EAT MEAT. AS LONG AS PEOPLE HAVE kept records of what they eat, they've made it clear that they will eat as much meat as they can. Meat is at the top of the planetary food chain; it is necessarily a food for the few and the rich, but it has always been the most desired of meals. In the Middle Ages, that rarity was expressed in how much could be wasted: whole herds, entire flocks. (A portion of the list for a banquet given by King Richard II in 1387 reads, "14 salted oxen, 2 fresh oxen, 120 fresh sheep carcasses, 12 boars, 14 calves . . . 50 swans, 210 geese, 50 larded capons . . . 1200 pigeons, 144 partridges, 96 young rabbits . . .")

Only a few people make it to the top of this pyramid, but for the most part, Westerners have been these few. Until the 1600s, meat was readily available in Europe even to the poor; rich or poor, there was plenty of land and relatively few people. This ended when the population reached a certain critical mass. Meat and grain prices went up; hunger was widespread for some time, and then the nutritional economy came back into balance—a lot of meat for the few rich, little meat for the many poor.

Meat-eating is itself a solution to overpopulation, even as overpopulation largely eliminates the eating of meat. A lot of meat in the diet means a lot of animals on the land eating a lot of subsistence grains, and this equation leads directly to the starvation of agrarian people. The historian Fernand Braudel hypothesized that the success of Asian cultures was due in part to their largely vegetarian diet, which allowed populations to grow large and spread across an efficiently managed expanse of land. That these populations were largely vegetarian only because they didn't have the grain base to support a meat diet is the other side of this suggestion.

In all this long history of meat-eating, there is a parallel history of solemn concern. People have been almost as occupied with what it meant to eat meat as with getting the meat in the first place. Eating meat is, traditionally, a matter of ceremony, sacrifice, and ritual gratitude. Eating a lot of meat, as Europeans and Americans like to do, has always been seen as a dangerous act, an act fraught with the possibility of psychic and spiritual ruin.

Vegetarianism, too, has a long history, particularly among the religious. The Enlightenment was marked by a wave of Christian vegetarians who saw meat as a coarse, primitive food, representative of feudal and embattled times; they believed civilized people avoided flesh. "These were of course problems and controversies of the elite," notes Massimo Montanari. "When exhortations for nutritional rationality and perhaps vegetarianism reached peasants or workers, the effect was grotesque if not ridiculous."

The European Renaissance, that enlightened emergence from the Dark Ages, put an end to such silliness as praying over a dead deer. Today we prefer the casual approach. Many Americans like to think of themselves as religious, but only in ways that don't interfere with the day's plans. We've never had a coherent sense of ritual, and we've never wanted one. The sacrifice and ceremony tribal people felt was required with meat-eating was not so much lost in the technological and industrial revolutions as it was deliberately destroyed.

This is not a fey reference to the distant past; the same concerns and suspicions are with us today, buried under nutritional campaigns and acrimonious arguments over animal rights. Underneath, we're quite superstitious, I think, but conventional wisdom, the attitude we share publicly with one another, has always been that it's best to march into the future and throw the past away. Only in modern times have large numbers of people been able to eat meat with regularity, and we've tried to do so as much as possible without noticing the thousands of years of history that hitched along. Americans have always eaten a great quantity of meat. An 1851 recipe for "bean soup" calls for six pounds of beef. American carnivorousness was simply another European habit, but Americans found they could take it to an unimagined degree because they had conquered a country unimaginably large. The hills, shores, and plains were sparsely populated and filled with game of all kinds, with fish, fowl, and beast. When these wild creatures were mostly eaten up, the empty expanse beckoned to herds of livestock, flocks of domestic birds, even farms of fish.

By the 1940s, large quantities of meat were part of the daily American diet even for the poorest people. Through the war, rationing or not, finding a way to get what was seen as a vital, muscle-building, strength-enhancing nutrient was central. (Whale meat—"the tenderest whale steaks come from young California gray whales"—was one suggested way to do this.) Rationing limited citizens to only 125 pounds of meat per person a year—a half-pound every day. (Soldiers ate more than twice that much—360 pounds each per year.) Food rationing continued in Britain until 1954, and the English were long limited to a pound of meat per person per week. But having access to many times that much meat was seen as hard deprivation by Americans. When the war was over, they couldn't wait to dig in again. Meat, said Betty Crocker in the 1950s, was "the star of the show," the "center around which the rest of the meal revolves." After the war, ranchers rapidly increased the size of their livestock herds, farmers poured grain down the animals' mouths, and their customers bought meat literally by the thousands of tons—while the rest of the world, recovering from the same war, largely starved on roots for two winters running. Half a century later, it's still true: Beef is back, I read in *Bon Appetit*, in *Gourmet*, in *Food & Wine*. Beef and pork and chicken, every manner of fish, game from buffalo to venison to elk.

When I was a child, we ate meat three times a day; the rare times when we didn't reflected a rather dire financial downspin I learned of only much later. One of my father's best friends was the town butcher, and I saw him almost every day. I went with my mother so she could pick up a few chops and some hamburger and a roast for

Sunday, all to be wrapped up in neat white packages by jovial Mr. Bryan. I also went there with my father, through the back door, while he made his regular rounds of back doors around town. I would stand on the sticky yellow sawdust powdering the wood floor, listening to the meaningless talk of adults. When one of the men in long stained aprons opened the freezer door, puffs of frosty air crossed my face and I could see the long room where the carcasses hung, swinging gently as they were brushed aside. That room, that cold breeze fragrant with blood and the steel slice of knives, defined meat for me at a very young age. I'm grateful for it; even today, I can recall that delicate perfume in a six-year-old's nose, full of wonder and questions never asked. Even today, standing in front of a supermarket case of neatly wrapped packages of chops and steaks, I remember the halves of cattle, the hooked lines of gutted pigs, the racks of whole chickens still slowly dripping. I know what meat is, even when I don't want to know.

I certainly feel hunger for meat at times, and wonder if there are unknown, even unknowable, nutrients in flesh. Sometimes I crave it, and most especially when I'm sick, as though we can trade life for life. The act of eating meat is marked, for me, by those hours in the back room of the butcher shop. Like all children, when I suddenly made the final, vital connection between animals and meat, it tore through my life like a quake, a cataclysm, ruin—as it should. I felt a childish, terrible loss. I didn't eat meat for a long time, and then I did again, wiser.

Here in America, meat is the quintessential ingredient. Perhaps it happens in all technological cultures, perhaps it is our own peculiar superstition, but Americans approach meat in a uniquely careful way. We don't like to see the animals, know the butchers, raise our own. We prefer our meat shrink-wrapped behind doors, and that means out of sight and smell of the factory farms, rivers sterile with pig manure, and automated slaughterhouses that allow us to eat so much meat so cheaply.

Well into adulthood, I tried to make myself believe that eating meat was unnatural—that any appetite I have for meat is conditioned, not innate. The way we Americans go about raising animals and making them into meat is so often inhumane that I wanted to believe our hunger was not entirely human. But all this history I've been reading, my ever-growing awareness that much of what I've wanted to reject in my culture is the deeply desired wish of billions of people—all this has made me change my mind. I've come to believe that the appetite for flesh is quintessentially human. Eating meat isn't necessary, and it isn't necessarily right, anymore than a lot of other human impulses are right—but I think of it as an impulse of the race nevertheless. My refusal to look clearly at meat, at meat-eaters, at meat hunger, was a refusal to look at something essential about people themselves.

EATING IS OFTEN REACTIVE—DEPENDENT ON circumstances beyond our control, broken into times of *enough, not enough, more than enough*. Meat, while central, is only part of a complex equation. In cycles of prosperity, people eat foods exotic to them, foods that aren't locally grown or commonly eaten. People eat excessive amounts of food in prosperity, too, and spend elaborate amounts of time preparing it with ever more complex tools and methods. In times of abundance, people eat less produce and fewer grains, more highly processed food, along with more meat, more fat, more sugar, more salt. In times of scarcity, eating becomes far more plain in every way. People eat locally grown and unprocessed foods, prepared with little fuss—even cooked for less time, to save fuel. People eat whole grains, more vegetables and fruits. Along with the meat, out go the fat, sugar, and salt.

These foods are human currency, jewels to be traded among the rich. Salt and sugar have always been valuable, used as money, as pawns, as power. Fat is the special treasure, the diamond, the rare and delightful goodness all people want. Fat—lard, oil, butter— keeps people alive in the worst conditions, comforts them when all is well; fat is a representation of wealth itself. Fat bodies are rich bodies—they are bodies as heavy with *meaning* as they are with flesh.

One of the most notable and peculiar elements of how we eat today is the upheaval of this historical truth. Only now do the rich eat lean and the poor eat fat. *Only now*—here is something really new, untried, unimagined. Fat cats living lean. Beef is back—but it's that expensive, unnaturally skinny beef we want the most. ("Gobble gobble—without the guilt," reads an ad for turkey in *Sunset* this holiday month.) The rich still spend an inordinate amount of money to eat the way they want to eat, of course. Ostentation just has a thin silhouette today.

Until the propitious meeting of modern food processing and nutritional evangelism, the poor were often as not actually better nourished than the rich. Nourishment as we define it now is largely about leanness, deprivation, resistance. Nutrition is microscopic, rational, quantifiable—measured in triglycerides, the body-mass index, micrograms, International Units. This view is also new, because for a long time, nourishment has meant something opposite—a matter of comfort, security, emotion. To be nourished was something one couldn't measure, only experience. Now we have it down, quite literally, to a science, and don't mess with those indefinable feelings so much anymore. I never cease to be surprised at how little attention is paid to joy and appetite in conversations about health. We know that relaxation, happiness, companionship, and the physical act of laughing actually make us healthier, help us live longer, better. Why do we forget these things when we design our healthy diets? What are the best things we've ever tasted? "I don't eat foods anymore," a dietitian told me a few years ago. "I eat nutrients." I eat nutrients, too, but I want them in a simmering broth of companionship and ease. I want them free of shame, held out in an open hand. The best thing—it's not only flavor. It is a declaration of pleasure taken freely, embraced. To anyone measuring life in calipers and scales, pleasure is alarming, a slippery slope into dangerous desires.

The diet of medieval peasants of Britain will sound familiar to health-conscious Americans today: lots of bread with a bit of butter and cheese, lots of plain vegetables and fruit, and a little beef and fish now and then. That's how poor people ate, out of necessity, not choice. Montanari points out that those medieval peasants who lived in the least "commercially developed areas" of Europe were generally more secure and had better nutrition than those in "more intensely urbanized or agriculturally developed ones." The latter, dependent on market economies and the vagaries of distant politics, depended on a few local foods and had little variety in their diet. They didn't forage like their supposedly less lucky rural kin. In the same way, slaves in the American South ate poorly, but because they ate wild greens and fruits as well as the staples they were given, they sometimes ate better than their owners, who lived long periods on little more than dried corn and salt pork. This has certainly changed. Wild greens and berries are gourmet staples, and salt pork is poor food.

PEOPLE ATE MORE MEAT AND LARD IN 1839 than they did in 1939. But butter consumption climbed, and sugar consumption skyrocketed in the same period—from 13.1 pounds per person per year to 95.5 pounds. Meat consumption has steadily climbed during this century. Whenever we ate less butter, we replaced it with different kinds of fat, like margarine. From 1909 to 1976, fresh fruit consumption dropped by more than half; flour and cereal consumption dropped by half. The amount of sugar we ate continued to climb. A growing economy meant a growing marketplace of food treasure. What most people eat today—when they have a choice—is the same as what people have always eaten when they have had the choice—meat, fat, sugar, and salt.

The promotion of a low-fat, low-calorie, limited-meat diet has been with us off and on ever since the twenties, in spite of what people actually ate, wanted to eat, hoped to eat. But dieting is a relatively new behavior. Except for the odd religious ascetic or political prisoner here and there, people haven't normally engaged in deliberate weight loss. Victorian women dieted—to show their control over appetite, to be wan and faint. But slimness alone wasn't the driving force until recently—until, in the scale of human history, just this minute. "Pleasures too widely shared quickly lose their allure," says Montanari. When European food supplies became more abundant and secure in the nineteenth century, food abundance was no longer a conspicuous sign of wealth. The poor had always been distinguished by their "*want* of fat," and when they no longer wanted fat so badly, the rich no longer enjoyed fat quite so much. "It is no surprise that the food revolution suggested new models of behaviour for the elites." As meat, sugar, and fat became easier to obtain and thus popular with the masses, these long-valued items lost favor with the rich. When most people could get enough calories that thinness no longer meant poverty, when fewer people were starved thin, thinness became a desirable quality. The slim, fit look in fashion now is an expensive one, requiring work, attention, and, above all, time. Only the rich can afford that lean silhouette now.

"The rich are thus doomed to prepare the future life of the poor," says Braudel. He refers here to the entire social pattern by which once-desirable items become uninteresting as soon as they are abundant. The junk food once thrilled to by the emerging middle class is now one of the most conspicuous portions of the diet of the American poor. Sugar and fat are still signs of wealth to the poor; the last people to give up such symbols are those who have no other money. What was once poor food is rather expensive now. The prosperous eat whole grains, barely cooked vegetables, odd fruits, and wild fish and game, some of them imported from all over the world and others grown specially for this small economic niche. Today the poor live on fatty, salty, sugar-laden foods, imitations of meals eaten by the wealthy of the past. A Big Mac is a shadowy symbol of a rich baron's feast.

"While it may be that to eat lightly is healthy, only those who eat abundantly (or at least are able to) succeed in thinking so," writes Montanari of modern European patterns. "Those who are truly hungry have always wanted only to fill themselves to bursting. . . . Only a wealthy society can afford to appreciate poverty."

To choose a special diet of any kind is at least a little venal by nature, anyway; to pick and choose and reject food costs money and takes time. The fear of fat in food, which is the fear of *being* fat itself, is complex and irrational. It is existentially layered, filled with metaphor and the primitive animal fear of age and age's ugliness— the fear of time flying by.

A radio show: "Vegetable Chronicles: A look at cultures in southern Italy, rural China, and rural Mexico where traditional low-fat diets are associated with dramatically low rates of diseases common in America." Invading the world with our junk, we take in return the supposed wisdom of mythic rural people. We think these materially poor people have a secret. (They *must* have a secret—otherwise, they're simply poor.) The "forgotten" and "discovered" cultures we periodically celebrate seem to know something we've lost. Of course, not having diseases of prosperity like certain kinds of heart disease doesn't spare people from the many other diseases brought on by poverty. It may be true that a moderate, relatively low-fat diet with limited animal fats is best for human longevity. But cultures don't choose to eat such a diet. They simply do not—no population, no people, have chosen to deny themselves the comfort and safety of rich foods. Individuals may choose such a life—but cultures are condemned to it. All of history tells us this.

The gourmet chef Alice Waters, a proponent of "light" and "local" cuisine, loves mesquite charcoal—mesquite charcoal that "is made in a time-consuming manner by the Yaqui Indians in north central Mexico." A subset of this high-and-low cycle of food behavior is how the rich emulate the poor in carefully stylized ways. Polenta, succotash, dandelion greens, and quail—once despised, now revered, for exactly the same reasons.

A new restaurant opened in Portland not long ago called Fiddleheads, and it's won all kinds of awards. The cuisine is "inspired by the First Nations People of the Americas" from top to bottom, Arctic to the southern tip. The owners, I read at the bottom of the menu, "are honored to be members of the Conceptual Design Team for the Smithsonian's National Museum of the American Indian." When I ate there, the specials were a vegetarian menu inspired by "The Northern Continent" ($28 per person): roast apple and pumpkin soup, wild mushroom stew, cornmeal cakes. The "Celebration Menu for a West Coast Winter Moon" ($35 per person) included "Imu Style" steelhead with "buckskin cake, spit-roasted Okanogan venison with savory huckleberry half-glaze." The recommended wines were a Chateau Ste. Michelle Canoe Ridge Chardonnay ($59.75) and a Columbia Red Willow Vineyard Syrah ($48).

We ordered off the regular menu: wild rice and corn fritters with crawfish and ginger remoulade, juniper grilled venison with chestnut beans and sweet peppers and onions, braised Clatskanie rabbit with barley and cilantro. (We skipped the "tatonka"—buffalo—raised on a farm in a fertile Oregon valley.) Fiddleheads, like so many new restaurants, is a noisy, postmodern pastiche, all strong colors and chunks of metal and tree branches and Native American art and Native American–inspired iconic art pieces. We ate within inches of other diners and shared the conversation of everyone else in the room—the buzz of cellular phones, the murmur of pickup lines, birthday parties, business dinners. The food came in big white bowls, gratifyingly heavy and earthlike, and our knives weren't sharp and dainty things but dangerous-looking fake Bowie knives.

The food was all right—not great, not bad. But I felt sick there, sick and sorrowful and ashamed. It was not the fact that my hillbilly ancestors came out here to the Pacific Northwest on the tidal wave of genocidal conquest and helped dig up, despoil, and depopulate the land. It wasn't the sense of indisputable victory that comes from eating the spoils of the conquered on their own land. It was the complete lack of irony and self-awareness that weighed on me that night. It was precisely the "celebration," the "inspiration," the comfortable atmosphere so satisfiedly beyond reflection, beyond consequence.

8

ANGELO PELLEGRINI, IN HIS IR-
ritatingly vast leisure, was a cook who grazed on
local pastures without longing for anything more than the bounty
they gave him. Pellegrini was a bit self-congratulating in his grand
good luck with life, but he had the patience of the happy eater.
Instead of the sour odor of entitlement, his food smelled of anticipation, the abiding reward of time.

Angelo Pellegrini has several seductive suggestions for handling
the crop of fall tomatoes. He especially likes conserva, or tomato
paste made by hand. To make conserva, you take a good homemade
fresh tomato sauce,

add more salt to the sauce as a preservative, spread it in a shallow
pan, screen it against flies, and put it in the sun. Stir it as necessary to expose the moist underside to the sun. In two or three
days, if the temperature has been in the high seventies or above,

the color will be a dark burgundy, and the concentrate will be dense enough to shape with the hands, but first oil your hands to prevent sticking, and then shape into a ball or patty. Press this into a sterilized jar, screw on the band, and store in the refrigerator. That will be your vintage conserva for the year. The salt and the oil will prevent spoiling. . . . A third of a teaspoon of conserva, diluted with a bit of hot stock, will do wonders to the family stew.

When I read this, in the early fall with my bare feet stretched out before me on a deck warm with golden light, I am thrust into conflict. What a simple gift it is to pick tomatoes in the warm September sun, to slice and stew them, to enrich them into paste in the same sun. But we live our days otherwise. We are told by faceless authorities to bleach countertops every few days and avoid raw eggs as though they are malevolent creatures—to bring into our lives more chemicals and less delight. We are told not to take potato salad to picnics, never eat another real Caesar salad or sprouts or peanuts or sushi. Fear salmonella, fear botulism, fear *E. coli,* fear the lethality of desire. Clean with the vigor of the ideal 1920s housewife, rid the kitchen of "germs," make life spotless.

I found it difficult to trust Pellegrini or to honor the centuries of experience that have tested his methods. We are the successful descendants of eons of fermentation and rot, but that century-old fear of the invisible has seized us again. The mildly ironic concern with health we felt a decade ago, when age first seemed to point its quavering finger at the boomer generation, has turned to panic. Asked what food will be like in twenty years, the chef Jean-Georges Vongerichten talked about a "sterile environment" for cooking. "The older I get, the less I want anyone handling my food. When I'm served a complicated-looking dish, I think, 'How many people have touched this?' "

Bacteria were identified as a cause of disease in 1876. It was a terrible prospect, this ghostly and unseen enemy, and one ordinary people had to take entirely on faith. Then the deliberate adulteration of food supplies was exposed—an especial scandal in milk, long considered a vital food. The realization that food could be corrupted—that food could not be *trusted*—helped lead people to put their faith and fear in corporations. Brand-name products, which were after all promulgated specifically as being reliable and eternally the same from day to day and year to year, seemed far safer than the open bulk supplies they'd used before.

"Self-service packaging lets you inspect a whole counterful of tempting fresh fruits and vegetables. And when they're packaged in sparkling cellophane, you know dust and dirt are sealed out . . . garden freshness, nutrition are sealed in." The well-dressed housewife in pearls and heels picks up her iceberg lettuce in its squeaky plastic wrap without getting soiled, and smiles. I've inherited an entire set of beliefs about food and disease based on silly pictures like these—irrational, illogical beliefs, but almost always there.

The strange thing is that we all know processed food is more dangerous—in part because of our own blind trust. Rat feces, hair, and insects are the acceptable corruption in food, what can't be avoided—there are federal standards for these. But everything from flame retardants to dioxin finds its way in to the brand-name food supply. Rice and broccoli and tea leaves and just about everything else are soaked in pesticides. Beef floats in hormones, chicken in antibiotics. Just about everything we eat floats in a soup of

preservatives and dyes and thickeners and softeners and other additives. We know about mistakes. We know about mad cow disease.
We know there are unknown chemicals out there in the plastic wrap
and foil cartons, in the laboratory, in the next new thing.

But what do we fear? Not the cow's truncated and painful life
or unmarked death. Not the cow's slowly decomposing flesh. We
fear the tiny *E. coli* that might grow within. Every step of the food
chain we've created in this country dirties our air and soil and water.
But in order to eat what we want when we want, to keep the variety and quantity and low-fat nutrition and most especially that elusive "quality" we crave, we invite ever more laboratory inventiveness
in. Why are there days when I worry about organic tomatoes cur-
ing in the sun?

People have always had a difficult time separating their science
from their philosophy. In the development of nutrition, all the anxiety of a changing world is felt. Nutrition may be an exact science,
and it may not, but its expression in the culture is almost entirely
subjective. From the beginning, the science of nutrition was tainted
by the belief that people "should" behave in a certain way toward
food. Perhaps this is inevitable, this wish so many of us carry that
knowledge will lead behavior. A surprising number of nutrition scientists have stated over the years that food choices must be based on
rational information and not on desire. In nutritional science, any
food that fails to qualify as good under the prevailing system is out-
lawed. Then only outlaws eat that food.

Until the middle of the nineteenth century, there wasn't any
rational understanding of nutrition—not in the sense of Western
scientific understanding. No one knew for sure what healthy eating
was. (Many people *thought* they knew, of course, and some of those

beliefs have been borne out later by science.) Most people believed that all food was of essentially the same quality—an "undifferenti-ated mass" of fuel, in Harvey Levenstein's words. For the poor, the problem of food had always been the simple one of getting enough of it. If you couldn't afford the meat and cake you wanted, bread would have to do. If you couldn't buy bread, you ate gruel (and longed for lard). For the rich, the problem of food was more com-plicated, one of taste and fashion and virtue. For some of the rich, food meant pleasure and the only problem was where and when. One could—and many did—live simply on meat and cake and not give it too much thought. For others, food was a problem of self-control in the face of plenty, of simply not eating "too much," how-ever much that was.

As the inchoate science of nutrition developed through the middle and late nineteenth century, scientists began dividing the "undifferentiated mass" of food into protein, carbohydrates, and fats. Nutrition-ists announced that it did matter, after all, *what* one ate—but what mattered was the nutrient density of these different substances, the relative efficiency in caloric energy of different foods. White bread was considered more nutritious than vegetables because its carbohydrates are denser. (Well into the twentieth cen-tury, nutritional scientists have worked at promoting the whole-someness of white flour over whole wheat.) Some nutritionists discouraged the poor from eating vegetables at all, suggesting that they spend their limited resources on packaged foods instead because of their denser caloric load. The fat in meat was thought to be more nutritious than the meat itself, because it held more energy.

Certain foods also were thought to cause people to lose control by creating cravings for alcohol and sex. In such a way do we still think white sugar is peculiarly dangerous, especially to children. Other foods helped people gain control over these appetites. (In such a worldview, abundant food supplies were dangerous.) The growing nation needed an energetic workforce, obedient school-children, and harmonious families. Eating in the most healthy way was, like the making of a happy home, a citizen's duty.

With the advent of basic nutrition came the concept of malnu-trition. (Even today there is no clear agreement about how many people are malnourished or even what malnutrition is, exactly.) It seemed patently obvious that poor people were malnourished because they were poor—not just because poverty and crowding limit food choices, but because bad food choices create the kind of people who end up being poor.

So began evangelical nutrition, nutrition as social work. A vari-ety of food-based social experiments took place around the turn of the century—cooperative kitchens, at-cost cafeterias for urban workers, even take-home services to provide hot meals for the poor. They were their own worst enemies. Malnutrition was caused by ignorance, and health a matter merely of education, not any redis-tribution of wealth.

For many reasons these experiments failed, but they were prophetic; they marked a flood of impending social change. The growing lack of spare time and the new concern with nutrition, along with the pressure of advertising, created a huge market for many new kinds of processed food. Conveniently enough, people came to believe at this same time that heavy, elaborate food was bad for the health. Home economists advocated simple, bland meals— easy enough to make when you can buy soup in a can. Both the symbolic and the real importance of home-cooked food as a source of nourishment and comfort were being let go.

Most nineteenth-century cookbooks emphasize fresh and local ingredients because that was all most people could get. When packaged food became common, new cookbooks (some by company public-relations writers) changed to reflect the new products. Suddenly, long-standard recipes called for canned foods instead of fresh. Fresh food—"raw" food—was simply not as good. This idea really sank in for a while; I find it popping up in strange places. In 1939, Prudence Penny recommended improving homemade soup "which is lacking in strength or flavor" by adding a can of commercial soup. During World War II, when half of the nation's produce came from victory gardens, one cookbook writer said, "When you've run low on stamps for processed vegetables, you are sure to find some fresh ones to substitute. To extend your purchase of canned or frozen fruits or vegetables, combine with some fresh fruit or vegetable that happens to be abundant . . ."

The earlier transition to processed food had led directly to an increase in vitamin-deficiency diseases like pellagra throughout rural areas. Conglomerates were making the same headway into farming as they had in milling and the transportation and packaging of food, decreasing variety, controlling choice. The transition to white flour, the increase in sugar consumption, and the monotony of many rural people's diets all added to the problem, but the biggest problem was belief. Some of the most nutritious regional foods were rejected in favor of processed, mass-produced foods precisely because of the perception that packaged food was the basis of a modern and elegant diet. Local, indigenous food like small game and wild greens were variously dismissed as "poor," "nigger," or "country" food, unacceptable to the middle-class ambitions of poor whites. Even country farmers came to prefer canned hams to local fresh ones.

Vitamins—discovered one by one from 1911 on—had even more of an impact on what people ate than the discovery of bacteria a few decades before had. By the 1920s, nutrition was the rage among the middle and upper classes, and a new cycle had begun—the promotion of a low-calorie, low-fat, low-protein diet that could provide enough of the "vital amines," or vitamins. Notes Levenstein, "Invisible, unmeasurable, and tasteless, obviously important but with little knowledge of exactly why, vitamins and minerals were an advertiser's dream." Even today, there is only general agreement on what various nutrients do, and little agreement at all on how much of any one we need.

Nutrition became ever more a middle- and upper-class obsession. The idea that one should eat for health and not pleasure was once again embedded in the common wisdom. Slowly people began to realize that processed food was often nutritionally weak, putting food processors in a terrible bind—one solved at first by the hiring of scientists as corporate shills (even Jell-O was good for you, one fellow explained) and later by reluctant fortification. Certain kinds of fortification, like the addition of riboflavin to white bread, were eventually made mandatory. Restaurant menus began carrying calorie counts and "vitamin ratings." Fresh fruits and vegetables, juices, and iodized salt were, in the new advertising mania—which could not let any opportunity for directing choice go by—promoted for their nutritive and even curative properties—properties as vital to business and social success as good hygiene.

In the late 1970s, George McGovern's Select Committee on Nutrition and Human Needs released a set of dietary goals; the response was, according to Warren Belasco, that "one pro-agribusiness group pointed out the potentially disastrous results if consumers actually bought more fresh fruits, vegetables, and whole grains: manufacturers of canned, frozen, formulated, and dehydrated foods would suffer from 'major adjustment problems.'" The guidelines were subsequently softened to the point of meaninglessness.

Nutrition represents the future—a future that may seem uncertain and unpleasant to the poor. In World War I, canned food was sent overseas, and citizens were encouraged to eat fresh fruits and vegetables and homemade soups instead. Millions of people had to reduce the amount of meat, wheat, butter, and sugar they ate, and depend instead on coarse grains, eggs, cheese, nuts, and fresh produce from home gardens. The Depression, which saw the advent of free surplus food distribution and food stamps, actually brought unexpected improvements in the nutrition of the very poor. But during World War I, many rural poor experienced an economic boost from various war industries. They chose to spend their extra income on precisely the scarcer, more expensive foods they didn't get enough of the rest of the time—meat, canned foods, sugar.

Again, during World War II, Americans had to give up more than meat. "What was the most difficult lesson you had to learn as a child or teach your children? Wasn't it sharing?" So says Marjorie Mills, author of a World War II ration cookbook.

Ration stamps improved the diets of the poor by guaranteeing them a measure of protein and enriched foods in the diet. The middle and upper classes saw rationing as deprivation and an excuse to lie, cheat, and even steal. Victory gardens provided about 40 percent of the nation's produce by the middle of the war. Many people consumed more fresh vegetables, fruit, and milk, a greater variety of foods, less meat, and used the healthier cooking methods of their grandparents. According to Levenstein, Americans ate more vegetables in 1945 than they ever had before, and more vitamin C than they have ever since, and they hated every minute of it.

Today, though, it is once again the wealthier classes that fret over nutrition, over getting not food but food chemicals. I am skeptical of the plague of food "allergies" abounding today, the endless "intolerances" that sometimes seem a thin disguise for dieting, a thin description of despair. Roland Barthes predicted some of the postmodern obsession with microscopic nutrition in 1961 when he said that nutrition science made for a world where "food is henceforth *thought out*, not by specialists, but by the entire public, even if this thinking is done within a framework of highly mythical notions." Modern nutrition, he added, was no longer an ethical science, as it had been in the century before; in the late-twentieth-century concern with nutrition was a concern with "values of *power*." A good diet is good business now—a cagey mind, the energy to win and prosper. We've replaced virtue with victory.

The natural-foods movement had profound effects—subtle effects, for the most part. The more overt change was the rapid mutation of *naturalness* as a food value to *lightness*. This change allowed processors full rein. By the 1980s, people had lost much of their temporary concern with the wholesomeness of food and traded it for avoiding fat, cholesterol, and calories. Many people have come to believe that their lives depend on tiny daily dosages of certain chemicals. Even while we obsess over adulteration and

micronutrition, this negative attitude guarantees that all kinds of
stuff is going to happen to our food, bad stuff. These days, anything and everything is acceptable in the name of achieving low-
calorie, low-fat, low-sodium goals, in the name of the difficult
coupling of convenience and taste. (Do you want to know? Wood
pulp extenders in bread. Aspartame. Olestra. Do you really want
to know?) Once upon a time, food processors held out soy and textured vegetable protein as the solution for a hungry world. Now
these are the profitable base of low-fat meat products for the worried executive.

Looking to the future, corporations plan on "functional" foods,
superenriched and almost medicinally loaded with supplements like
psyllium (and perhaps to be regulated medicinally by the FDA).
Space Food Sticks returned, long after we thought they were gone.
The future will be nanoistic, invisible, an infinite horizon for labo-
ratories and factories and barely differentiated brand-name promotion.

I believe in the value of cruciferous vegetables like broccoli and
brussel sprouts, but I believe more in the intelligence of the body
and the inevitability of decay. I wonder why we talk so much about
omega-3 fatty acids and beta-carotene and so little about anxiety
and deprivation, kindness and joy, about the long-term effects of the
day-to-day struggle to be recognized and loved. The "French
Paradox"—that the French eat a diet relatively high in cholesterol
and saturated fats but don't develop heart disease at anything
approaching the rate of Americans—has long been discussed as a
question of food chemicals like flavonoids and tocotrienols.
Relatively little credit is paid to the entirely different attitude the
French bring to the table—one of pleasure, leisure, and (no small

matter here in terms of bodily health) *deserving* to eat well. There is
a mystery in metabolism and in the hungers our body feels, in our
cravings and dreams. I suspect there are nutrients we cannot see,
cannot measure, essentials that can't be synthesized and packaged.
The best thing, the most living, present, desirable thing I can taste
is only now, now, now. There is nothing certain here, no reliable predictors. I don't want there to be predictors——I want to be surprised, inspired, renewed by food. I want to eat with no idea, no
idea at all, what to expect, no idea what will happen next, what taste
will turn my head, change my mind, next. To eat with ease and joy,
to eat with the wholehearted belief that what one eats is good, to
eat with trust——this is a great secret.

THE INDIVIDUAL IS ONCE AGAIN FIRST AND
forward. The youth revolution first seen in the twenties, and its
vibrant revival in the sixties and seventies, shrank in the eighties
into something else. We call health "fitness" now. A minority of
Americans eat healthy food and exercise regularly, but sociocultur-
ally this is the leading image of consumption and success. The constant presence of lean, mean, athletic, and perpetually young white
people in our shared images renders all the rest of us invisible. Wages
fall, security drops away, the rich grow richer and the poor poorer,
and at the same time——and not coincidentally——the image of happiness gets richer, leaner, younger, and farther and farther out of
reach. We laugh at the bemused housewife of midcentury, caught
between Betty Crocker and Betty Grable, but we are caught
between teenage models and marathon-running CEOs, and we buy
it, we buy it all the way.

Words like *labor-saving, leisure, freedom,* and *economical* are early examples of a degradation of language forced by social change, something T. J. Jackson Lears calls the "collapse of meaning." For close to two hundred years, how things look has been becoming more important than how things are. Advertising offered less and less information and more and more messages of desire, more blurring between lies and truth—shadows thrown and lights carefully cast to create false impressions. By the early twentieth century, slogans, jingles, free samples, and mascots were everywhere. Words like *natural* and *homestyle* appeared as new disinformation; in Waverley Root's phrase, these are the kind of words that deliberately "evoke but don't inform." Canned foods were a return to "home cooking," while raw and bulk foods were labelled "unwashed."

More recently, the words changed again. The food technology industry first co-opted *natural, homemade,* and *fresh* from the natural-foods movement, and then corrupted their meaning by adding *light* and *low*. In the 1980s, New York's Rainbow Room offered a "fitness" menu guaranteeing the diner fewer than 500 calories and a bill of more than $30. There is a trend in kitschy and old-fashioned cookbooks, a return to the past, but it is not what it seems. "The classics," says a food magazine, "lightened and reinterpreted, are reappearing." Endless recipes are "reinterpreted" and "refined" and "intensified" and especially "lightened." Lightened, buoyant foods of flight, foods of the rarefied, the few.

"Butter! Give me butter! Always butter!" This was Fernand Point's cry. Point, a famous haute cuisine chef, said you shouldn't eat in a restaurant until you'd seen the chef; he believed that if the chef was thin, the meal would probably be poor. A very fat man himself, he added that in all fairness, "before judging a thin man, one must get some information. Perhaps he was once fat." Point approached life on the side of delight and the power of appetite; he had an unpredictable and often dramatic sense of humor and didn't suffer fools. He is someone I would like to have known. I would like to have waited as patiently as I could at a small table while he cooked for me. He seems from his writing to have been a man free of apology, sure of himself, his time, his work. The great passion for la grande cuisine was, he said, "pitiless"—and he loved his mistress as few of us do now, even those whose lives are cooking. *Food & Wine* recently interviewed Ferdinand Metz, the president of the Culinary Institute of America and one of the keepers of the highest culinary standards in this country. Metz says he eats only super-low-fat, light food. He recommends making a soufflé with skim milk and substituting cornstarch for the eggs. Other cooks, like those of the French Culinary Institute, offer similar recipes "favorable to your waistline," but they are changes that betray the meaning of soufflé at least as much as calling frozen peas "fresh" betrays the meaning of *fresh,* the very meaning of peas.

I came across another Betty Crocker cookbook not long ago, one called *Old-Fashioned Cooking*—"tried-and-true, old-fashioned classics" that had been repaired for modern life: low-fat, low-salt, low-calorie food like a photograph of what Grandma used to make. "Old-fashioned cooking," I read, "means delicious recipes that simply can't be improved." Yet they've been improved: "Excessive amounts" of fat and salt have been removed, and microwave and Cuisinart instructions added, "while remaining faithful to the essence of the traditional recipe." The result is clam canapés consisting of canned clams, a package of cream cheese, dried dill weed, lemon juice, and squares of sandwich bread. The result is Sour Cream Biscuits: "2 cups baking mix / 1 cup dairy sour cream."

I find this again in *Fashionable Food: Seven Decades of Food Fads*. Sylvia Lovegren writes in her introduction, "As much as possible the recipes in this book are true to the originals. They have not been updated for modern tastes, except occasionally to reduce the amount of salt, sugar, or fat." These are the unavoidable changes, she adds, alterations that "had to be" made. Lovegren changed recipes to reflect current and ever-evolving beliefs about nutrition even while writing a social history, without wondering what it means to rewrite the source of our history.

The Betty Crocker Test Kitchens, a warren of basement rooms, is in a sprawling complex ten miles west of Minneapolis at the corner of General Mills Boulevard and Betty Crocker Way. When I visited there a few years ago while writing a story for *Saveur*, Marcia Copeland took me down the hall to the Pennsylvania Dutch Kitchen, where several coffee cakes waited, warm from the oven. Copeland and Jeannie Kozan, the team leader for Dessert Mixes, wanted to demonstrate the perilous balance between speed, nutrition, and flavor that haunts recipe development.

The classic Betty Crocker sour cream coffee cake is so good it has the rare distinction of being in every edition of Big Red, but it's not exactly diet food. Every recent survey General Mills has done points out the intense desire on the part of consumers to have their cake and not eat it, too. Consumers tell market researchers, without hesitation, that what they want is low-calorie, low-fat, easy-to-make foods that taste just like what Mom used to make. They will pay a lot of money for anything that seems to offer this combination.

On the counter before us were three versions of the sour cream coffee cake: classic, low-fat, and very-low-fat. We perched on stools, looking out a fake sunny window on a fake sunny barn, and gently cut off small slices. "How do you make a classic recipe light?" I asked. Kozan said, nibbling, "The number of changes the consumer can handle is as few as possible." The changes made are largely substitutions and simple elimination—a lessening of the original, in literal terms.

The lightest (and by this I mean the *lowest*, the fewest calories and the least fat) of the coffee cakes is not bad, a little rubbery and dry. But the three cooks quickly agreed it had poor texture, poor "fork resistance," not enough flavor. Another miracle deferred. We moved on to the moderately light version, which was softer and moister and seemed perfectly acceptable to me. (This particular recipe did make it into the most recent cookbook.)

But then I tasted the "classic" version. Suddenly, it's cake—yellow, moist, delicious, one of the best bites of cake I'd had in a long time. But before I could reach for more, they led me down the hall to the Cape Cod Kitchen to taste Christmas cookies. Outside the window there, a bright blue ocean crashed eternally on a sunny, rocky shore.

So here we go through the looking glass to this, the best of all worlds—old but new, traditional but modern, tasty but healthful, old-fashioned but easy, packaged but fresh—everything we want life to be. All the paranoid, melancholy longing for a bite to eat I've suffered, and all along I just wanted to do this—rewrite. Reduce the fat and salt, take out the tears and anger, delete twenty pounds, eliminate the guilt, the factory farms, and ugly packaging, that last bit of regret. And add instead a few homilies and a kind pat on the hand.

· · ·

DURING THE DEPRESSION, FOOD SURPLUSES were destroyed more than once while people stood in breadlines. "Indeed, no sooner did the Depression strike than a wave of reducing diets swept the middle class," writes Harvey Levenstein, citing everything from the Hollywood Eighteen-day Diet to the use of enemas, thyroid supplements, and amphetamines. While millions went hungry, the middle and upper classes were largely able to eat as well as they liked during "the greatest economic crisis the nation had ever seen." Yet many chose to eat as few as 600 calories a day in order to lose weight. The new emphasis on youth and streamlined, uncluttered lines, new warnings about obesity and health, all had an effect. But Levenstein also thinks it was simply impossible for people to believe there could be starvation in a land of abundance. Starvation in America? How could it be?

Americans are lively defenders of the right to leisure time and toys and vacations, and lively judges of what they see as other people's indulgences. But it remains that the behavior valued most in a world of abundance isn't creative use of that abundance but resistance to it. "The danger and fear of plenty have replaced the danger and fear of famine," writes Massimo Montanari. Modern dieting, he adds, has "reticent penitential values" in the face of unexpected plenty.

According to surveys, about half of American households have at least one person on a diet at any given time. Dieting is normal— more normal than eating what you want to eat. How many of us now live on various versions of Lean Cuisine during the work week and pay premium for a plate of swordfish and greens on Saturday night? (We have the sauce and dressing on the side—of course.) Stouffer's Lean Cuisine (now a Nestlé product)—is little more than smaller portions for a higher price; the consumer pays for the corporate mother to dole out the proper foods in their proper amounts. A man told me he's never had to worry about his weight, he can eat whatever he wants. "People resent me," he said. "They don't want to go out to eat with me." He paused. "It's *lonely*."

If an alien landed here, it would see a strange world—a world with much food and many starving people. Most of the starvation is forced on whole populations by power brokers and distant agendas. But what could visitors from afar think of the hundreds of thousands, the millions of healthy, wealthy people who starve voluntarily? Who go at least a little hungry all the time? They take on the mantle of hunger with pride and self-satisfaction, complaining of the deprivation, seeking sympathy.

The marriage of desires—between sensual pleasure and the pleasure of denial—is a tense marriage. We buy asceticism at a decadent price, spend thousands of dollars a week to be supervised eating fewer than a thousand calories a day, hands slapped if we stray. Starvation, paid for with hard work. But both indulgence and sacrifice are limited to the privileged few who can afford to throw away what others literally die to have. If I take any comfort in the painful dead end in which we find ourselves, it is the rather petty one that very thin people with reduced body fat are people who have been in a self-induced famine for a long time. And they didn't have to do this—there is no reason to do this. The next time a real famine comes along, dieters are going to lose. They have nothing left to give.

My own life has been marked by a perilous and disturbing terror of my own body—a pendulum swinging, inexorably, forward and back. I ate too much, I ate too little, I dieted for dieting's sake—simply to resist, to conquer food. I dieted because I did not deserve not to be hungry, to hunger, to yearn. I made food both fetish and taboo; I felt secret appetites and attended to them in private, with shame, while the words of television commercials and magazine headlines echoed in the shadows.

To the extent that my mother disliked cooking, she was fond of eating sweets. She was perpetually dieting in a casual random way, though she wasn't heavy. She made no sense of it and didn't seem to mind even that, relishing her Mounds bar after the Saturday grocery shopping was done and eating a bowl of ice cream every night. "It's really ice *milk,*" she would say. "Not so fattening." She bought box upon box of AYDS diet candy (I'd eat half a dozen at a time when she wasn't looking) and diet breakfast milk shakes and Hershey's chocolate syrup to pour on top of her ice *milk* while she watched television.

I didn't diet like that. In my twenties I starved, I took pills, I picked at tiny portions of dreadful, frozen, reconstituted diet food. I fasted. In my thirties I mostly worried at food, skipping meals and snacking when no one saw. Dieting is credit and debt. For many years I caught myself wondering if I could "afford" to eat something, if I'd "earned" it through activity or earlier deprivation, if I "owed" more denial. When I was dieting I would haunt the kitchen hour by hour, gazing, grazing, tracking, noting—keeping the books. Now that I no longer diet, I sometimes forget to eat, look up from work or play surprised by the clock. When I eat, I try to eat with relish and attention. But I can't always do that; eating became more than sustenance and less than nourishment the longer I worried about eating this way. It became something else, not quite metaphor. More symptom. I still tend to eat certain "bad" foods with half-averted eyes, flinching, haunted.

I write today as a woman who dieted "successfully." I lost quite a lot of weight, and kept it off for several years. I was thinner at twenty-eight than I was at puberty. I look at photographs of myself from that time—I see the cheekbones, collarbones, the apricot-sized breasts, the tight jeans. The tight smile. The dead eyes. What I remember (besides the counting, besides the scales and measuring cups and careful, constant planning and the hunger) is sadness. I had come to believe that I was unhappy because I was too big, and when I was smaller and still unhappy, I could not for a long time figure out what was wrong. When I finally started to relax, and the weight gradually, inevitably, returned to my body, another kind of weight slowly rose off me and disappeared.

Dieting utterly disrupts one's relationship to food, to all food at all times. Eating takes on a sinister power and food an animate spirit—mostly malevolent. The way one thinks on a diet is the way people in famine think about food—obsessively, with great care—but turned upside down. Instead of being desired and out of reach, food is desired and within reach, but just as potently remains fantasy.

Dieting is about being good and bad; the eater is either obedient or naughty, compliant or resistant. (Dieting was once considered a sin simply because it is rooted in vanity.) Food is good or bad for you—but more important, in eating any given food, *you* are good or bad. When I dieted a lot I liked being hungry because it meant I was being good. A childish dichotomy, but one that can take up the whole world for a time.

Dieting is control. The word *anorexia* is rooted in the Greek *orex*, meaning appetite, desire, to reach after. Anorexia means literally not to do so—not to long for, to stretch out in need for, not to reach, not to want. And when we finally can't control our desires, we can control what our body does with food—we can vomit, take laxatives, have surgery, swallow pills, exercise into oblivion. We can always find another way to say *No*.

Processed diet food is successful because it allows us to relinquish control for a moment, to be, in a tiny way, uncontrolled. It doesn't matter that a frozen diet dinner doesn't taste good, doesn't satisfy hunger, and lacks any nutrients to speak of—we eat them because they allow us to eat without thinking, without planning, without keeping the books. Michelle Stacey, in *Consumed*, her book on modern American food, says they let us be children. "To talk about simple moderation—good, satisfying food in normal amounts—is to talk like an adult, a parent . . ."

In the thin joke of chronic dieting, people conspire to pretend that what they are eating is actually delicious. (Spas advertise their hedonism without a wink. The Golden Door recipes are "sybaritic" and "sumptuous," the Rancho La Puerta meals are "flavor-packed.") If you diet all the time, like many women do, dieting is often vaguely masked as a sensible approach to health. The customer nods and smiles and says, oh, it's *good*, isn't it good? Of course, it's dreadful; no one can make 800 calories taste like 2,000, and even if the miracle of modern chemistry breaks through with the final equation, no one can make 800 calories and 15 grams of fat *feel* like 2,000 calories and 40 grams of fat. The body isn't fooled.

Robert Farrar Capon, an Episcopal priest, remembers his big uncles as "sacred groves, as *places* in my history." The "diet-mongers" who force such uncles to slim "dwell only upon what they would like a man to conform to; they never come within a hundred miles of knowing what a man *is* . . . dieting is wrong because it is not priestly. It is a way of using food without using it, bringing it into your history without letting it get involved with your history."

In such a way does dieting become a profound reduction of self-hood. When we shrink the body from shame at its size, we are literally *reduced*—encaged by our failure. Anger, demands, selfish insistence on personal freedom, escape, resistance—lost, put aside, inside. Our bigness disappears not only in fact but from sight, disappears inside, and we become inside-out people. All our weight and shape and meaning are withheld—all that anger, that insistence, those demands. When I was thin the emptiness in me felt bottomless. I don't mean the hunger. I stopped being hungry, or stopped minding. The emptiness I felt, the hollowness, was psychic, spiritual—it was the opposite of feeling big, strong, safe. I had gotten hungry for the sake of others, for their opinion of me, and so the hunger I felt was a bottomless hunger, one that could never be satisfied.

Recently, a new fashion in soap has appeared: great chunks of translucent perfumed soap made to look like food. Peach bars filled with candied "fruit," and chocolate bars and coconut cream bars, aromatic of the grocer's. They are sold individually by weight, like good cheese. Instead of real food we buy false food, products to soothe and pamper the "self"—that is, the body, in its long days of hunger.

Dieting is hatred—of self and others. Women, fat and thin both, hate fat women. We hate one another, say cruel things to and about one another, judge, cut apart. We sympathize with one another but the battle is about survival. In such a world, as Sally Cline says, eating disorders are an "extreme but *orderly* response."

I catch myself thinking, *I should lose a little weight.* I catch myself spiraling downward; I catch myself turning toward an ill-tasting frozen dinner because it promises "under 300 calories"; I catch myself denigrating my own *experience* of happiness. I remember that I actually am happy and that I do not need to turn helplessly through this spiral; I remember that there could hardly be anything less important in the world than whether or not I lose a few pounds, and I feel like I've caught my breath after being held under water, pleading for air.

It is a chronic disease, though: To this day, there are certain foods I do not allow myself. Such divisions down the middle of the world are the core truth of dieting. There are foods I like and almost never touch—good, fun food like doughnuts and milk shakes and onion rings. Most of the food I don't allow myself to eat is the sort of thing one might say has *no redeeming value.* But there's nothing consistent about it. I cheerfully make and eat brownies, pies, pizza, rich and creamy sauces. I find myself contemplating doughnuts, looking at one single doughnut on a plate, and I hear shrill voices chorus together in my head, voices crying out, *calories, fat, nasty, bad. Bad girl; mustn't touch.*

Other voices tell me what to do at restaurants, at parties, at the grocery store. Go ahead, laugh—if you don't recognize this. I go to the grocery store. I buy all kinds of things—vegetables, juice, toilet paper, bread. But what I want are potato chips. Will I buy them? Won't I? Yes. No. Yes. I grab them on the fly as I approach the register, refusing to think clearly, not looking, and then, back home,

I don't eat them. I just keep the unopened bag in the cupboard. This is grotesque behavior. But even this behavior isn't what I think of as the real sickness—it's not the eating or not-eating, the buying or not-buying, not the wanting or not-wanting that matters. Not even the shame about eating or the shame about being ashamed. The sickness I want to be shod of for good is the continual *thinking-about-food* in all these joyless ways. I want back the room dieting has made food take up in my life without regard for pleasure—the terrible space this grotesqueness fills.

Several years ago, I consciously stopped dieting—and sometimes not dieting was as hard as the dieting had been, harder. The entire question of whether a person is "too big" (or too small) is rarely asked in objective terms—objective measures for such things simply don't exist. Some very big (and very small) people defy the apparently objective medical criteria behind which judgment often resides. Even these criteria change frequently. To ask such a question—Am I the "right" size?—of oneself or another is to ask only whether one is too big or too small, too tall, thin, dark, or light, to meet another person's standard. I weigh myself only once or twice a year, and my weight has been the same for many years, about eight pounds more than I weighed in high school. This is, in the general scheme of female physiology, normal, healthy, nothing to worry about. My weight stays the same through illness and holidays, vacations and surgery, in happiness and sadness. And still—*still*—I think, *If I just cut back a little I could probably lose a little weight.*

The act of dieting is the act of creating a mental world of struggle, a struggle most people expect to lose even as they begin. In the last few years, an anti-dieting movement has slowly gained strength, empowered by a great deal of careful research showing that almost everything we think about dieting and food attitudes and weight is wrong. The journalist Laura Fraser, in *Losing It*, a tour through the dieting industry, describes a world clearly outside logic and outside ordinary human experience. By the time the reader passes through the strange environments inhabited by Weight Watchers, Susan Powter, and a host of self-styled thinness gurus, the world of dieting has ceased to make sense. She ends with a discussion of what it means *not* to diet—new gurus giving power back. Viewed in the whole context of obsession with ounces and inches, anti-dieting becomes the truest pro-life philosophy I know.

Some of the most important research has been done by Janet Polivy and Peter Herman, who have carefully studied the mental world of the dieter for more than twenty years. The dieter, Polivy and Herman write, is occupied continually with food and meals and lives in an "entrenchment of dichotomous thinking." In their article "Dieting and Bingeing: A Causal Analysis," they propose that "dieting causes bingeing by promoting the adoption of a cognitively regulated eating style." In other words, dieting makes you so obsessed with food that you eat too much. Polivy and Herman have found that "non-dieters eat less when they are anxious than when they are calm . . . Dieters, however, eat small, diet-maintaining amounts when calm, but eat somewhat *more* when distressed . . ." Nondieters lose weight when depressed; dieters gain. Nondieters eat less when drinking alcohol; dieters eat more. Depression and alcohol are "disinhibitors" for dieters—these and other factors interrupt the fragile mental control dieters must constantly exert upon themselves.

Polivy and Herman did an experiment wherein several men

starved themselves down to 74 percent of their starting weight on a very-low-calorie diet. "When food was later made available in unlimited quantities and the men had returned to their initial weights, they exhibited a persistent tendency to binge, gorging at meals to the limit of their physical capacity. Such behavior was never observed in these men prior to their 'diet' experience." Not only that, the men weren't overweight to begin with, didn't "need" to lose weight. They were part of an experiment and under no social pressure of any kind. This is what Polivy and Herman call "counter-regulation." Dieters diet until the diet is interrupted and then they give up completely and overeat.

In another experiment, the researchers gave people "preload" milk shakes. Some shakes were low in calories and fat grams, some were rich. The subjects were sometimes told the truth about what they were drinking and sometimes not. Only their bodies knew for sure if the milk shake they'd had was a "diet" drink or real dessert.

When a self-declared dieter thought she'd had a diet shake, she ate little of the rich treats offered later. When she thought—correctly or not—that she'd drunk a rich milk shake, she gorged on the treats. This happened again and again. The sense of having "blown" the diet for the day was followed by "lusty eating," say the researchers. Dieters responded to the food psychologically. On the other hand, people who said they didn't diet responded *physiologically*—their bodies balanced the fat in their diets by regulating their appetite for it.

Much research supports the fact that many, perhaps most, people can't wholly regulate their eating. The body insistently regulates itself. Secretly fed low-fat diets, people unconsciously seek out fatty foods later, in one study after another. There may be a purely biological response to dieting involving a disrupted sympathomimetic and endocrinological system. Polivy points out that "restrained eaters salivate more than do unrestrained eaters in the presence of attractive food cues . . ."

This research reveals a world already quite familiar to me, one I am nevertheless glad to see validated this way. It is so hard to explain, and its distorted logic is so often displayed as the prevailing point of view. Physiological reactions aside, Polivy and Herman believe most of the behavior is cognitive. Dieters respond to their perceptions; nondieters to the facts. Moreover, the crash of cognitive control is socially specific. Dieters binged more when they thought they were unobserved. If they had an official observer, dieters acted much like nondieters did all the time, neither restricting nor indulging. "Unfortunately, such socially induced 'sensible' eating lasted only as long as the observer was present," note the researchers. When the observer pretended to be another experimental subject, the dieters followed her carefully, eating more only if she did first. Dieters ate least of all if their companion claimed to be on a diet, too.

A few years after this experiment, Polivy and Herman published a survey article called "Diagnosis and Treatment of Normal Eating." Their deliberately paradoxical title was the point: Chronic, often obsessive dieting is now the normal way for many people to eat; in certain segments of the population, far more people are actively dieting to lose weight than are not. "It is now 'normal' for individuals in our society to express concern about their weight and to engage in fitful attempts to change it," and so "the meaning of a phrase such as *normal eating* is no longer obvious." This is only a rumor, but I'm told by a good source that there's a sign in the women's bathroom of a leading fashion magazine that reads, PLEASE DON'T VOMIT HERE.

Polivy and Herman propose the possibility of a continuum of disordered thinking. Based on their own and others' research, Polivy and Herman believe that dieters lose the ability to understand both hunger and satisfaction. Normal boundaries between cognitive, social, and bodily desires exist only in the "*undisturbed* organism"— not in the overeater, who is unusually sensitive to external cues, and especially not in the dieter, who has created an artificial boundary closer to hunger than satiety. That boundary is a painful one, almost constantly present, and it is frail, requiring continual vigilance. "In fact, the sorts of disinhibited eating that the dieter fears actually arise from dieting itself."

When one exercises a continual (as opposed to occasional) restriction on any natural desire, one loses the ability to make rational decisions about that desire. This is one of the paradoxes of living in a human body, this need to give up control at some point and trust in an invisible and immeasurable wisdom—part biology, part something rather more ethereal, perhaps. Constant conscious control makes us the puppet of physiological systems we barely understand. The only way out of the downward spiral is to stop basing one's hungers entirely on nutrient dosages, calorie counts, and what the person next to you will think. I needed to learn, and continue to learn, to listen to my own appetite for food, and I am always surprised. There is newness here, curiosity, the unexpected. I am still learning what satisfaction is. I am still learning that trusting in the often irrational pleasures of the body is not only normal but wise.

A few years ago in New York City, I ate dinner with three women

I know there. It was a lot like a Polivy and Herman experiment. We met in the restaurant of a trendy midtown hotel. All three of my friends came from work and they all were wearing black—short black skirts, black tops, sheer black stockings, and black shoes. Their hair was neat and carefully combed and pulled back. They all were thin. I was the contrast, the out-of-towner, out of touch—my unruly plumpness, my loose long hair, my pink blazer and blue jeans. We talked throughout the meal about their pressured lives, the impossibility of it all, their stressful jobs, the crazy city full of noise and tension. "Oh, if I don't get out of town on the weekends, I go out of my mind!" said one.

Anyone who looks at so-called women's magazines now knows how to order in restaurants so as to protect one's special dietary needs: no oil, no sauces, dressing on the side, steamed vegetables, grilled everything. We used to go out to a good restaurant in order to enjoy a chef's unique creations; now we go out and try to avoid them. That night, we ate up-to-date eclectic cuisine of some kind or other, all shellfish and portobellos and bits of pasta—I ate, they dabbled. Everyone oohed and aahed at the dessert tray, and each of us ordered something off it. But when the desserts came, I was the only one who ate. The other women poked and sipped and stared, and stole a few bites of my crème caramel. Their reward was the virtue of resistance, the tight spring's long-held tension still holding. Denial is what some women have come to desire most, and that's nothing new. Certain emotions are dangerous to people who live by denial, by need and hunger. The relaxed happiness of a good table is one. Another is gratitude, in any form.

I find it difficult to explain the twin position I seem to occupy in this scene. I am inside and outside at once. I am watching four women around a table, three of one world and a visitor from another—so clearly foreign, so unable to fit in. I am watching the strangeness of a rich, noisy, seductively vibrant city I love, which demands so much of people, and the smaller worlds within it where codes of dress and conduct and appearance are strictly, harshly enforced. And I am inside, nervous, aware of my differences, my inability to meet the standard these other women meet every day. And we all are living in times so detached that "lighten up" is used when people are more thoughtful than their fellows want them to be. There is no way to point out these self-contained contradictions and not be guilty of something or other.

I ate my dessert, all of it, and I ate in a glaring spotlight, a complex concoction of feelings. I ate my dessert because I had wanted it, but it went down hard. I didn't feel guilty about their hunger; I resented it. But what I felt besides resentment was shame. Shame at my bigness, the big space I took up in my chair, the lack of restraint in my hair and my clothes and my desire. I felt shame not that I ate dessert but that I failed at not eating. I failed not to *want* too much.

THESE DAYS, THERE'S ENOUGH OF A BACKLASH against endless dieting that the most successful diets are in disguise. They are camouflaged in a fog of claims about health, endurance, and success—Barthes's predicted "values of power."

The modern cycle of disguised diets began in the mid-1980s. An early proponent was Sabine de Mirbeck-Brassart, a Frenchwoman with roots in the Cordon Bleu of Paris, who started the L'Ecole de Cuisine Française Sabine de Mirbeck in East Sussex, England, to develop Cuisine Santé. Santé, she wrote, evolved in part as a "way to accommodate today's stressful and sedentary habits," and was "especially evolved to satisfy the concerns and desires of the most health-conscious gourmet," especially the one who had grown tired of nouvelle cuisine's tricks. Cuisine Santé was an early runner in the race of postmodern diets: elaborate, rather expensive, time-consuming, and beautiful dishes with almost no fat, no sugar, and very little salt. Like nouvelle cuisine, they depend on "poaching, steaming, sweating, braising and casseroling," but almost everything in Cuisine Santé is literally reduced: low-fat yogurt in place of cream; herbs instead of salt; white meat instead of anything else. It is an elaborate, expensive, time-consuming, beautiful way not to eat very much. Santé has been supplanted by the recipes of the Canyon Ranch spa, *The Golden Door Cookbook* (less than 20 percent of the calories from fat) and *The Rancho La Puerta Spa Cookbook* (less than 120 calories a serving), and a parade of other fussily defatted gourmet diets.

Then there is the Zone. Barry Sears made a mint with his Zone diet. Sears (never mentioned without the modifier "Ph.D.") disguised his in the cloak of health and complicated "biochemistry." The Zone, says Sears, helps everything from premenstrual tension to diabetes and multiple sclerosis, is better than both vegetarian and the American Cancer Association diets at preventing cancer, and improves "civility." Sears bases his diet on an elaborate set of hormonal and genetic equations based on what our humanoid ancestors supposedly ate—meat, vegetables, fruit. "Neo-Paleolithic man was a prolific hunter, actually reducing many species to near extinction," writes Sears. "In locales where hunting was good, people stopped to gather fruits and fiber-rich vegetables. So lean meat, fruits, and vegetables were the preferred menu . . . To be genetically correct, man needs a modern version of a Neo-Paleolithic diet, a diet that's based on his current genetic makeup. That's exactly what a Zone-favorable diet is . . ."

A "Zone-favorable diet" is not for slackers. It requires careful ratios of "blocks" of nutrients at carefully controlled times of the day in specific caloric amounts. The official Web site has a page called "Master the Zone (For Advanced Users)." For the rest of us, "the new ZonePerfect QuickStart Kit is the quickest and easiest way to enter the Zone. *Perfect* for Zone newcomers!" There's a lot of talk about glucagon and eicosanoids, hyperinsulinemia and what Sears calls the delta 5 desaturase enzyme "(which is really the gateway to the Zone)." It takes a calculator to figure out how much protein you should eat each day, using lean body mass, activity level, weight, and a few mathematical factors. Food is a drug in Sears's view; we medicate ourselves, and it's a complicated science.

Carbohydrates are bad in this pastiche of history, fantasy, and legerdemain. Neo-Paleolithic man didn't cultivate grains—so Sears dictates no rice, pasta, cereal, tortillas, bread. On the other hand (and this alone helped line Sears's pockets), fat is good. Fat, that is, in tiny amounts, like a single macadamia nut or one-third teaspoon of olive oil. Meat is really good—but only in small, low-fat, skinless forms. There are many contradictions and innumerable exceptions to this foundation based in "genetic makeup." You can eat egg whites but not yolks. You can't eat carrots, potatoes, mangoes, or papayas. You can't eat dark chicken or chicken skin. You can, however, eat tofu, Eggbeaters, and "protein powder." Sears goes on for some time about our inability to handle lactose well, but allows low-fat cottage cheese and yogurt. It is truly hard to imagine our ancestors, roving gangs of nomads with "bone structures of world class athletes," walking away from a carrot or skinning the chicken breast.

What do you eat on the Zone? Not very much. (That's a funny thing about diets.) In order to keep that all-important ratio of carbohydrate to protein just right, Sears emphasizes that the absolute maximum anyone should eat in a day is 1,700 calories—and that's for very active men. The original Zone diet allowed only 800 to 1,000 calories a day for many women. "Many complained of hunger," explains a Web site page devoted to proving that the Zone is not a low-calorie diet. Now the minimum is all the way up to 1,100 calories a day.

This means that lunch is perhaps three ounces of skinless chicken breast, two cups of broccoli, one-half of a medium apple, and nine olives. For dinner, three ounces of tuna, one cup of cucumber slices, one cup of zucchini, seven cherries, and a teaspoon of canola oil. At bedtime (very important prior to the long fast of sleep), four ounces of plain low-fat yogurt. And sure, you can go out for dinner—where you annoy your server and the chef and make a nuisance of yourself by ordering a low-fat entree but eating only a portion of it, and having a small glass of wine and half of a fruit dessert.

Sears and his adherents spend a lot of time making the point that the Zone is not a diet. It's a drug-delivery technology, it's medicine, it's evolution. The Zone is about health, energy, and disease prevention. It's "a testimony to the power of food in controlling hormonal response." It's a lifestyle. Zone energy bars, Zone fitness consultants, Zone dietitians. Zone oatmeal. Ready-to-eat Zone meals. Zone skin cream. The Zone's adherents are thrilled to find out that meat and fat are not wicked after all, and then obediently eat so little of either they lose weight, and then make that last, vital leap of imagination—meat and fat must make you lose weight. The credibility is there to be had. Sears made money on the Zone and even seems to believe in it, though the whole Zone empire has collapsed into a competing set of entrepreneurs, most of whom have shut Sears out in the cold. Regardless, the Zone was never about "peak athletic performance"or Neo-Paleolithic bone structure.

I tried to follow the Zone for a few weeks while I was reading the book, and it was all so drearily familiar: the almost instantaneous obsession, the careful shopping and planning ahead and looking ahead and wistfully looking back, the barely felt sense of guilt when I snuck a bite or two of rice, my growing aversion to bread and pasta, the sudden, daily concern with my body which wasn't, after all, very different from day to day. I've dieted so many times before, I've done Dr. Atkins and Dr. Stillman and Weight Watchers and Diet Center and Jenny Craig—and the Zone was just another one.

I first became interested in the Zone after reading a couple of histories of the human relationship to food. It wasn't the fact that here was one more diet aimed at the "Porky Pig" shape of Americans—Sears's image, not mine. It was the way this diet was all trumped up in scientific smoke and mirrors about evolution and human history, a lot of it incomplete or just wrong. Human beings evolved not just as nomadic hunters and gatherers running down the herds and picking fruit off the trees they passed, but as lethargic cave dwellers struggling through long periods of famine. Sears believes that "lean meats, fruits, and vegetables were the preferred menu" of our ancestors. But I believe that our ancestors preferred simply to eat—whatever they could find, everything edible they could find. Preference was not at issue. The most important mistake, I think, in Sears's philosophy is the idea that our endocrinological systems are so delicately attuned to every gram of carbohydrate and protein that a slight variation in schedule can make us sick, that we've developed as picky creatures who think far ahead about the consequences of our appetites. But we're simply hungry animals, happy at a full plate. When there wasn't enough food, our ancestors went hungry—not just at bedtime but for days, weeks, and longer. That's not only ancient history but the near past. The fact that women tend to deposit fat around their hips, thighs, and belly is a manifestation of evolutionary success. A little bit of fat *is* health and fertility. It's no secret that the ideal we strive for now is one of a sterile and even asexual woman, a hungry woman, a starving woman past the point of worrying about languid pleasures and the slow ministrations of love.

In his 271-page book *The Zone*, Barry Sears does not mention famine a single time. What he does is tell his readers again and again, in a hundred different ways, how to eat to get the body we evolved to protect ourselves from having—that lean, mean, hungry look.

9

MY PARENTS AND GRANDPARENTS, their parents and grandparents, wanted the new. "What has drawn the Modern World into being is a strange, almost occult yearning for the future," wrote Wendell Berry in the 1970s. "Just to *reach* the future, assuming the future will inevitably be 'better.'" In spite of brief spurts of nostalgia for a simpler past, this is what Americans have always wanted—until, quite suddenly, that momentum came to a skidding halt while I was growing up. What was modern and new was suddenly dreary and old; what had been old was suddenly new. The halcyon past was our future; the terrible *now* rejected for an imaginary (and improved) *then*. The past was a lost horizon to us, just barely far enough away it couldn't be tested for truth, and therefore irresistible.

What seemed to be wrong with everything in the late 1960s was what was new with everything: technology in almost every form, the steady accretion of American power and wealth in fewer and fewer hands, the separation between people and the physical world around them. All the food we had grown up eating, liking—the Space Food Sticks and the Tang and the multivitamin promise of Jet Age microefficiency—was the end-point of 150 years of processing, complicating, and controlling the raw state of food. Longed-for, welcomed—and suddenly we didn't want it anymore.

Every generation rejects part of the previous generation's traditions, at least for a time, but do many reject a culture's entire cuisine out of hand? A loud and visible minority of Americans did. We rejected the food and the entire web of expectations and hopes it represented. It was probably that much easier to walk away from the newly constructed world of the American fifties than it would have been to walk away from a naturally evolved tradition. We had no evolved traditions, didn't know how to read the buried texts of our history. Still, in Warren Belasco's words, "it took a substantial act of disaffiliation to forgo familiar cooking."

I began my retreat from the mainstream American foodway in 1970, a frustrated thirteen-year-old who had to watch Vietnam protests and Woodstock on television because I was too young to go. I was loudly vegetarian then and ate plain noodles at home in conspicuous sacrifice, and snacked on fruity yogurt and Sesame Snaps. I thought this was "natural food." I left home at sixteen (the door slamming behind me) to be a student at an alternative college program, a Summerhillian experiment in student-directed learning at a college in southern Oregon. A lot of us who ended up in that brief educational refuge were dropouts of one kind or another, self-styled teenage poets, hipsters, dreamers, ragers. So of course many of us were vegetarians, or claimed to be when anyone was looking. We began to play with what it meant to manage our own lives, and one of the first things we did was start complaining about the standard cafeteria fare we bought with our room-and-board payments. The powdered scrambled eggs, soft white bread, and orange macaroni and cheese smelled of all the lost comforts of home, but we resisted. We fought the siren call.

A group of students solved the problem, and they did it in the remarkably straightforward way problems sometimes get solved. They designed a vegetarian cafeteria line—designed the menu and the budget, found the staff, wrote a plan, and convinced some administrator it was worth a try. Then they actually made it work, all with the college's bemused blessing.

Late at night we went to George's Coffee Shop across the street from campus and ate huge bowls of chili heaped with cheese and raw onions, mounds of French fries covered in ketchup, thick black coffee. But during the day, Scott and his assistants cooked a different sort of thing altogether. Scott was one of the older students, tall, round, and ponytailed. He had experience as a fry cook, and he happily fed us stir-fried vegetables and fresh whole-wheat bread. We lined up in proud defiance three times a day by the institutional glass counters of the cafeteria, dishing up eggplant parmigiana, bowls of brown rice, bean soup, while the hundreds of other dorm students dined on ham sandwiches and Tater Tots. There were days when I would have liked a few Tater Tots, or even some ham, but the sense of separate belonging was a potent fuel. I was one of a tribe standing apart, marked and defined by its labor for food and its mundane rituals, and this satisfied a much greater appetite.

So the past became new. "These are early days too, but of another era," wrote Ita Jones in *The Grub Bag*. "In the cities, mountains, hills and desert, communes have flowered and reached into the past, bringing forth handicrafts, beautiful ways of doing and making things, art forms on the verge of dying, and discovering ways of living in peace of mind, even if bombs do hang over our heads."

All things seemed possible then, intoxicatingly possible. The success of that simple cafeteria line was my first experience in the shared thrill of the realized manifesto, the thrill of change. For me, for a lot of us, it was also a daily source of discovery about food. I ate my first vine-ripened tomato there, my first composed salads, my first brown rice and crisply stir-fried vegetables. I learned to anticipate food in an entirely new way.

We enjoyed a lot of private jokes. Reinventing cuisine was the cosmic equivalent of playing with our food; we were stirring the peas and creamed chipped beef together in the school cafeteria. While Ben and Jerry were still getting stoned and only dreaming of Chunky Monkey and Phish Food, we were laughing over "library paste sherbet" and "lima bean fudge ice cream." The naturalist Euell Gibbons drawled across the television, "Ever eat a pinecone?" and my dormmate Carol crowed back, "Ever eat a *rock?*" and it was very funny. There were infinite possibilities when one stepped outside convention, together.

For a brief spell, a group of us played with macrobiotics, late in the fading bloom of that trend. Macrobiotics, wrote its modern guru, George Ohsawa, was " the biological and physiological application of Oriental philosophy and medicine, a dialectical conception of the infinite universe." We didn't know from dialectics. To us, macrobiotics was just new and exciting and foreign, mysterious, promising; it was a brief but sincere conversion. "You are all sanpaku," we quoted wisely, examining each other's corneas and the dark circles under our eyes, and for weeks lived on plain brown rice and mu tea until the edges of the world began to soften.

Brown rice was as expressive of our tribal identity as our clothes and hair, as central to the nascent ethnicity as matzo and tortillas are to other cultures. Brown was altogether better than white. "Darkness was funky, earthy, authentic," wrote Warren Belasco in *Appetite for Change*, "while whiteness, the color of powerful detergents, suggested fear of contamination and disorder." Thirty years ago, the shiny streamlining of food and a century of whiteness gave way to a grubby love of the natural, the dusty leaf and slightly buggy lettuce of the local garden, the gritty co-op floor and big bins of beans, rice, and nuts reminiscent of the lost general store. That was health, that closeness to soil and growth. Soil and compost were a different kind of dirt than the adulteration of the conglomerates; clean was a matter of purity, not color. Everything from jewelry to hair was thick, clunky, textured, multihued, and layered, everything jangled and dangled and intertwined, antiwhite and antishine and very unstreamlined.

We did our "substantial act of disaffiliation," but we also committed substantial acts of reaffiliation. We didn't simply reject our family food. We created our own, and in doing so adopted one another as family. We made up new foods, from the ridiculous to the sublime. Carob-honey fudge was almost as bad as the tofu carob cheesecake that kept showing up at potlucks. But the sublime! Feta cheese and spinach pizza; breads, breads, so many breads; chocolate-orange ice cream. Fluffy, nutty brown rice. Like yogurt, ginseng, and Tiger Balm, brown rice was at first strange and redolent with other places, other times, other ways—other than this, other than what we had begun with—and in time became as familiar as Mom's macaroni and cheese. In many ways, this new cuisine was as rigid, homogenous, and familiar as our parents' had been, as any Old World pattern. A lot of it wasn't remotely new, either, but the community around it was.

While I toyed with George Ohsawa, other friends discovered Adelle Davis, Helen and Scott Nearing, Francis Moore Lappe. We read *Small Is Beautiful* and *Walden* and *Seven Arrows*, and it was like discovering fire. By 1973, these were standard works, old school. But nothing feels like seventeen years old, like breaking out into the world in the giddy, passionate, rigid certainty of youth. It was a painful and feverish time, the same fever a thousand generations have had, of course, but it wasn't all talk. Things got done.

In *Appetite for Change,* Warren Belasco defines three important elements of the natural-foods and organic-farming movement. First is avoiding processed food. Second is awakening to the joy of cooking and eating, especially together. Third is the "organic paradigm," which addressed the larger socioeconomic questions of production and distribution. Together these three elements formed "an alternative food system with its own ideology, staples, and supply lines, a countercuisine. . . [a] social complex of alternative production, distribution, and consumption: country and city communes, organic gardens, co-ops, alternative restaurants and stores . . . The staples of the countercuisine tended to be low in fat, calories, and additives, but they were rich in nutrients, taste, and symbolism when understood and used in the social environment."

General social resistance had met up with the rather musty world of health-food stores long before I found either one. The latter was the almost direct descendant of nineteenth-century health fanatics like Sylvester Graham and John Kellogg, dim and dusty storefronts with shelves of vitamins and supplements, the occasional crystal and pyramid, the racks of pamphlets detailing the pending apocalypse. This food network already expressed an unconventional and skeptical view of the establishment, albeit rather narrowly focused. It was the health of the individual's body that mattered to Graham and Kellogg and their descendants most. When activist hippies looking for cheap food landed in this fertile, sparsely planted ground, it bloomed. Suddenly it was the body politic whose health was at stake. The big difference between the food purists of the nineteenth century and the organic food activists of the 1970s was this broadening of the question itself. "Strange as it may sound, some of the public's disenchantment with the food supply can be traced to the breakup of the American Communist party in the 1950s," writes Harvey Levenstein, making the connection between the New Left and the SDS and the blossoming influence of a generation determined to reinvent each thing they found. Health became a matter of the massive structure of food production and distribution as much as a matter of personal survival. In the 1970s these two battlegrounds—the individual and the global—could no longer be separated even in theory.

By 1975, when I moved to Eugene, Oregon, to join a flourishing counterculture community, I'd studied a little of the appropriate technology movement, which took the notions I'd begun to apply to food and applied them to energy use, building, sewage, transportation, and more. This was the life I wanted, the life I thought possible only for the asking. I was at the tail end of a time of new ideas, and entered a deeply and complexly theorized way of seeing the world that remains with me today in all my compromises.

I was too young then to fully grasp the interpenetrating network of established powers. Wendell Berry wrote the essays of *The Unsettling of America* in that same period of time—a cogent and discouraging critique of modern agriculture. "It is impossible to mechanize production without mechanizing consumption," he wrote, "impossible to make machines of soil, plants, and animals without making machines also of people." That agribusiness and the medical establishment might have a mutual interest in controlling people's food preferences was a startlingly big idea, but it made a deep kind of sense to me right away, makes sense to me still.

It has long been the hope—an inchoate hope, in many ways, but there nonetheless—of the intertwined concerns of agribusiness and food processing to eliminate individual control over the food supply, and distracting difference inside it. Clementine Paddleford came to Oregon some time in the 1950s and visited a huge plum orchard on Bull Mountain. She wrote, "Mr. Lasselle, President of the newly founded Purple Plum Association, said that up to the year previous, these plums, when canned, were sold under 23 different names, such as tart plums, red Italian plums, Idaho prune plums, fresh Italian prunes . . . Now all the packers by co-operative agreement use the Purple Plum name."

Vertical integration was the other key. Washburn Crosby, which became General Mills, succeeded by controlling not only the raising of wheat but the processing, transporting, and selling of wheat in every conceivable form, from Bisquick to Betty Crocker's muffin mixes. What General Mills did with wheat, other companies did with cereal, produce, snacks, putting more and more of the steps of the food chain into self-referential loops.

The tilth movement, a national grassroots effort of small farming, organic gardening, and soil improvement, was in part a class revolution. Like all good revolutions, it was led largely by the children of the ruling class, and is still, in state after state with tilth associations offering everything from soil testing to food distribution. *Tilth* means the act of tilling the land, it means that tilled land itself, it means the state of good soil—and it means the state of *being tilled*. Being cultivated. Tilth politics became core to how I saw the world—that every cent paid for food, every bite eaten, every package opened, every single thing thrown away mattered. What we ate could influence national policy. "Think global, buy local," we said, while the United States sold a quarter of its grain crop to Russia and the oil crisis contributed to food shortages around the world. What we eat is a political act, an act we commit every day. It has a universal and infinite power when harnessed. Tilth politics is based in the belief that the personal experience of appetite not only is political but cannot be anything else, cannot be otherwise. I still believe this, though I don't always act like it. The tide pulls hard. I compromise. I buy time. I buy gratification. I rationalize. I deny. I turn away. I turn away.

Large corporations had come to control the American body and appetite, the American way of buying, selling, and living, in part by directing that appetite, in part by following its every twist and turn, ready to pounce. Eventually I grasped the fact that however one defined the problem, the solution would have to be local. I could see that what I ate, where and from whom I purchased my food, how it was shared or hoarded, how waste was handled, had instantaneous as well as long-lasting effects. I could see that each small act was part of one large whole—a whole motion, a wave, a *movement*. Eating in a healthy way—a "whole" way—meant I had to ask a number of what seemed at first irrelevant questions about the rest of my life:

what kind of clothes I wore and where the fabric came from; how animals were treated and used; how I used birth control—not just to prevent pregnancy but as a matter of what women were willing to do to and put in their bodies, their female earth-symbol bodies. The network ranged far and wide, from my mouth to my uterus to my kitchen to my heating bills, into my livelihood and congressional district, my air and water and kinship with distant people. "Food for people, not for profits." It was real, it was serious, it was scary and fun. For a while, it was easy.

From 1969 to 1979, between five and ten thousand alternative food co-ops were established. Mine was Growers' Market, which began as a cooperative buying scheme to get wholesale prices but which eventually soared into a remarkable organization serving hundreds of households. For several years, my weeks revolved around the Wednesday-and-Thursday schedule at the Market, a cavernous warehouse with offices above. On Wednesdays in the dusty office, people tallied the orders thrust in the doorslot by dozens of walking and bicycling customers. In the warehouse, other volunteers sliced cheese and bagged flour. On Thursday mornings, the produce buyers rose early and went to the local warehouses and negotiated over case prices for spinach and cauliflower, grabbing bargains where they could be found. All day long on Thursday, people pushed carts up and down the aisles and filled each individual order—five apples for this house, two dozen for that one. Then one by one the families and couples and communes and individuals came and picked up their orders and stood in line, saying hello, paying the bill, going home until the next week. I lived with several other people in a rundown house, and what we couldn't buy at the Growers' Market we bought at the New Frontier, a neighborhood grocery store gone funky, with the motto "Tofu to TV Dinners," and that was all the shopping we ever did. For years, I didn't think about eating differently from the way we ate then. The air was always fragrant with virtue—in the scent of simmering garbanzo beans, frying tortillas, baking bread—fresh-baked bread from home-ground flour, with homemade butter from raw milk.

The counterculture made mockery of the values of wealth and poverty, embracing the used and the secondhand in every part of life. The effort to avoid using money was sometimes extreme. People didn't always want to acknowledge how much federal money (community development and job development grants, mainly) went into some of the nonprofit businesses we used. Nor did we find it all that easy to have no bosses, no employees, to make every little decision in an endless and sometimes maddening group process. But for a time you could get by with very little, and many people did.

In 1977, John Hess wrote, "Women simply do not make soups anymore, and the stock pot has disappeared." He was mostly right, and a little wrong. By then I'd been cooking soups in stockpots for years, raising vegetables in a backyard garden, buying very little of anything ready-made. Hess was notoriously pessimistic about food in America, but he credited the counterculture movement with making "enormously promising steps toward revising the taste of our food. . . . They are our hope. But their biggest handicap is that they are cut off from our past . . . It is desolating to see thousands of middle-class youngsters trying to farm, trying to cook, as if they had to reinvent the wheel."

For years I didn't realize how old a lot of our way of handling food was. We were trying to pick up what our parents and grandparents had happily put down. After all, bran was big with Dr. John Harvey Kellogg's nineteenth-century food faddists. So was dry whole-grain cereal—a version of which he called "granola."

When I read the 1943 book *Cooking on a Ration*, the recipes were tenderly familiar to me. They read like *Vegetarian Epicure* and *Moosewood*. "Mother has to cushion the shock of transition from steaks," says the author, addressing women suddenly bereft of endless meat supplies and canned peas. She describes instead how to make soufflés and ramekins, frittatas, and bean casseroles, Lima Bean Loaf and Asparagus Shortcake. She talks about seasoning with mustard, fresh herbs, lemon slices, flavored vinegars, and freshly ground pepper; how to make salads of apples, celery, and dates; how to use watercress, chicory, and capers; how to bake molasses cookies and macaroons made with shredded wheat. The way we were eating was, on the practical level, just ordinary rural eating, farm eating minus the meat—the homemade, simple, creative food known to times outside the twentieth-century technological miracles.

I had a baby in 1978, and nothing much changed for a while. We still ate beans and rice, rice and beans. I got tired for the first time— grown-up tired, bone tired—but I kept cooking simple, fresh food from scratch because that had become normal to me, it was familiar and important. My son was a whole-grain soy-milk baby, and he was as healthy as a genetically engineered warrior. But accommodation had already begun, in me and all around me.

The *Whole Earth Cook Book* of 1971 reads like a religious manifesto: a textbook for the "exodus from institutional bondage we are all called upon to enact" so that we can be part of "the restoration of kinship with the Whole Earth." The recipes are simple and plain, food for "the zeal of atonement" a younger generation has taken upon itself. The *Whole Earth Cook Book II,* published just four years later, looks much the same and is fundamentally different. The second edition is largely dedicated to low-cost and simple food—simplified not for any aesthetic reason but to accommodate "today's busy schedules." The recipes call for canned food and quite a lot of meat—including veal. There is even advice for the "weight conscious."

The community was changing fast, dispersing through age and a weariness with voluntary poverty, through divorce, sexual politics, and the harsh reality of child-rearing, through maturity and a macroeconomic climate difficult to fathom. Federal development grants dried up, and CETA money disappeared. The New Frontier burned halfway down. Growers' Market's orders declined as people began to work longer hours and saving time began to matter more than saving money. One of the founders, a dear friend who had welcomed me to his world in all my irritating zeal, died of cancer, and his death seemed as unjust as any death could be.

I moved to a larger city, finally finished college, got married again, and in 1986 adopted two more children. Working part-time and doing volunteer work turned into a full-time job and three small children in a small rental house. My bicycle became two used cars, the co-op afternoons became the supermarket on the way home from work. As I slowly put down the *Vegetarian Epicure* and *Moosewood,* I usually picked up *Joy of Cooking* instead, trying to learn how to cook, ironically enough, in a more convenient way. The influences ran every which way, like paint spilling. In 1978, the year my son was born, the new edition of Betty Crocker eliminated Beef Wellington and added more convenience foods, but also whole-wheat flour, beans, and rice. The ends were coming toward the middle, and somehow or other what I cooked for dinner began to look a little like what my mother had served me not that many years before.

To cook for a family, I found, isn't the same as cooking for a commune, or like cooking for fun, or like cooking to save the earth. My eldest son, adopted from an institution when he was nine, saw love only in the big portions of meat and platters of French fries he was denied when he was small. A plate full of flesh was his own symbol of prosperity, the way it has been for the hungry as long as people have been eating, and he was happiest when he could throw half of it away like a rich man. My birth son, who'd been fed organic food in the womb, was weaned onto a soy milk and brown rice diet, who never had a cold or cavity, hit the age of ten and refused everything but peanut butter and hot dogs. My daughter, just to complicate things, liked beets, Brussels sprouts, and turnips, and wouldn't eat pizza at all.

Three children, three different schools, long winter rains, long commutes and never enough money, too much weariness and lonesomeness. I was trying to write a book in a cold basement late at night, living always under the weather and under the gun, and so it goes. Cooking for my family sometimes felt like a guarantee of failure. It required me to give up the whole dream of summer afternoons baking bread with happy children, canning the berries they picked in the autumn, and the surprisingly ordinary fantasy of a family sitting together in the evening. When I read Peg Bracken's *I Hate to Cook Book* last year, I could tell that a lot of her recipes wouldn't be much good. But several sounded at least as good as some of the crap I ended up making for my kids in the 5:45 P.M. low-blood-sugar rush of whining children on a rainy winter's day. I was pleasing no one, myself included, with my failed attempts to serve stir-fried vegetables and bean casseroles and spinach lasagna. If I'd cooked Bracken's Beef à la King or Chicken Rice Roger, we might all have been a little happier at the table. I would have felt a million ways guilty—but I felt guilty anyway. Guilt was my constant friend, as it was supposed to be; I was beginning to feel just what "role strain" meant.

Half from sympathy and half from exhaustion, I gave up on making the kids sit down for dinner as they grew. They snacked their way through the afternoon and skipped dinner altogether, much as I had at their age. Several years ago, when I bought a microwave, it was a kind of surrender, a kind of peace. I was restless and lonely in a new way, and a bit distracted by my own desires.

They lived for years on the same frozen pizzas and tamales and individual-serving-size boxes of pasta that made my mother so happy when I was that age. They have been obnoxiously healthy all these years, lean and muscled and cavity-free, and mostly they ate their meals standing up in the kitchen and in their rooms and walking out the door, scattering crumbs in their wake. My mother is gone, my sons are grown. Instead of Mounds and *Lost in Space*, my daughter and I eat microwave popcorn and watch *The X-Files*, but it's not that different in the end.

Much was lost, much stayed the same. But many things did change. All kinds of bread bakeries and tea merchants and farmers' markets thrive. The People's Food Store, a co-op here, goes on in a small, steady way, uncompromised. Organic farming is officially sanctioned. In regions like the Northwest, where both farming and a taste for something new have long thrived, organic farming is a reasonable way to make a living for many people. Hippie berry farmers and conservative cattlemen combine forces to protect open land from urban development. My mainstream grocery store carries tofu, brown rice, whole-wheat bread, and soy-milk ice cream now, because these aren't strange foods anymore—they've infiltrated slowly into American lives. The basic ideas of tilth, the importance of local control of land, and the danger of centralized agribusiness make for surprising bedfellows in a world where the most conservative small farmer struggles to get by. The idea that bodily health and environmental health are interconnected is no longer a radical thought. Much was lost, but much was gained.

Warren Belasco asks, "What if living lightly meant watching resources, not waistlines?" The current fascination with light ("lite") and lean and low-fat foods has elements both in tune with and in opposition to the natural-foods movement. How this fascination translates into what we buy could go both ways: Americans' fear of fat has led to a widespread willingness to put up with central control and high-tech food processing. But it's also created new markets for small produce farmers and raw foods. I think it is quite telling that people who profess to "need" lean meats, white chicken, and oodles of fish because they are "light" and healthy don't seem excited about tofu and other traditional soy products. Tofu is inexpensive, low-fat, cholesterol-free, and a good source of protein. It's delicious when prepared well. But it's not very sexy. And it's not meat. There is more at work here than concerns about health.

So far, people who partake of one system—extreme processing—seem to partake of the other—raw and organic—as well. Maybe in the end that's the best solution a country this size can find.

Now and then I have dinner with a few of the friends who stood in line with me at the dormitory vegetarian line. We've been friends for twenty-five years, and we laugh at the bald spots and crow's feet, and we eat really good food together. We barbecue and make pies and elaborate salads. We share old, private jokes. We are doing good work, too—in carpentry and design and urban planning. But we live apart, singly and by twos, with separate mortgages and bills and never enough time. Whenever we get together to play bad croquet and share platters of that good food, we promise to get together more often, cook together, eat together more. We will buy land together, we say, retire on it together, plant gardens, bake pies, share the labor of the tribe. I know that we won't, but it is such a nice dream.

Last year, I went to the silver anniversary of Growers' Market, which has fewer orders than once upon a time but a loyal membership after twenty-five years. I came into a sea of tie-dye and dreadlocks and patchouli, dirty-faced toddlers in overalls and braids running between the adult legs, women in handmade patchwork skirts and men in Tibetan caps and torn jeans, standing in line before a banquet of barley-mushroom casseroles and bean dip. All these quiet, polite people with their intense, politicized conversation were about twenty-two years old. They were the children, and the grandchildren, of my friends from Growers' Market. I spied my friends one by one at the tables around the edge of the room, dressed in plain button-down shirts and khaki pants, amused and relaxed and happily eating again.

THE CUISINE OF UPPER-CLASS EUROPE, AFTER various eruptions here and there, gradually settled down from the extreme excess of medieval times into la grande cuisine. This was most powerfully realized in France, where it was called haute— "the name the French give to cooking designed for kings, million-aires, and conventions," said one wag in 1927.

Sidney Mintz rejects any concept of national cuisines; he believes true cuisine is regional and in continual evolution and "discourse." Mintz does think that most true cuisines develop a "high" form: a "refinement of the aggregate foods, styles, and dishes of a collection of regions, a skimming off of representative foods" that are then substituted for and combined endlessly. Part of what makes haute so high is that this refinement is limited to the privileged— however privilege is defined. "When one thinks of *la grande cuisine* one cannot think of money," said one chef; "the two are incompatible." "An haute cuisine need not have geographical roots," continues Mintz. "Its social character is based on class." And that class, as always, is defined as it always has been, partly by specific foods available for one reason or another only to the few.

However natural or derived, the formal cuisine of France was well developed by the mid-1700s and had been formed into prescribed menus and recipes by the end of that century. What came to be called haute cuisine in this century is a complex and rigid code of technique and ingredient, limited to the dedicated chef. ("*La grande cuisine* must not wait for the guest; it's the guest who must wait for *la grande cuisine*," Fernand Point liked to say.) One learned to cook through a long apprenticeship, learning the solutions derived by the experiments and practice of past masters, much as one learned mathematics. Some considered cookery to be perfected at this point, a finished art. Invention and creativity were frowned upon; consistency and attention to detail were praised. The code of haute cuisine was concrete, preformed: One "ought" and "should" and "must" cook "only" by particular techniques and with "indispensable" ingredients, as the few collections of haute cuisine recipes are wont to explain. It is "more learned, more focused, and follows stricter rules" than any amateur method, writes Jacques Pépin. "Cuisine is not invariable like a Codex formula, but one must be careful not to modify the essential bases," said Fernand Point, thus defining the Codex.

In 1903, Auguste Escoffier published a cookbook with 2,973 such recipes. Escoffier brooked no dissent; in his world stock is king and sauce is queen (157 recipes, with another seventy-eight for aspic). He felt the need in his cookbook to "reveal the groundwork" for correct cooking, "although this has already been done again and again, and is wearisome in the extreme." Escoffier was the director of the kitchens at both the Savoy and the Carlton hotels in London. One can almost see him, a temperamental man of barely contained impatience, struggling to explain to his English patrons the vital importance of the stock and why he must take so much time on the reduction. Overseasoning was "absolutely deplorable," and he wished not "to preach"—but he did, nevertheless. There was no reason in Escoffier's world to cook at all if you didn't cook correctly, and that meant cooking like him.

American cuisine took its own course—a disgustingly crude course to most visiting Europeans. That course was redirected again and again without settling in to a single recognizable stream, by the newly ascetic emphasis on nutrition, the Depression, two world wars, and a maddeningly fast pace. Not many Americans outside the upper class knew refined European (that is to say, French) food until after World War II. Americans began to travel, Henri Soulé opened

Le Pavillon in the style of Escoffier, and John Kennedy put a French chef (a bad one, many said) in the White House.

Then, in the mid-1960s, the "gourmet chefs" began to appear— on television, in the women's magazines and in newspaper supplements. Celebrity chefs offered elegance in a tarty "You-can-do-it, too" package. This is surely a kind of elegance possible only in the United States, where it isn't an oxymoron but a promise. André Soltner, Jacques Pépin, Pierre Franey, and others came to the United States. On television, cooks like Julia Child and Dione Lucas deconstructed one scary, foreign pinnacle of sophistication and created a new, local one. The bar was raised on what could pass for "fine" food, but the standard of haute cuisine itself was lowered in the process with an unending series of shortcuts and substitutions. The cookbook *Instant Haute Cuisine* was published in 1963, a year after Julia Child's television show *The French Chef* began.

John and Karen Hess's influential 1977 book, *The Taste of America,* is a long rant aimed in part at fifteen years of celebrity chefs. John Hess despised most of the famous cooks of the time and almost all the famous cookbooks, including the Time-Life *Foods of the World* series. (This last opinion was shared by many and various culinary stars.) Hess never seemed to run out of examples of plagiarism, contradiction, the egregious use of brand-name foods, and just plain errors committed by the big names of American "fancy" cooking. He was especially offended at what he saw as the ignorance many experts displayed about the history of a particular dish. He wanted them to know the provenance and meaning of the food they cooked, and instead they seemed ever willing to steal from and rewrite the past. In his genuine and deeply personal distress about the direction of American cuisine, Hess's criticism became so extreme that his carefully supported and often shared concerns were lost in a sea of hurt feeling.

James Beard was an early culprit, according to Hess. Beard was an impulsive showman who loved attention and loved to eat and loved to be loved. He seems to have evoked strong feelings in everyone he met. Betty Fussell calls him a "Paul Bunyan folk hero . . . a cross between Bacchus and Sydney Greenstreet." He was best known for being "fun," for breaking all kinds of rules and conventions. He could write a straightforward recipe and freely imparted the kind of background explanation useful to the working cook. Beard had a great love of finger food and good drink, of the sensuality of food, and was always, in body and voice and words, showing off his own appetite. "When you cook, you never stop learning," he counseled. "Improvise, invent, experiment."

Beard's career, in all its chameleon colors, has been broadly influential to American cuisine: his cookbooks, his classes, the James Beard Foundation and its eponymous awards, the Beard House in New York City where up-and-coming chefs strut their stuff before critical diners all are central to changing cuisines. Appropriately so: Beard was quite opportunistic, rarely turning down the chance to make a little money and be petted for pushing a product. Whether he did this from a crass desire for profits or a more subtle need for flattery depends on who is asked; either way, he was what you might call flexible in his approach to fame and its uses. Hess rankled at the fact that Beard had "toiled for such clients as Planters peanut oil, Green Giant, Nestlé, Restaurant Associates, and Pillsbury . . ." Worse still, to Hess, was that Beard would compromise the historical accuracy of a dish to accommodate a brand name.

Craig Claiborne, by contrast, approaches food and restaurants as a kind of eating scientist. At the beginning of one of his cookbooks, Claiborne writes, "I would say that the most important thing in learning to cook well and with love is a sense of organization." For all his many uses of the word *love* in relation to food, though, Claiborne has never seemed a bon vivant. He is a fastidious model for the diner, serious about food, an autodidactic sophisticate like a lot of his readers. He is also a connoisseur, a collector of fineness in all forms, and had a huge influence on what Americans considered "fine" dining. Claiborne is remarkable in what he doesn't say; his autobiographical writing is painstakingly free of real personal information. He can list every ingredient in a meal, but won't tell you a word about his companion. He is a man with few limits on his movements in every realm, and has long enjoyed a degree of freedom so unusual that he seems to have forgotten what it is like to live otherwise. Elizabeth David, he writes, "will make you hunger for another trip to Italy, no matter how recently you returned." Escoffier's work taught, he notes, "a few of the finest cooks I know, those who do not read French." People simply believe Claiborne, who has always seemed so professional—tidy, precise, passionate about standards. But John Hess considered Claiborne a boast and a brand-name promoter much like Beard, with little real understanding of food or cooking.

Dale Brown, in the Time-Life *American Cooking* volume, disdains nineteenth-century recipes with "those meaningless terms" like a pinch, a fistful, or "cook until done." I wonder where he's been. Elizabeth David was famous for her maddeningly brief recipes, many without set amounts beyond "some" or a "handful." Read Fernand Point, one of the modern masters of haute cuisine, on gratin d'oeufs: "Prepare a mixture of thick cream, a little *béchamel sauce*, and a little *hollandaise sauce*. Slice some hard-boiled eggs, place them in the sauce and heat. Season with salt and pepper. Spread the eggs and sauce in an ovenproof gratin dish and sprinkle with some thinly sliced mushrooms which have been cooked in white wine . . ."A lot of American cooks go batty reading recipes like this; they don't have much real cooking experience, haven't even seen real cooking, and have never developed the instincts of experience. Such disconcertingly loose instructions hardly seem like recipes at all to someone used to measuring careful quarter-teaspoons and following package directions.

Haute cuisine is rigid and constructed, but it is based in precisely this assumption of considerable skill and experience on the part of the chef. The Cordon Bleu, when Julia Child studied there, didn't use any recipes at all. Perhaps one reason Americans took to the new celebrity chefs like Child—and later to the often simplified recipes of nouvelle cuisine—was that instead of an assumption of skill, they assumed ignorance at least and incompetence as often as not.

Julia Child first learned to do basic cooking—while living in Paris—from the 1943 edition of *The Joy of Cooking,* which takes for granted that there are no stupid questions in cooking. *Joy* tells the reader that no one is born knowing how to do much of anything in the kitchen, and unprepossessingly reveals a fine mass of vital information about ingredients and methods. Julia Child took this as her guide and decided that for English speakers to learn French cooking, they would have to learn French methods from the very beginning in much the same way.

Child's several volumes on French cooking are in a style far from chefs like Point and Escoffier. Child knew that out in the real world, functioning adults might not have any idea how to make supper,

because for a long time she herself hadn't known. She tried to anticipate every possible question of the amateur cook, and some of her
recipes read like novellas. (Her critics still claim her techniques
were poor.) Child could hardly have been better suited to her role
as television's mascot for good food and pleasure in cooking, with
her clown face and confident heart. She was a purveyor of possibility above all. She is, still, one of the most trusted and beloved
women in the United States; she has an ability to encourage without patronizing, almost unknown in fine cuisine. Her biographer,
Noël Fitch, calls her "the first to marry California and France." This
wasn't a marriage just of ingredients but of style, too.

Anyone could learn to cook if they put in the time, she claimed
over and over again. It was just time, and that time was considerable. She wasn't exactly speaking to the middle-class housewife with
three children—let alone women like my mother, who had three
children and a career outside the house, too. Child was speaking to
women and men who wanted to cook not only well but in depth,
people willing and able to put in serious kitchen time for years.

Restaurant critic Jeremy Iggers thinks that until Julia Child
came along, we Americans were "innocent" eaters, rollicking stu-
pidly but happily in some white-sauced casserole of ignorance.
Iggers goes so far as to compare Julia Child's coq au vin with Eve's
apple; Julia Child, he suggests, played Satan in the 1962 Eden that
was America.

John Hess, however, said little more about her than that Julia
Child was "exceedingly fond of aspics." He saw her as a lover of fussy
foods like pastry crusts and crepes, tiresome clichés that weren't
particularly good eating. She sometimes relied on canned and
processed foods and once asked Alice Waters to stop going on about

organic produce in public because it worried people. Plenty of people stole from Child, but according to Hess, Child now and then cavalierly passed off as classic recipes her own bastard concoctions.

John Hess despised Claiborne, Beard, and Child as corporate shills, freely calling them poseurs and plagiarists. But to Hess, and a few other cranky resisters, their great collective sin was that they were bad cooks. In his book, Hess spends many pages and citations discussing why a certain sauce can't have flour in it and why it's a travesty to add sugar to bread. He dissects recipes, thrusting and parrying so vigorously I can almost hear him shouting, "En garde!" as he skewers the upstarts and interlopers messing with good food. But far fewer people have read John Hess than have read the paragons who put flour in sauces made with canned stock and added sugar to their bread, and in the end, Hess's quixotic battles disappeared from sight.

None of this touched me directly. I knew no more about gourmets, the right fork, fine dining, or coq au vin than what I gleaned from *Life* magazine. Mom's fanciest foods were her New Year's appetizers and the occasional Sunday dinner beginning with half an avocado stuffed with canned shrimp, followed by roast beef. And these certainly seemed like fancy foods to me, used as I was to Thursday-night hamburger hash and Spam mixed with a box of dehydrated potatoes "oh gratten." I was a young woman before I went to a truly "nice"—meaning dressy, expensive, and intimidating—restaurant. I am still, and perhaps will always be, something of an anthropologist in the presence of haute cuisine. Certainly I look at culinary fashion with a jaded eye. That doesn't mean I can't be easily seduced by the lure of rarefied culinary secrets. Writers like Hess may be correct or they may not, but they often have the effect of reminding me how untutored my own skills seem by comparison. They fog the question a little with the breath of the mystical and sacred.

While Americans watched *Cooking with Julia* and learned how to make quiche from James Beard, France wasn't standing entirely still. Haute cuisine was gradually opening up, changing to accommodate more local and fresh ingredients in standard dishes while struggling to keep the methodology precise.

These were changes long in coming; Elizabeth David had spent decades influencing English home cooks just to try fresh, local, simple foods. Meanwhile, Americans went to France and the French went to Japan. In *Empire of Signs*, Barthes describes his enchantment with the "infinitesimal" aspects of Asian cooking, the efficient and ritual preparation without a single wasted gesture, and especially the rawness, the freshness, the "virginity" of Japanese cuisine. He declared himself to be "on the side of the light, the aerial, of the instantaneous, the fragile, the transparent, the crisp . . . the empty sign." Barthes's heady, slightly fevered reaction isn't unique, and it was probably predictable—Barthes, after all, wasn't one to accept a rigid and codified system in anything, including food. But he had company. Haute cuisine seemed, to more than one cook who discovered sushi, tempura, lacquer trays, and the tea ceremony, so used up—so *cooked*. Barthes saw the dinner tray as a finished work doomed by its nature to be made into something new, something else. Food has fluid boundaries; the eater is both artist and destroyer. Dinner is "destined to be undone, recomposed according to the very rhythm of eating: what was a motionless tableau at the start becomes a workbench or chessboard, the space not of seeing but of doing." Japanese food in particular seemed to be "a written food," a story with a mysterious conclusion, uncertain narrative, a far more interesting story than the finished art of the French chef. Barthes felt he'd discovered a way of cooking that seemed analogous to eating itself—a deconstruction, an *exhaustion* of the essence of food, and in his parsed, occasionally giddy prose he unknowingly described the strange future of American high dining.

Under such influences, French cuisine quickly—as cuisines go—adopted more raw ingredients and overtly architectural designs, until the most carefully designed dishes became comments on cuisine itself, as much about the idea of food as the food itself.

The term *nouvelle cuisine* first appeared in 1973. Nouvelle was the product of younger but still formally trained chefs—not so much a sea change as evolution in technique and ingredients. Jean and Pierre Troisgros trained with Fernand Point, author of *Ma Gastronomie*. But when they came into their own, the Troisgros brothers largely eliminated "the more complicated formulas . . . that are burdensome to make in a home kitchen." Instead of Escoffier's pages of fresh stocks, they used only a few, and suggested making extra to freeze. But otherwise the Troisgroses wanted to rely, like other nouvelle chefs, on fresh ingredients, like "good housewives" who shopped every day at the local market. Theirs was "a *rapprochement* to that of the *ménagère*, the French home cook." (Today, more rapproachement. I found this startling statement in a recent *Food & Wine*: "In a quest for perfect produce, Eberhard Muller of New York City's Lutèce goes to extremes; he grows his own.")

Nouvelle began eliminating excessive decoration and formality, both on the plate and in serving patterns. (Even at the turn of the century, Auguste Escoffier was praising Russian service for *eliminating* excessive fuss at the table.) Garnishes almost disappeared, and just as the gingerbread had fallen off houses and furniture and clothes to be replaced by long low lines and simple angles, food became its own decoration. Nouvelle chefs seemed to discover the tilting of the earth on its axis as though it was a new idea—everything was "fresh" and "seasonal" again, with a great trumpeting.

"It is not well understood, especially outside of France, that *nouvelle cuisine* is a creative point of view toward cooking, not a codified repertory to which a *nouvelle* label is to be applied," wrote the Troisgros brothers. "Codification is exactly what the new chefs abhor, and if the menus in their restaurants sometimes list similar dishes, this is for the reason, also new, that they exchange information about their experiments, sharing ideas in a pioneer spirit."

Haute cuisine split in three ways—a true grande cuisine, still alive; what is called Continental cuisine, a shadow of classic cooking served in big hotels, which advertise their commitment to "fine dining"; and nouvelle. By the end of the 1970s, a new cuisine was solidly in place, deliberately light and undercooked in the tradition of everyone from Christian ascetics to John Harvey Kellogg—but still snobbish, expensive, and difficult for the amateur to pull off, as all good fashions are. The growing urge for something authentic helped fuel the trend—and this was also an old hunger, as old as the century, when people first began to cry out against the artificial and mediated in their lives even as they succumbed to it.

A surprising number of nouvelle's new ideas were actually old. Vinegars flavored with chili, horseradish, tarragon, and raspberry, among other seasonings, were common in the 1800s. So were condiments like walnut catsup and caper sauce. The common medieval fashion of cooking meat with fish or with fruit is one example—today's fresh taste is duck with oysters; chicken with anchovies. The influential *Silver Palate Cookbook* has Glazed Blueberry Chicken; Rock Cornish hens with a stuffing of apples, grapes, parsley, and orange zest; and the inevitable roast suckling pig of the 1980s rubbed with limes and decorated with kumquats. Bobby Flay's *Bold American Food* includes a smoked pork loin with apricot and serrano chile sauce, and a squab dressed with blue corn and chorizo stuffing and served with a cranberry-mango relish. (The last, he added, was "very much a fall item," as though it were a lipstick color.) The great medieval spice cupboard of cinnamon, allspice, cardamom, nutmeg, and ginger is the fashion for flavoring everything from tenderloin to monkfish now. Decorating dishes with flowers, the artistic gilding and coloring that sometimes giddily marked high-fashion cuisine in the last century was pointedly done in by nouvelle chefs who opted for lean lines and raw (albeit sculpted) looks. Today's chefs champion "new" garnishes like spun sugar ribbons and shaped meringue and chocolate leaves and flowers this minute. Next, a spare look, a frankly sculptured look, returns—distant descendant of medieval excess.

In nouvelle, taste was only part of the infatuation. Rawness itself seemed to have its own almost mystical power (as it has always had for ascetics)—an antidote to the corrupt urban environment. Of course, nouvelle cuisine can succeed as a product only in just such an urban environment, and many of the ingredients required to turn these raw materials into their brilliant finished forms must be imported and are both processed and far more expensive than local ingredients.

Nouvelle cuisine came from France to California and then spread, mutating as fast as a cold virus until the original intention to remain true to the technique and philosophy of haute cuisine while using fresh ingredients had given way to invention for invention's sake. The food was not really the point after a while. The plates, the tables, the rooms, the chefs, the descriptions, the surprises—these were the point. Nouvelle lives were being served.

RAYMOND SOKOLOV, WHO KNOWS A GOOD DEAL more about high, low, and in-between cookery than I do, calls nouvelle cuisine a "hypermenu" made possible not only by easy international travel but by easy access to the literature of long invisible or sheltered cuisines. "The essence of the new cookery is its openness to unprecedented combinations of food known to no traditional cuisine," he writes. "Even if today's cross-cultural cooking is a form of culinary sacrilege, it is also the latest phase of a Darwinian process . . ."

Darwin knew, of course, that not every mutation will succeed—that is the point of mutation, as it were. Unexpected leaps in form are simply experiments with the future, and they don't all work. By the 1980s, when invention was itself the goal, cooking was throwing off new forms right and left. One of the codes of nouvelle cuisine is the opposite of haute—a deliberate and even authoritarian melding of local ingredients with global methods, local methods with global ingredients. (Perhaps James Beard was the first nouvelle chef in America. Betty Fussell quotes him at a cooking class twenty years ago: " 'What you cook is a reflection of *you*,' he tells us. 'Don't be afraid to try new combinations.' It's the cook that unifies a meal, not a country or a culture.") Now so-called "regional" cookbooks for various "American cuisines" influenced by nouvelle ideas require such oddball and decidedly nonlocal items as coconut and lemongrass, saffron, hazelnuts, and mahimahi—importantly, this far-reaching flavoring of local basics is what nouvelle has become.

"It is a style, but it is a sly style," writes Raymond Sokolov, "a forest of symbols and allusions." More than a style, less than a philosophy, nouvelle cuisine is simply another code, and one somewhat harder to obey because its rules are hidden. (Roland Barthes understood these semiotics—but he was a linguist.) Nouvelle cuisine uses words like *fresh* and *natural* as code words just as Carême used "à la provençale" to refer to a sauce of tomato, olive oil, and garlic. Certain ingredients have long risen and fallen in favor in nouvelle cuisine—shiitake mushrooms, swordfish, the ever-changing panoply of fresh greens, the endlessly "discovered" produce and spices of small foreign cuisines. An evolving pantry of unusual ingredients is to nouvelle cuisine what sauces were in the old school—adjectives neatly fitting the dish and the diner into their proper slots.

Ken Hom, one of the early proponents of the odd new French-Asian-American-Pacific cuisine, said that his own form of cooking is "an unforced, natural blending of ingredients and techniques borrowed mainly from China, France, and America. On occasion ideas from Japanese, Italian, and Mexican cuisine also come into play."

Nouvelle is, perhaps inevitably, ironic, "a parody or perhaps a pun based on the old culinary code," in Sokolov's words. He sees wit here, an intelligent comment on culture taking place in the mundane world of the dinner plate. Much of the humor is self-referential. But some of the jokes fall flat. No cuisine, no combination of cuisines, is completely artificial. People have been mixing up together whatever they can get their hands on, figuring out what tastes good together, without regard for borders, as long as they've been eating. But while there may be excellent places for Chinese, Italian, and Mexican methods and ingredients to meet—and I'm not convinced this is true—such a meeting can't be, as Hom specifically claims, unforced.

The cook Karen Lee proposed, as examples of "nouvelle Chinese," jicama and dandelion salad, wok-charred Norwegian salmon, pork chops with spicy tomato sauce, and bouillabaisse with black bean aioli. Such things do not evolve through gradual trial and error, through ordinary encounters with newness. They are the products of financial opportunity and calculating research. In fact, Lee readily admits that her editor suggested she come up with such recipes—sometimes taking a classic recipe and "drastically altering it so as to render it inauthentic and deliciously original."

Part of nouvelle cuisine has always been the very pretense that such dishes are natural discoveries, inevitable, that this method is natural and spontaneous, in a way—nouvelle as the free, wild destiny of great food. But for the most part, nouvelle was simply "inauthentic and deliciously original," and sometimes even delicious.

Nouvelle cuisine has become, in its way, the haute cuisine of the new century. It is now absolute in its continual change. That change, these days, is a fanatical focus on the "delicate, light, flavorful, and fat-free," in Pépin's words. Escoffier's bones are dust now, and nouvelle can be discovered, quantified, and defined, in spite of the insistence of many of its purveyors that this isn't true. One of its essential methods—one of its limiting boundaries—is the very merging, inventing, and experimenting with boundaries used to prove that nouvelle is open-ended. This is just a way of burying code. Two apparently contradictory things occur, a kind of culinary dissonance. In the name of one of the newest trends—regionalism—I can't call my soup "clam chowder" if it doesn't have clams and potatoes. But in the name of globalism and invention and, yes, humor, I can do anything else I want with clam chowder—in fact, to be really on the edge, I have to do something, well, edgy. (Raspberry coulis on the side, perhaps.) To go past the edge, I can leave out the potatoes. I can even leave out the clams, and call it "clam" chowder.

Alice Waters is often held up as the paragon of California cuisine, the most influential American purveyor of elegant, "light," and, above all, local cooking. "Her philosophy of always using the highest quality, fresh, seasonal ingredients, grown and harvested in an ecologically sound manner, has made her the mentor of a generation of adventurous cooks," reads the commentary on a Web site devoted to her. Waters herself said, "I would like the cooking at Chez Panisse to be perceived as straightforward and basically unsauced because I believe that is a very healthful way of cooking and eating."

Alice Waters wrote an underground food column in the late sixties. But her 1967 degree from the University of California at Berkeley was in French Cultural Studies and she was influenced deeply by French cooking. "We all believed in community and personal commitment and quality," she wrote in her still-popular 1982 *Chez Panisse Menu Cookbook*. But what she really wanted was "to eat certain foods of a certain quality."

Chez Panisse was established in the late sixties in Berkeley, and remains a hybrid of French, California, and Japanese culinary styles. (Waters is the owner, not the chef.) Waters has always claimed to be freeing her staff and customers from the establishment of corporate food processing and agribusiness, to be "totally self-sufficient," as her goal. In her writings, where she is fond of exclamation marks and phrases like "wonderfully fresh" and "perfect little lettuces," she extols kitchen gardens, local ingredients, hands-on techniques, and small farmers. But her recipes are a long way from a pot of communal garbanzos. Some are simple, others extremely time-consuming. Most are expensive to prepare. One of her more frequent comments is to note that a certain ingredient is "expensive but worth it."

Waters likes plenty of meat—beef, veal, pigs, ducks, lamb, and wild boar. She likes to render her own fat, make her own sausages. (If you don't have bones left over while making stock, she advises, "you will have to buy an extra little beast.") She adores suckling pig (that is, piglet) and fish of all kinds.

As for produce, she admits to be "fortunate to be in California, where we have a long growing season and easy access to major food markets." Fortunate, indeed: She once bought three cases of green beans and had her assistant Judy Rodgers (now the owner of the Zuni Cafe) pick through them to find thirty individual beans small enough to meet the standard for her salad.

Alice Waters is doing some important work, especially with schoolchildren and gardening in what she calls the Edible School-yard Project. In a recent *New Yorker* story on her attempt to open a restaurant at the Louvre, a French chef who admires her says, "There's something crystalline about her—an extraordinary purity of spirit." But if hers is a cuisine for "the people," if this is light or local cuisine, I'm missing something. There is nothing in her books for the mainstream; it's elitist to the point of absurdity. (Marinated Quail Grilled with Sausages and Bay Leaves; Pig's Ears Breaded and Grilled with a Mustard Sauce; Cardoon, Cannellini Bean, and Artichoke Ragout; Risotto with White Truffle and Pork Kidneys; Curly Endive, Radicchio, and Fuyu Persimmon Salad.) Dinner for two at Chez Panisse on Friday and Saturday nights is $138, not counting tip, tax, and, of course, the wine. Waters has regulars, loyal customers who dine there weekly—an elite peopled by celebrities. She also sells posters.

Her recipes call for a drift-net's worth of seafood: Gulf Coast red snapper, Hawaiian shrimps, Louisiana crayfish, Oregon salmon (before it was fished nearly to extinction), Eastern shellfish, Maine lobsters. The success of her recipes depends on many such exotic or imported ingredients: Swiss chocolate, salt-packed anchovies, tropical fruit, French lentils, mesquite charcoal, cognac, caviar, Italian arborio or Indian basmati rice, French and Italian olive oils, Spanish wine vinegars, "partially cooked foie gras in a block" flown in from France, French butter, French tinned goose fat—but only "in the fall." Then there are the wines, usually French. On one page extolling the pairing of food and wine: "a St. Péray, a Côtes-du-Rhône . . . a young Château Suduiraut . . . a 1966 Château Léoville-Las-Cases . . . the charming elegance of an older Bordeaux." For one dinner: "Drink a light cool Italian red with the shellfish, a Barbaresco with the risotto, and an old Barolo with the pig." Truffles are the symbol of it all.

"There is simply no substitute for fresh truffles. They should be used as close as possible to the time they are plucked from the ground . . . Considering the travel time from Europe, fresh truffles may remain fresh for only a few days." Black truffles are fresh only twice a year; white truffles—"extremely perishable"—can be had from the fall through early January, from Italy. Fresh and local means fresh *somewhere*, but not necessarily *here*. And, boy, does it cost.

All this food needs to get eaten, preferably in public, and the rigidity of formal dining we associate with haute cuisine has given way to a more subtle rigidity of informal dining. Diners now face a strange forced casualness of manner and dress coupled with an explicit formality reserved only for the plate itself. Food is dressed up in a new way now (dressier than the diners), while we banter with one another without apparent regard for old social conventions of rank and intimacy. The rituals of nouvelle cuisine, be it "spa," "California," "Pacific rim," or the new hybrids called "fusion," are maturation rituals. One discovers first fire and then the wheel, absorbed with one's own experience as we were twenty-five years ago eating brown rice and drinking mu tea. Flouting convention easily becomes a new convention on its own.

Nouvelle is a kind of chain restaurant reaching all the way around the world, now—a franchise cuisine like "Chinese American" or "Mama's Italian," where you always know what to expect. You know the decor and the lingo and what to wear, you know the slang as well as you know *BLT* and *over easy*. You know how the servers will talk and how they expect you to respond. I sometimes experience the modern restaurant meal as an oppressively constructed world built to a rigid code with a hidden key. You know if you belong or not. Waiters introducing themselves to customers supposedly began as a way to give customers the sensation of being independently wealthy—the waiters were to act as temporary personal servants. But what it has become is a sign of false intimacy, intrusive in a way that's exactly opposite of professional servants. In our postnuclear world of individual plates and private satisfactions, each of us precisely separated from the other, anyone who would rather not chat on a first-name basis with total strangers is out of date.

Nouvelle cuisine is now as predictable as Continental. At one restaurant (all black and white with drawing paper and crayons in a dish on the table), we eat moussaka with Gruyère cheese, a "Caesar" salad thick with cucumbers and tomatoes, grilled salmon on a Greek roll with wasabi aioli. At another (a warehouse with cement walls and exposed heating ducts, distressed metal, and big wooden color blocks on the wall), we have chili shrimp corn cakes with spicy red pepper aioli and cold golden beets. At a hundred, a thousand restaurants now, I can expect these things, the aiolis and the greens, the sea bass and the horseradish, the newest replacement for mesclun, the vinegar sauces and mustards, the sheep feta and blue corn in ever-evolving combinations. Nothing new: In an essay in *Food & Wine* in 1978, Justine de Lacey complained about how out of hand nouvelle cuisine had gotten when she was served "the same *salade folle* (al dente green beans, foie gras, truffles, and an occasional crayfish tail) five nights in a row" on a trip to France.

Last year, I was in Los Angeles for a few days and met my friend Bernard for lunch. We ate at the California Pizza Kitchen in Marina del Rey. Each employee at CPK wears a name tag with his or her birthplace listed: Josie—Chicago; Tom—New Orleans; and so on. (Juan could claim only Mexico.) CPK is to nouvelle cuisine what the Best Western is to haute cuisine. The room was loud, crowded, all bright edges and clean glass and bad acoustics. Bernard ate a barbecued chicken pizza, and I had a portobello mushroom pizza. We shared a walnut, Gorgonzola, and greens salad with balsamic vinaigrette. The food was good; the company fine. The next day I flew to San Francisco and went to my friend Laura's apartment, where she cooked me lunch. She served a walnut, Gorgonzola, and greens salad with balsamic vinaigrette, followed by angel-hair pasta with heritage tomatoes and corn and basil and freshly grated Parmesan. It was very good. That evening I went to see my friend Don, and he made me dinner. I was having a wonderful time, and we ate a walnut, Gorgonzola, and greens salad with balsamic vinaigrette (with slices of nectarine on top), and angel-hair pasta with tomato sauce and freshly grated Parmesan. So good. Good friends, good food.

Early the next morning at the San Francisco Airport, late for my plane, I felt a great hunger, a kind of starved and panting desire. I bought a doughy, hot English muffin overflowing with gooey processed cheese, and ate it all, every bite. And that was really the best of all, the best thing I'd ever tasted.

JEAN-FRANÇOIS REVEL, WHO CAN TAKE SEVeral pages to explain what couscous can and can't contain and still be called couscous, believes all cuisines are either regional or international. There is nothing in between. A true international cuisine includes "local dishes with the tang of the soil . . . basic principles . . . the capacity to integrate, to adapt, to rethink, I will say almost to rewrite the recipes of all countries and all regions, or at least those that are amenable to such treatment . . . [it] must remain extremely flexible."

Modern French cuisine is, some argue, the only truly international cuisine, because only its methods and recipes have infiltrated other cuisines and absorbed the methods and recipes of other cuisines so thoroughly. Revel thinks so. (He is French himself, of course.) He calls French cooking, and the italics are his, an "international *culinary art* . . . a body of *methods*, of *principles* amenable to *variations,*" and a complete antidote to the anonymous Continental menu that *"transports the picturesqueness* of a regional dish without *transposing its principles."*

Nouvelle was supposedly moribund by the mid-1980s—no longer new, no longer entirely surprising. We were getting used to this transported picturesqueness. Nouvelle was almost, horribly, *old*. The Japanese-inspired French cuisine had given way to French-inspired California cuisine, which gave way to increasingly odd combinations like Wolfgang Puck's French-Chinese and Ken Hom's Chinese-California style. And these have now given way to what is usually called fusion and to the strange eating style that combines fat-free diets with occasional big-dinner nostalgia.

Revel describes yet another historical cycle in food: the continual tension between how we value tradition and how we value imagination. Many successful restaurants today call to mind small, independent diners of the past—but only of an imaginary past far enough away most of us can't remember if it's true. A thoroughly unschooled longing for history and tradition is colliding with our jaded palates and high expectations, crashing headlong into the massive traffic jam that is upscale cuisine today.

Fusion is not a new cuisine but simply a gradual mutation of nouvelle cuisine. Sometimes its sum is more than its unpredictable parts, and sometimes it is far less, inharmonious and self-conscious. Fusion cuisines proceed on the stated philosophy that a chef can "evolve" ethnic and traditional cuisines with new ingredients and combinations of tastes without changing the "identity" of the ethnic source; such sudden changes instead "enhance" the "essence" of slowly derived cuisines. Words like these, along with *punctuate* and *declare* and *locate,* occur frequently in discussions of fusion cooking. The intent is linguistic—Barthesian, in a way—making wide-ranging taste into a kind of postmodern story.

And what is this story? It has jets in it, lots of jets; mobility in every direction; migration and emigration and immigration; a celebration of multicultural diversity of imagined cultures. Our story is a messy one, full of digression and disappearing plot lines and shaggy dogs. At first glance, it's a rich epic with layers of subtext and endless new characters, a rapid-fire mix of high and low elements, new and old points of view, infinite. Up close, I wonder if what I'm really seeing is a very simple story, all ABCs and pretty pictures—everything subsumed into one time-worn plot.

The variant ingredients on a fusion menu, says one food writer, "lose their national identity and become something like the diet for a culinary One World . . . one can hardly predict where the separating semicolons should go." The future, according to Ruth Reichl, is going to be "increasingly eclectic, with more Asian, Indian and Latin-American ingredients turning up on the table"—it will be good eclectic, fun eclectic. "Think global, buy local," as we used to say. In the newspaper this week, I am startled to find a restaurant column with that title: "Thinking global, buying local." But it's simply the ironic title for a story about the opening of a new restaurant that "fuses Caribbean, Asian and Mediterranean flavors, relying heavily on local ingredients." What flavors, what locality? "Crispy mango duck lacquered with a coffee and hot pepper glaze," a beef tenderloin "sandwich" of filo, caramelized apples, dried cherries and figs. Global, local, or some place of the imagination?

In the last few months' worth of the major food magazines, I find reference to the damnedest things: goat cheese–onion naan with mango salsa; Beef Wellington tamales; mashed avocado with lily bulbs and lotus root chips; fresh boysenberries with black-currant-tea créme anglaise; cranberry beans and pea shoots in sherry-hazelnut vinaigrette; feta-stuffed rack of lamb with pumpkin-seed crust and chipotle sauce. The now-standard pantry lives on: wild mushrooms, goat cheese, garlic, fennel, cilantro, smoked turkey, mustards, lemons and lemon juice and lemon zest and lemon vinaigrette and preserved lemon, the wonder of ancient maize in the form of corn on the cob and corn oil and polenta and grits, man-goes and arugula, and everything grilled and lightened in thin sauces made without cream or stock. Seafood, of all kinds, in enormous quantities, an ocean's worth.

There is something soothing, soft, balsamic to this food: It is anodyne to jaded psyches. Our painful adulthood requires baby veg-etables and soft terrines and sweet purees. Striving, accomplished lives are comforted by the clean flash of grilling and the bath of poaching. Crowded days require thin, runny sauces for palliation. Everything is light—the way the food of the prosperous is supposed to be—flying, buoyant, rarefied, light. Local—sort of. *Fresh*, of course—except for the myriad imported flavorings, the wine, the necessary ingredients that one can't find at home. The sophisticated American palate still depends on processed food—white truffle oil, salted anchovies, fermented black beans, crab paste, balsamic vinegar. What makes ours a truly global palate is that we don't really know where any of this stuff comes from: We don't think of the globe as being a sum of parts, but as being one thing—"elsewhere." Source is insignificant on a global scale because everything is equally distant, equally foreign, equally available. Who needs to know the meaning of a tamale when it's a Lean Cuisine tamale—or a

Monterey Jack and couscous tamale, like the Canyon Ranch spa makes? Fettucine Alfredo, tabouleh, and gnocchi come in boxes now, with authentic-sounding brand names and foreign-looking labels from God knows where—as often from Wichita as Ceylon. Cutting-edge cuisine has to go that much further. The American way of eating is a way of eating the world, eating up the world: contained, eternal, self-referential.

The edge of cuisine now is yet another amalgam of high and low, heavy and light, old and new. Regionalism and globalism pass through each other and sometimes both seem to disappear in the process. We have Charlie Trotter and Rick Bayless brand-name lines—processed, convenience products—sauces, dressings, salsas. This year's annual Fancy Food Show featured expensive stoneground nut oils, packaged "nouvelle cuisine" sauces, a variety of ethnic condiments ranging from syruped ginger to white anchovies, and tuna noodle casserole. The newest rediscovered cuisines are thoroughly Old World: Macao, Sri Lanka, Sardinia. Classic Indian cuisine is being "fused" now: oxtails braised with cinnamon and cloves, tandoori with grape chutney, salmon raita. To read cultural historians like Harvey Levenstein, Waverley Root, Reay Tannahill, and others is to see that there is nothing special to fusion, to global cuisine, except the speed with which these combinations now occur. Each trend leaves a mark and many trends repeat themselves, but none is the end.

One reaction to the sometimes extreme forms of fusion around today is a return to "tradition," away from the experimentation and globe-hopping. "Simple" and "classic" and "beloved" dishes of the past are back, albeit many lightened of fat and sugar and salt, sped up and intensified and "reinterpreted." This is the "new American" cuisine, where less is more, simplicity is maturity, and fanciness distracts. Delmonico's reopened in New York City, featuring lobster Newburg and baked Alaska. Beef is back, back, back; once again we are permitted to engage in suckling pig and tenderloin in a quiet atmosphere of luxury and abundance. Emeril Lagasse, a current television cooking darling, fills the necessary niche of the outlaw, the bad boy who gives us permission to indulge. He's not afraid of the old quartet of richness—meat, fat, sugar, and salt.

Casual "picnics," "patio parties," and "suppers" are new again, preferably made up from expensive, carefully prepared food served on china, with expensive wine in crystal goblets on the grass, luxury treated with feigned inattention. A few of us are rich, and a lot of others are playing at richness, like people always have. (This, too, is tradition; we struggle against boredom with the same old things.) The "newest must-have for the acquisitive cook," I read, is the outdoor wood-burning stove, at a cost between three and four thousand dollars, and a "continual supply" of hardwood logs.

I RARELY GO TO MCDONALD'S; I RESIST FOR many reasons—but sometimes I want nothing as much as I want a hamburger. I am seized by the palatable texture of those long-ago trips to A&W, seized not just with the obvious desire to be in that past, to be that child, but with a physical desire for the precise paradigm of comfort that a good hamburger can be.

There's a disparity between memory and reality, between imagination and experience—between advertising and life. I went to McDonald's and bought a meal—fries, soda, burger. I ate my limp fries, watery soda, and tepid burger, with its filler meat, cold hunk of iceberg lettuce core, and watery slice of tomato, under bright and humming fluorescent lights at a soiled plastic table. If my childish appetite had been satisfied, I might have overlooked the bleak environment. If I'd been given that old-fashioned feast of fatty meat, rich cheese, sweet sauce, that medieval banquet—the oily mouthfeel of fats, the warm fullness of salt, the brightness of sugar. I expected the food to satisfy something young and greedy in me. But this was bad meat, bad fat, bad salt, bad sugar, badly done.

Not long ago, I bought Velveeta, Wonder bread, and Miracle Whip. The solid yellow rectangle in its neat silver wrapping is like a solid block of my elementary-school career, with no need to refrigerate before opening. I made my childhood toasted-cheese sandwich as an experiment, with my daughter as the guinea pig. She's been raised on sandwiches made from whole-wheat bread and local whole-milk cheddar and homemade mayonnaise.

I fried the bread lightly, spread one slice with Miracle Whip, and piled on the Velveeta; put the bread together and fried the sandwich again, squished down flat with a spatula until it was brown and melting.

I cut the sandwich into triangles and gave one to my daughter and took one for myself.

She chewed meditatively and smiled.

"This is *great*," she said. "How did you make this?"

The generation between us, between my daughter and me, has taken to diners—luaus and lounge lizards and cocktails with little umbrellas in them, a cuisine distant in its gummy warmth. It's hip to be square, for sure, to seek, as Jane and Michael Stern suggest, the "essential dinerhood of the dish." In one of their books, the Sterns make fun of the 1950 fashion for theme parties—

"Polynesian" barbecues, in particular. Then they give careful instructions for how to put one on—proper music, pseudo-Hawaiian games, Tiki lanterns, the pineapple-sticky sauces—without seeming to realize that a parody of a parody begins to seem a little like reverence. Mashed potatoes, pupu platters, meat loaf, and tuna casserole are their own delights—but the cool irony with which they are presented as something "current," something somehow "new," dispels any real pleasure.

When the expensive dinner out pales, when the linen and china seem just a bit too much and the Tiki parties lose their thrill, we turn to a different past, not so much to the food of childhood as to the lost hopes of childhood. We who were raised as the dining room disappeared into a parallel world of fast food—we have dinner parties, lots of them. We buy old houses, we're "old house people," we like big dining rooms and oak dining tables and good cookware. We have "antiqued" walls and "distressed" furniture, prefaded jeans and vintage shops and toy replicas. We have entire catalogs and stores devoted to reproductions of everything from lunch pails to light switches, stamped tin ceiling pieces to reissued Hardy Boys mysteries, glass doorknobs and weathervanes, so we can restore our old houses to their authentic origins and somehow, in the midst of it, restore our lives.

JOHN HESS SAID TWENTY-FIVE YEARS AGO that Americans had forgotten how to eat—they had forgotten what food should taste like, what good food is. Prolonged exposure to bad food had destroyed their critical palate just as exposure to invisible radiation would destroy their bone marrow. He blamed personal factors, like impatience and the infatuation with "sophistication" and the trend in brief, uncritical travel. He blamed societal factors, too, like the industrialization of food production, the homogenization of brand names, the advent of labor-saving appliances, which encouraged long-term storage and quick fixes. He blamed a lot of things, but mostly he blamed the bad food we ate.

If we ever knew how to eat—if we really did forget—have we learned once again? When I go out for a meal now, I have a choice not only of Thai, Mexican, Vietnamese, northern Italian, southern Italian, Japanese, and Catalan cuisines, but of good Thai, Mexican, Vietnamese, Italian, Japanese, and Catalan cuisines. I can go to grocery stores and buy most of the ingredients, even the fresh produce, required for many of these cuisines—the green papaya and galanga, chipotle, and annatto powder; bortega and cranberry beans. So what? Hess would say this isn't enough, isn't nearly enough. He went so far as to say that enjoyment isn't enough. To truly know how to eat means knowing source and root, history and culture. One can't judge the quality of cassoulet or pad Thai until one knows where cassoulet and pad Thai are from, how they developed, what they meant in that place and time, what purpose they filled in the lives of people who ate them, what their *truth* is. Only then can you know if it is a "good" cassoulet, an "authentic" pad Thai, or simply an imitation.

All through this discussion of various "cuisines," I hear the reader protesting: Who cares? What matters more than whether the food is any good? In fact, a number of fashionable chefs have defended their fusing and shifting of ingredients and methods by making this very argument—taste it, they say, and then tell me I shouldn't mix these elements. If it's good, it works. I think this is a fine line to walk. I do like a lot of this food, in fact. A lot of the food I've been holding up for inspection here is in fact quite good. I have no idea what goat-cheese-and-basil pizza is, in any Hess-ian sense of knowing, but I like it. I really like walnuts, Gorgonzola, and greens salad with balsamic vinaigrette. The combination of sweet potatoes, caramelized endive, green peppercorn sauce, and rare duck breast doesn't leap logically out of any established cuisine I know about, but if chef Alfred Portale says they work well, why shouldn't I try putting them together? I know that "whether or not you like the food" is currently one of the abiding rules of cuisine; every food magazine pushes appetite as the best guide, and claims that the best chefs are driven by nothing but their own keen and sharpened tastes. But the buried code says that if we don't like the food, that is our failure. It is philistine not to be charmed by the new, for its newness; it is coarse not to share the same keen tastes as the chef.

We are more sophisticated these days, but not more mature— maybe less. Americans are spoiled, which is not the same thing as worldly. Jason Epstein, writing in *The New Yorker* last year, praised the current "culinary transformation" of America, with the growing abundance of choice in markets and restaurants, and the "spontaneously awakened undreamed-of refinements" of taste and sophistication among ordinary people. This last I argue against. We are exposed to more, obviously, but I don't think we understand more. We cook better than we used to, but we also cook less, far less, and for very different reasons. The foreign cuisines we enjoy on our outings are the result not of a chef's inventiveness but stolid, often boring, lengthy effort by ordinary, hungry people over the course of centuries. We are more adventurous than those people, perhaps, but also far more jaded, flocking around trends like starlings swirling together in the sky.

Most of us taste our first lemongrass and cherimoya and mahimahi in restaurants, carefully guided by menus and waiters. We are prepared by a wide-ranging media to go to certain restaurants and try certain foods. That is, new food, new cuisines, new tastes are mediated just like everything else in our culture; they are passed along to us through a series of hands, through the middlemen of many kinds.

Depending on which media we consult, trends and new tastes filter into our range more or less quickly, but they invariably arrive, no longer exactly new. Of course, new foods aren't "new" at all— they are tried and true, proven safe and desirable, new only to our own small world. Few of us will ever be driven by hunger to eat something we've never seen before, the way the early American colonists were. Instead of risky, our new experiences are chosen, sought after, sold as the "next big thing"—a most familiar and old-fashioned idea.

Harvey Levenstein notes that the natural-foods movement was partly about finding a way to be "real" and "authentic" with food, because culinary trends had long been about technological invention and cuisine removed from its source. Foreign food seems more authentic to us than our own, more a product of coherence and slower times, just as foreign ways always carry the scent of sincerity. The market for exotic tools and utensils, specialty cookbooks, spices, and ingredients is largely a market of hardworking, affluent people seeking a kind of truth they imagine is there to be found. A tribe, as it were. The new trend of regionalism is partly an attempt to find the same sense of authenticity we find in foreign foods in the foods that our own recent ancestors ate in the places we live now.

Levenstein points out also that dominant cultures adopt the cuisines of weaker cultures only when the food is no longer strictly associated with the very weakness that made them available—undeveloped technological bases or poverty. Usurped cuisines "also tend to marry colonial foods, flavors, or methods to foods that are of high status in the imperial centers, giving us curried beef, shrimp, and even lobster . . ." Which foods are chosen to be usurped is purely a matter of status; chicken feet and snake meat are common and valued in Chinese cuisines, but neither made the transoceanic shift because we associate them (however wrongly) with poverty and desperation. Levenstein suggests that French chefs had plenty of opportunity to learn Vietnamese traditions from immigrants in Paris long before they discovered Japan but that class distinctions made such a thing unthinkable.

We like to eat the cuisine of foreigners in two ways—traveling and one step removed. What Americans don't and have never liked to do is enter foreign subcultures and eat foreign food among foreigners in our own country. Most cultures don't assimiliate foreign cuisines until the foreigners themselves are assimilated or, at best, out of sight. Foreign foods are most popular where they are most unusual—and that means where they aren't in daily use, made ordinary. In other words, foreign foods are accepted into mainstream cuisine, into fashion, to the extent that they are separated from their true foreignness—from the daily life of the people to whom the food is nothing special at all.

Food is one of the safest ways we can feel we are celebrating difference without feeling actually threatened by difference.

Americans eat Japanese food but heartily resist the forms, gender roles, and social ranking intrinsic in a Japanese meal. (If we don't resist them, we play with them.) The food without the culture is our doorway into difference, and as far as most of us are willing to go. The seemingly infinite variety of world foodways meet and are absorbed here in the melting pot, which means they *melt*—and then they absorb each other, merging and blending into new cuisines with no roots at all. Traditional dishes born out of necessity—season, locality, climate, economy—are transformed into dishes without basis in region and season, in what people do, need, revere. Americans are psychic colonialists, taking hold of whatever we touch, and all our conquests are tinged with sorrow for what is lost in the taking.

Yes, it's a big country, full of variety. Never have so many different people from so many different places eaten more different kinds of food in one place. I can eat Thai, Mexican, Italian, or Greek for dinner tonight. So can you, in just about any American city. So can all the Thais, Mexicans, Italians, and Greeks who have migrated here. In Thailand, Mexico, Italy, and Greece, they can eat Big Macs. But never have so many different people from so many different places eaten exactly the same food in the same place, either—billions and billions served. At Taco Bell and Happy Panda and KFC, the differences disappear even while the illusion of choice remains.

I spent three days in a small city on the west coast not long ago, eating all my meals in restaurants. In the course of three days, meeting friends at the restaurants they chose, I ate vegetarian eggs Benedict and "Cajun" eggs Benedict and eggplant Parmigiana, fishball soup, baba ghanouj and a cheese omelet, gumbo and deep-fried tofu, sushi, and an Arch Deluxe. The drive itself was a bold experiment in freeway eating, filled with strange, greasy salads and sloppy sandwiches and spinach-filled tamales. I stopped at Taco Bell on the way home and bought a "Mexican pizza"—two fried flour tortillas filled with hamburger and refried beans, covered with melted cheese. I bought it from a polite, teenage Mexican girl; behind me a half-dozen young Mexican men stood waiting for their turn to order.

A thousand sociologists, anthropologists, and historians have pointed out that what we eat as children is one of the most potent forms of identity and community alignment. What are we to make of our own global pastiche when we consider our children? American food is big, meaty, and abundant. American food is low-fat and frozen. American food is the mall's food court potpourri. American food is the ethnic family-run restaurant down the street—and it is Grandma's cornbread, too. All and none. Betty Fussell says with good cheer that American cooking "defies definition, appalls the tidy minded, and delights the muddlers and mixers." She thinks Americans like to be "where everybody is. . . . Eclectic is a pale Greek word for the chaos of where everybody is."

What eclectic means for many American children today is a little of everything and nothing much. When one grows up able to eat almost everything, anything, whenever one wants, how does food memory grow? Traditionally people eat the same kind of food all their lives. We don't. Whether it's an expression of our identity as trendsetters or just a symptom of our groundlessness, baby boomers eat their childhood foods only as an ironic comment now.

I asked my Japanese friend Mikio what he thinks of the foods his mother made for him when he was young. I expected to hear about tempura, delicate desserts, bowls of steaming soba. But he remembers deep-fried sweet doughnuts, macaroni with ketchup and onions and canned corned beef, fluorescent-green drink powder in ice water. My friend Megan, who was raised by somewhat Bohemian parents in the 1950s and 1960s, grew up eating quiche on a regular basis, a fact she found quietly embarrassing at the time; her sons prefer Ritz crackers. Annie Rose, my Mayan daughter, was born in Guatemala in an ancient maize culture. She loves peanut-butter sandwiches and midnight bowls of Wheaties. In Mexico she eats sopa de lima; in the Bahamas, conch fritters; in London, papadum and tuna sandwiches. In Hawaii, sushi, late at night and watching with rapt attention the rapid ministrations of the Japanese chef folding and wrapping his wares. When she is my age and feeling nostalgic, what will she hunger for?

We have a global cuisine that is neither authentic nor wholly new, neither regional nor a true blend. Perhaps this, after all, is the best expression of our broken world—a world of people confused between the bewildered celebrations of multiculturalism and their choice of race and religious wars.

CELEBRATE DIVERSITY, say the bumper stickers. But the point of all multiculturalism is not to celebrate (or even notice) the true differences between us but to prove that we're really all the same. We "celebrate" diversity by pointing out in myriad ways that under the skin, under the differences in color, language, religious belief, sexual mores, point of view, politics, body shape, ability—underneath, in other words, every single human quality that makes us different from and interesting to each other, there is no real difference. Even our food can be made the same, by being made different, by being brought together into one.

What we call fusion, what we call global food and something

new and very different, is nothing more than faux global, only a new
kind of homogenization. Perhaps Taco Bell will replace the taco
someday all over the world. Taco Bell, or an Alaskan codfish taco
with mango salsa, no matter—the result will be the same. Costco
has opened four stores in Asia and is already building more. In
Taiwan, Costco sells frogs and live fish, but it sells them in big, ugly
warehouses in really big quantities, because that's what Costco
does. We are eating and digesting the world—what will come out
in the end? "If you're traveling around, what are you going to have?"
Julia Child said in an interview not long ago. "I prefer the Quarter
Pounder, though, to the Big Mac."

DO I KNOW HOW TO EAT? DID I EVER KNOW,
have I somehow learned? There is joy in the long-evolved world of
high cuisine, in the slow turnings of society around and around the
special meal. In a world of commuter snacks and global hybrids,
something remains that represents careful eating of a certain
kind—something profoundly "civilized" because it is so directly
tuned to gentle pleasure.

A quiet day, a boon companion, and Genoa, a tiny, dark, hushed
restaurant near my home. At the half-dozen tables sit a young
couple in jeans, an old couple in dressy Sunday best, a man in a
tuxedo with a beautiful woman in what appears to be a formfitting
wedding dress. We take our time in near silence, beginning with a
glass of bittersweet red vermouth, complex. Then the waiter gently places a bowl of bagna cauda over our small candle, where it
warms and melts a little while I spread it on good bread. Then he
brings zuppa di cavolfiori, a subtle pureed soup of cauliflower and

leeks. An hour passes in the rosy light while my companion and I talk quietly, occasionally closing our eyes to taste, and it is like tasting history, eating the communal menu, which passes through time and across space. There are no secret wishes tonight—no secrets, because all the secrets have been shared. The smiling waiter brings us ravioli made of fresh marjoram and ground walnuts, then small plates of mussels in a dark, lusty sauce. The preparations are superb, the portions small and exact, each movement quiet, almost still. My companion eats a filet of Chinook salmon grilled with baby artichokes; I pick with delicate predatory hunger at a quail stuffed with wild porcini mushrooms. A cold bottle of Pinot grigio has disappeared, and almost two more hours are gone. We order dessert, and linger another forty-five minutes over pot de crème and hazelnut torte. I have eaten two bites too many, and dream all night of searching for a beautiful bottle of translucent olive oil.

10

GENERAL MILLS HAS HAD TEST kitchens for many decades, and the seven in use now look a lot like the pictures in the 1950 Betty Crocker cookbook. The Williamsburg kitchen is blue and pink, with flickering candle "flames"; the Arizona Desert kitchen is poppy orange; the Chinatown kitchen, all fake red lacquer and bamboo. Each has a particular use—Cape Cod is usually the province of the Flour and Bisquick team; Pennsylvania Dutch reserved for Dessert and International; California and Hawaii for the Mainmeal, Side Dishes, Snacks, Cereal, and Yogurt team. Each kitchen has a false window looking out upon a false view of a false landscape. All the views are sunny.

The purported mission of the test kitchens is the same as Betty Crocker's mission from the beginning—to "represent the consumer" and, in the process, sell products. ("It's really hard to maintain a business atmosphere around kitchens," says the director,

Marcia Copeland. "People have warm, social feelings in kitchens.") These are working kitchens meant to be as much as possible like the kitchens you and I use, a kind of absolute averaging of consumer needs. They are fitted with the most popular brands of appliances, the most widely used muffin tins and blenders, the top-selling oils, ketchups, and margarines. All the shopping is done at retail prices in grocery stores.

Marcia Copeland is a confident, tidy woman and was dressed on the breezy May day I met her in a navy blouse, red blazer, and match-ing Betty Crocker Red Spoon watch. She has worked here for most of thirty-four years and goes home and cooks dinner almost every night.

Copeland, a lifelong professional, carries the torch of Betty Crocker to millions of women, just like her predecessors. She was fired by General Mills when she got pregnant many years ago, but she forgave the company and eventually returned. She sits today in a bright office in front of a sleek computer, the screen saver a series of glowing neon balls. "Everywhere made you quit then," she told me. "But I can't imagine not working, I just can't."

Copeland directs a staff of forty, almost all women and divided into teams of technicians led by home economists. The teams spend much of their time testing products and recipes in these carefully stocked kitchens. A lot of it is "tolerance" testing—taking a Betty Crocker packaged mix of one kind or another and making it incor-rectly as many ways as they can imagine. Too much water, too lit-tle, too much oil, oven too hot, too cold, pan the wrong size, and so on, trying to imitate the common mistakes made by the con-sumer to whom they sell. Kitchen staff also go into private homes to watch people cook—this is how they know many people buy their battered, blackened baking pans at garage sales, and that a lot of people will use a coffee mug to measure. In real scratch cooking, even in Elizabeth David's or Fernand Point's more complicated recipes, this is fine. But it is a quality of packaged cooking that each step is prescribed, the cooking itself is a quantified act, strictly designed. In that world, creativity can be a disaster.

The same attitude that inspired Betty Crocker to tell grown women how to peel a potato prevails here. General Mills gets more than 600,000 queries a year to the various Betty Crocker help lines, and a lot of them have to do with following simple directions. An entire team of communication specialists focuses on writing recipes and package directions in such a way that they can be understood by people who don't speak English, who can't read, who have never cooked anything in their lives. Along with the most popular appliances, the staff at the test kitchens try to anticipate the dumbest questions. Betty Crocker doesn't lead fashion in food—she follows it, assiduously, and guides from the rear. These days, that means people who do not even know how to cook convenience foods.

"There was a ready-to-spread frosting mix," Kay Emel-Powell, the team leader for Dessert Mixes, told me. "We found that people took the plastic container and *put it on the burner*. And you can imagine! But that just taught us a lot about what people do not know. There are always funny questions, like where do I buy egg whites, or if I'm on the tenth floor of a building, do I have to use high altitude? Does oil mean *motor* oil? That's real." A century of ready-made piecrust, canned soup, and Minute rice means, unsurprisingly, that a lot of people have no idea how such things as piecrust and rice and soup are made. Part of the blame rests on Betty Crocker's cake-mix-dusted shoulders.

. . .

I NEED TO USE "CONVENIENCE" FOODS SOME-
times because I don't have time to cook. A roving cycle of desire and
need marks how we eat now, and especially how we cook. Everything seems to move too quickly, be a bit too much to absorb.
Cooking for others is now a special event instead of the most natural and ordinary part of our lives. I wonder if we've come to prefer the fast, weird food we grab on the run because it fits the other
mismatched parts of our lives. Setting aside why I feel so confusedly
driven to justify this behavior, I am still left with defining what it
means to say I don't have time. Not many people seem to have any
these days. The enormous Kellogg's conglomerate has had a few bad
years because of it. (Bad is relative. Kellogg's now holds only 32 percent of its market and made only $1.81 billion in the third quarter
of 1998.) A company vice president blames a recent decline in part
on what he calls "the bagel situation." People are in a terrible hurry,
he added. "Cereal and milk in a bowl is not convenient enough anymore."

ON AN ICY DAY IN JANUARY, I AM SCHEDULED
to lecture at a private school downtown. I walk to the bus in the
dreary rain, dodging cascades of ice crashing off the overhead wires
and shattering around my feet, and as I turn the corner I see my bus
pull away, early for the first time. When I finally reach the school,
the secretary tells me with harassed courtesy that their schedule
is in chaos and my lectures are canceled. I walk back through the
rain and catch the bus home—cold, wet, dull. It is January, the

hopeless time, and alone in my living room, watching the water tumble off my clogged gutters in silver waterfalls, I can think only of other climes—of hot and spicy lives, other lives.

So I decide to make curry, Thai red curry, starting with fresh curry paste. This is a big job, a slow job, and requires last-minute shopping.

I scan my recipes, make a list, grab my checkbook, and as I walk out the door, the telephone rings. It is my daughter's school; the furnace is broken and they're closing the building. So I continue out the door and drive the other way, a few miles in the dark, splattering storm, and find her with a dozen waiting children playing video games under the sleepy eye of the principal in a dim cacophony of beeps and the tinny shouts of cartoon soldiers. We promise ourselves we will do things differently, be different, choose differently, not surrender or give up or submit, not be overrun, and lie still, and we end up slogging alone in a car through dirty city streets to a run-down brick school where our most precious butterfly, our hope, is glued to the video game we promised not to allow.

My daughter and I toddle through the apathetic streets to a big Asian market in a bleak neighborhood in east Portland. Grocery stores are all the same in a way, down to the impulse candy buys near the register. Than Thao is like all the rest, with a lot of familiar items on the shelves—many bad, bad-tasting, bad for you. Here I can buy big green papayas the color of spring leaves; long, skinny, green beans; elegant stacks of fresh lemongrass; long, lavender Japanese eggplants. The meat counters are marked in script I can't read and filled with cuts of flesh I don't recognize, whole fish, squid parts, tubs of pig ears, another of chicken feet. Among the canned corn and beans and soy sauce are canned lotus shoots, chili paste, bags of pearl barley, bags of dried mushrooms, and flat sheets of dried cuttlefish and transparent noodles fine as hair.

At home, I chop galanga and lemongrass and garlic. My son, the high school dropout, works on the computer; my daughter watches television. The telephone rings. I help my son, and tell my daughter to turn off the television, and the telephone rings. And it rings again. And the doorbell rings; the man has come to clean my gutters, and the rain spills over the edges onto his head.

I work on my curry, chopping hot peppers and grinding cumin seeds and peppercorns, and listen to the radio. I learned how to make red curry paste from a stout American woman in a class held at an upscale Italian grocery. And what do I know of red curry paste? Nothing—rumors. I've never been to Thailand. I'm book-learned, self-taught, a poseur like all the others. I'll use Indian basmati rice grown organically in Texas. I'll add local mushrooms, hand-picked by immigrant laborers, and canned coconut milk from Thailand, and serve it all with slices of California limes. Such bounty—such choices. How lucky we are.

The phone rings and it's a friend, an old friend I've known for twenty years who lives only a few miles away, a friend I haven't seen in a month because we can't find time in our calendars. We schedule dinner for an evening two weeks away. Perhaps we will splurge on Catalonian tapas, or Indian grill, or sushi. So many choices.

The gutter man bangs his ladder against the roof, and I put the chopped spices and golden corn oil into the food processor and whirl them into an evil paste the color of a dirty tropical sunset, the kitchen shimmering in the drugged, smoky perfume. The telephone rings, and while I'm answering, the gutter man comes to the doorway to ask for a check, which I write with the phone pressed against my ear.

So I cook my red curry and make these notes, I talk to my daughter and do the dishes, and I know that I'm lucky, really lucky. I'm hungry—we all are so hungry, starved for ground, for some idea, any idea, of stability. But we hunger alone. As I set the table I know only that all up and down the street people are doing the same things, the same mismatched and lonesome things, under a river of water falling from the sky.

IN THE MEANTIME, THE "SLOW FOOD" MOVEment ("for the Defence of and the Right to Pleasure") has crossed into thirty-five countries with more than 60,000 members. The Slow Food Manifesto was endorsed in 1989, in language and organization deliberately reminiscent of revolutionary hymns and international treaties. "We are enslaved by speed and have all succumbed to the same insidious virus: Fast Life, which disrupts our habits, pervades the privacy of our homes and forces us to eat Fast Foods," it reads. "Our defense should begin at the table with Slow Food. Let us rediscover the flavors and savors of regional cooking . . ." This is dinner at Genoa, this is baking bread through an afternoon, this is a return to an imagined past we all share.

I like Slow Food, in spite of the fact that all this gentle persuasion is found on the Internet. I like the idea that the answer to our dilemma lies, at least in part, in "care, tolerance, hedonism, balsamic calm, lasting enjoyment," and similar delights. Slow Food doesn't just promote good food, well-prepared, but food grown in politically palatable circumstances, carefully tended, and properly raised.

But the movement can address only this one aspect of Fast Life, and only for those who can afford to take the time. Time to discover the Slow Food Movement, read the Web site and the literature, change the frenetic demands of a day filled with kids and work and bills and a million small troubles and dreams. Time to follow the instructions for how to have more time. Time to figure out how to spend less time working, since time is so palpably money now. Fast food is not the cause but the effect of Fast Life, and slow food is the result of that life changing, not the catalyst for it.

Processed and prepared food in such quantity and universality as we are used to now has a value all its own. Making food is now something machines do. A lot of cooking is drudge work—many of my recipes begin with a variation on chopping onions and mincing garlic, and sometimes I just don't want to chop another onion. I want to cook onions—onions someone else has chopped. (I'd rather be a chef than a cook, that is.) In such moments, I lose track of the importance of each swing of the knife, the comfort of repetition and the importance of doing each thing well—the joy of doing that, attending to these things. I'm just tired of it—because I'm just tired. And we need only look in a supermarket to see how much more precisely and readily food is prepared by automation, how much better it can look, how much easier it looks. Food magazines may be largely a product of stylists and photographers, but the message sinks in—the food, and the cook, should look good in the end. There have been times when I really felt like a pot-au-feu, a woman whose time is worth no more than a simmering pot on the stove. When time is money, how much you are paid for your time defines how much you are worth.

In my family as in others, in my life as in many lives, the tension grew until two distinct styles of eating now coexist in my household. Many of my meals are not really cooked. They are heated, warmed up, opened. (Sometimes I call packaged noodles and canned soup "headache food.") But my hunger for fresh foods and food society and the pure pleasure of chopping onions and kneading dough drives me to cook. Other people live on Hot Pockets and Healthy Choice dinners all week and feast on marinated BBQ extravaganzas on the weekends, or eat out five days a week and then spend Saturday making tortes. I am not as extreme as this, but the dissonance is certainly there, the lifestyle of the convenient gourmet. I've been doing this more than usual lately—grabbing prepared food at a deli, opening packages, cobbling together sandwiches or omelets at the last minute. Going out. I haven't had time to cook much lately; I've been busy trying to finish this book.

It is simply quite difficult to cook much while working or rearing children, in the way we do those things today—in a world where work and children are far from both home and kitchen. A painful irony of many women's lives is that only when they are both working and rearing children do they feel pressured to cook regularly. In a spare moment, I sort through catalogs that sell mascarpone cheese and demi-glace and wild mushrooms, pots and pans and almost infinitely expensive knives. This is another kind of food pornography: the stuff of a cook's safe anticipation. I can dream of the kind of cooking I would like to do if I had an entirely different life and were, in fact, an entirely different person.

What women really do, in Sally Cline's word, isn't cooking but *catering*—they do everything, take care of each detail of eating. Few men who cook, even in these somewhat more enlightened days, do all the work of catering that is taken for granted when done by women: planning, budgeting, making lists, driving to the store, shopping, loading the car, driving home, unloading the car, emptying the bags, packing and repacking refrigerator and cupboards, cleaning refrigerator and cupboards, starting new lists, looking through leftovers, making snacks, making school lunches, looking for recipes, substituting ingredients, cooking, setting tables, serving, managing the meal, feeding the children, clearing tables, putting away food, doing dishes, emptying the dishrack, wiping down the counters, sweeping the floor. Starting over.

Women cater and cook; men "prepare a meal" (and trumpets sing). We raise the preparation of food above drudgery only when it is done exceptionally. Cooking a complex meal on the weekend, perfecting a soufflé or a nice sauce over several leisurely hours, sharing the results with friends doesn't feel like drudgery. Cutting up the carrots for the daily pot-au-feu often does. We "show off" our skills on special occasions, to entertain and impress others, and the less we do it the more impressed people are when we do.

And I am still left asking myself why, exactly, it feels like I don't have time to cook. I want to cook and am simply doing other things. We all are working a lot—working at work, working at play, working at family and romance and sports and entertainment. There are not fewer hours in the day than there used to be. But what we consider basic, essential to those days, has changed. The gym. Soccer practice. Commuting. Getting the kids to ballet. Surfing the Net. "To live for the moment is the prevailing passion," wrote Christopher Lasch in 1978, "to live for yourself, not for your predecessors or posterity." Two decades later, living for the moment (and Lasch meant *for appetite*) has become a matter of nanoseconds and parking spaces, an increasingly small point of view camouflaged by immense detail.

We take advice on how to lead simple lives. Some of this advice seems intended as parody, but it's not. (The Center for a New American Dream suggests, "Are you concerned about this culture's encouragement of consumerism? Are you looking for ways to simplify your life? Just click onto www.newdream.org.") Simplicity has been reinvented as a new form of consumption, complete with its own magazines, its own stores, catalogs, and how-to classes.

What it comes down to is still preference; though it often feels otherwise, we choose almost everything we do. We are, as people have been for a hundred years, driven largely by other-directed anxiety. This has nothing to do with time, but we persist—individually and as a culture—in pretending time is the problem. When I say I do not have the time to cook supper, can applesauce, weed the garden, pick berries in the warm sun, I simply mean that I want to be doing something else a little bit more.

Confronting a world in such a rush only makes my personal decision of how to proceed in another direction more difficult. When I go to the grocery store now—and it gets harder to shop all the time in a world of conglomeration and merger—I am trying to balance many things. I balance my time with subtly haunting concerns about contamination and nutrition, with price, with emotional hungers for comfort and companionship, with strong political beliefs, and, somewhere in the fog, a love of cooking and food. I am eating more lunches of cheese slices and oranges, more suppers of scrambled eggs and carrot sticks. I find myself doing this not for any one reason like speed or nutrition, but as the only possible solution to the combination of all these concerns. I find it too easy sometimes to avoid thinking about the extra costs, big and small, involved in my own convenience, my own savings of a few dollars here and there. We aren't encouraged to think about it, *really* think about what it means to eat the food we are told we want to eat.

A recent newspaper story on local delis offering "gourmet grab-and-go" dinner choices contained the comment "Don't overlook your local supermarket as a resource for dinner." The author explained that "stopping at the store on the way home" just feels good—it makes people feel like they're cooking.

"Home meal replacement," or HMR, is one of the biggest new directions in food, an organized response to what the food industry calls the "meal-solutions dilemma." Research done by Pillsbury, General Mills, and other companies shows that people want to "participate to some degree in the cooking process," and "some even want to cook from scratch." But that doesn't mean what it used to mean, which is where Pillsbury and General Mills come in. (Marcia Copeland told me one of their recent surveys revealed that opening a can of soup qualified as "scratch" cooking to many respondents.) These companies (often in tandem with large supermarket chains) are marketing packaged whole meals made up of, say, precooked frozen vegetables, "teriyaki" sauce, and precut slices of raw chicken breast. Instead of sticking a whole frozen dinner in the microwave—which makes it seem as though you're eating a microwaved frozen dinner—the chicken can be cooked "from scratch" and the whole meal served "fresh" in just fifteen minutes. Reynolds is working in partnership with companies like Tyson and BestFoods to create meal packages specifically requiring aluminum foil. One supermarket chain in the Midwest is even trying "themed areas"—ready-to-cook meals and multiple ingredients divided into "Italian" and "Mexican" and "Asian" sections.

My nearest big warehouse store, a block-size building selling garden fertilizer, underwear, birth control pills, videos, hair dye, and groceries, has started offering HMR. They call it "honest to goodness homestyle taste and nutrition." (*Homestyle,* like *natural* and *wholesome* and *fresh,* is one of those buzz words that implies much while promising nothing at all. In this case, it suggests freshly cooked food, but doesn't make any guarantees about who cooked it or where.) The food comes in a variety of ethnicities Americanized for comfort—"a world of good taste." Everything from spaghetti to Chinese Broccoli Chicken is sold at "one easy price" per pound. If you buy nine dinners of at least one pound each, "your next pound of dinner is free."

I drive to the overgrown store and in one corner of the great white space find a steaming buffet table of meat, vegetables, and bright orange sauces. A small line of people clutch big plastic dinner trays, reaching past one another for a little of this and that— plain, fill-up food, dull as dirt. There is nothing I want to eat. I am tired, I am hungry, I am blue and getting bluer in the bleak light. The deals we make come at a terrible price; I believe they wound us, wound us deep and hard. We are injured when we buy crap, make crap, eat crap, choose to contribute to the making of a crappy world. I buy four and a half pounds of dinner at $3.99 a pound, at 6:30 on a dark, wet evening, pressed for time, because (I tell myself, knowing it isn't true) we have to eat something hot for dinner.

Another day, I take two hours to make dinner from scratch— browse recipes, ride bicycle to store, buy a few things, ride home in the falling light. To start, I make a roux—a quick boil of butter and flour turning golden in the pan, breaking continually into distinct, crackling bubbles that rise and burst instantly. The roux is alive, moves on its own accord, breathing. The sauce is silken, velvet, soft and solid at once, with sweet, biting chunks of vegetables and the lilt of garlic. I feel like an amnesiac given a sudden jolt—all at once, *memory*, and my life, my history, is almost in my hands. I have remembered . . . something, but it is elusive, incomplete. In front of me, warm and moving, the food is alive, full of spirit and power, gladness and heat. *I* am alive. I need be nowhere else, do nothing else, be no different than I am right here, right now, because there is nothing missing. I am, and will be, filled.

I'm listening to the radio, listening to Spanish flamenco music played live over the happy noise of glasses clinking and people laughing, and I am beset with a terrible sadness. So much of what has been valued by humans for thousands of years—family, friends, community, identity—seems missing from my ordinary shared past. I'm well aware that what I want, even what I seem to remember, may have nothing to do with what any people have ever had. But the dream is a strong one and not cured by my own happiness, by the islands of love and health in my life, by the exquisite things I've tasted.

My mother is long gone and my father still lives in the house where I was raised. He's not long for this world—he hasn't been for more than thirty years. I ask him questions about the past and he says he doesn't know. Sometimes he simply doesn't answer at all, and sometimes he starts to reply and the words fade out over the phone line, never to be done, which seems to be the most accurate answer of all.

The last time I was there, I looked through his pantry. This is a big pantry he built himself when he remodeled the kitchen—a deep cupboard with heavy, interlacing shelves on hinges. He lives alone. In his cupboard he has dozens of cans of Campbell's soup—pepper pot, tomato, scotch broth, vegetable beef, cream of mushroom, cream of asparagus, cream of celery, cream of chicken. He has cans of Dinty Moore beef stew and Chef Boy-Ar-Dee spaghetti and Spam, tiny cans of chicken and salmon, and bigger cans of shrimp and tuna, dried Cup o' Noodles and Cup-a-Soup, boxes of Minute rice and Uncle Ben's, packages of seasoning mixes in "teriyaki" and "sweet-and-sour" and "taco" flavors, boxed bread and muffin mixes, canned pie fillings, jars of applesauce, jellies, jams, and peanut butter. He has canned gravy and broth and stock, canned vegetables of every kind, canned peaches and pears and pineapple. He has boxes of tamale pie and Hamburger Helper and Tuna Helper.

All this food is old. I was hungry, and I prowled the kitchen, opening every cupboard, every drawer, staring into the refrigerator and the freezer. I finally settled on an individual-serving-size box of Froot Loops, but I couldn't manage a single bite; the cereal was so old it turned into gum in my mouth. Food, food everywhere, and not a bite to eat. That's when I realized everything is the same as it has been for years—*exactly* the same. It's not that he's still eating frozen stuffed whitefish filets—he just has the same frozen stuffed whitefish filet in the freezer that he had last time I was there. He has the same can of tuna in the cupboard, the same box of macaroni and cheese on the pantry shelf, the same half-full jar of pickles in the fridge that have been there for months, or years. Even the four different half-empty jars of Dijon mustard were there, dust-free and clean in the extreme age of neglected delight. I felt like I was standing at ground zero of the twentieth-century cornucopia, on a plain raked clean by the blast. This was ghost food. *Danger!* I thought. *Danger. Lost in space.*

I went to the grocery store and made him a pot of soup, lots of fresh vegetables and beans, but he said he preferred his fat-free instant Cup-a-Soup instead.

THE STEADY CONSOLIDATION OF FOOD PRODUC-tion into fewer and ever larger corporations goes on. Writes Warren Belasco, "In 1950 the largest fifty food companies had owned 6 percent of all food manufacturing assets, in 1963, 42 percent, and in 1978, 63 percent. . . . Between 1973 and 1978, the number of food companies declined almost a third."

By 1974, 90 percent of processed breakfast foods were controlled by four companies. About three-fourths of packaged bread and flour were controlled by four companies, and almost two-thirds of sugar and baking products. Campbell's sold 90 percent of the canned soup. General Mills, Nabisco, and Quaker all bought toy lines or toy companies in recent years, too. This year, Albertson's bought American Stores and became the largest food and drug company of all—almost 2,500 stores in thirty-seven states. A few months later, Kroger's bought my local warehouse market chain and became the biggest supermarket company in the country with about 2,200 stores in thirty-one states. When Kellogg's decided their cereal empire was threatened by the trend toward bagels in the morning, they bought Lender's Bagels.

Some of the consolidation has been by mainstream companies buying much smaller companies that make "health foods" of various kinds. Conglomerates have a vested interest in encouraging our daily confusion over what and how to eat; disordered thinking around food can only be to the advantage of companies large enough and shifty enough to change tack with each new breeze. Even as huge food companies merge, alternative co-ops have either gotten big or disappeared. Successful co-ops, like Co-opportunity in Santa Monica, run on millions of dollars a year in sales. Mrs. Gooch's Natural Food Store chain in Los Angeles is a $90-million company. The for-profit chain Whole Foods Market has sixty-eight stores and almost $900 million in annual sales. In an interview, Whole Foods's president, Peter Roy, said, "We consider all people that are selling natural and organic foods competitive with our company." Such an attitude is a world away from the nascent hope of early nonprofits, but well in line with America's history of food production.

Fast-food chains also continue to merge, and many now are entering into partnerships in what is called "dual branding." Fast food is an intensely segmented market, broken into "dayparts" like breakfast, lunch, afternoon snack, and so on. Dual branding allows two companies that serve different "dayparts" or offer complementary food to share one restaurant with side-by-side menus. Thus, Taco Bell and KFC, Dunkin' Donuts and Baskin-Robbins, Carl's Jr. and Green Burrito. (Most of these companies, too, are part of larger concerns.)

The national A&W chain, more than seventy-five years old, almost went out of business—1,700 of its outlets closed, including the one in my hometown, and the whole gestalt seemed too old and too small in a big brave world. The funky homeliness of Mama Burgers has given way to the more measured and carefully considered mechanics of McDonald's and Burger King, where nothing is left to chance.

But A&W is coming back. The chain was sold in 1994 to a group of investors, and the company is gradually expanding again, with plans to open almost 200 outlets this year. But this is not my mother's A&W. The company bought the rights to Dagwood and Blondie Bumstead and will now serve a Dagwood Burger. Instead of small-town drive-ins, A&W is focusing on college campuses and military bases, designing diners for the future. The design was deemed "contemporary nostalgia" by the new president, a concept, surely, whose time has come.

Many consumers respond positively to an image of corporate political correctness. This is another challenge for food technology conglomerates in recent years: How can you make processed food produced by the millions of cans and packages in huge factories look homemade? As early as the 1970s, clever manufacturers coarsened brown sugar so that it seemed more homespun and less refined, and packaged it in plain paper wrapping for that old general-store look.

By the mid-1980s, *natural* and *fresh* weren't the only words with interesting new meanings. *Handcrafted* and *rustic* had also taken on a flavor altogether different from their original use by the counter-culture. What had been a sincere if confused attempt to live in the relative simplicity of agrarian societies and small communities became a form of status. The attempt by many people to be satisfied with what they could make and grow themselves became a matter of acquisition. *Handcrafted* and *rustic*, like *artisanal*, came to define a lifestyle instead of a life, dedicated not to the local, common, and sufficient but to quality and uniqueness. Instead of making one's own crafts, the emerging market of the 1980s and 1990s sought to collect examples of the agrarian lives lived by other people far away. The grit and local flavor of early co-ops are now used by stores and restaurants to give a rustic impression without the actual mess of the co-ops themselves—just as ethnic restaurants evoke the feeling of fresh cooking instead of fast food, served with the aroma of the small village life impossible in the city where the restaurant thrives. Ethnic restaurants are as likely as any to use all fresh ingredients, too, because immigrant populations have more time—more cheap labor—than money, capital for buying ready-made ingredients.

These days, what I think of as a "natural-foods" store is a long way from what I used to call a "health-food" store. The latter is still around, small, dusty, scattered. But the natural-foods store is an uneasy blend of fresh and processed, local and imported, plain and gourmet. Once upon a time, the complex politics of food were often the first priority in such businesses, followed closely by healthfulness. Taste was a distant third, and convenience hardly a concern. Priorities are much less clear now. Almost all such stores are run for profit now, so profits, obviously, are the first priority. But what follows? Sometimes health seems the next most important value, but more and more this seems a superficial healthfulness based in appearance and strength—values of power, that is. It's confusing: What passes for health food is not always particularly healthy. But some gourmet foods are almost accidentally good for us, like organic "baby" vegetables. Sometimes taste seems most important, and when this is the case, taste is paramount, singular, and covers a multitude of sins. Sometimes convenience is the first priority, even in a so-called natural-foods store. Sometimes shopping is downright appalling.

A surprising number of people I know shop regularly at that ugly retail warehouse near my home, and others go to Costco and Wal-Mart for all kinds of things. I dislike that world of outsized shopping carts and gargantuan aisles most of all, its chittering fluorescent lights and the giant cans, giant boxes, cases of cans and boxes, fifty-pound bags. The deals. I know that in the abstract, many of the customers of such stores would stand up against certain practices: the destruction of farmland, the exploitation of foreign labor, shoddy manufacturing. I know they do, because my friends who shop there express liberal opinions about the interconnection between consumer choices and macroeconomics. Some are people who believe that every act has consequences, people who try to be kind and thoughtful. But when they realized they could save money at Costco, when they were caught up in the possibility of a bargain, a lot fell away. "Only an idiot pays retail!" a usually gentle woman said to me not long ago, discussing grocery stores. In the hypnotic urge to get a deal, to feel that in a world mostly beyond individual control one can beat out the system, such things as gentleness do fall away. A friend of mine calls the urge "atavistic," an almost primitive urge to fill the pantry with staples and be assured the wolf is kept from the door. But the mania to acquire is matched with the powerful need to get "the better" of something—a price, another store, another brand, another customer. With each purchase in such places, we contribute to the paving over of fertile fields, the closing of small businesses, and the destruction of livelihood—we contribute whether we see these things happen or not. We can't divest ourselves from the consequences of each act.

Decades after Clementine Paddleford came to Oregon and extolled the standardizing of plums on Bull Mountain into a single name, Bull Mountain is a bare hill covered in expensive subdivisions. But I can go down the street to Zupan's and shop for the same "heritage" plums once raised there. I can buy tiny purple potatoes, "antique" apple varieties, wild morels, broccolini, fresh fava beans—and Campbell's soup. Zupan's is a small, local grocery chain, and the one nearest my home is spread through the first floor of a remodeled dairy-turned-upscale-shopping-mall—because dairies aren't what they used to be, either. I shop there sometimes because it is the last locally owned grocery chain in the city.

Zupan's sells "quality." All the banners say it: "We Sell Quality." That means high prices, racks of good wine, $6.95-per-pound vine-ripened tomatoes, an "olive bar," black-tip shark, and imported red curry paste, spread more or less evenly between shelves of Campbell's soup, greeting cards, toilet paper, macaroni, ketchup, ice cream, magazines, and deli cases, under clean, bright lights in the hum of prosperity. Quality like this feeds the American appetite for variety, the deep, inarticulate belief that we deserve to get what we want and we deserve it now. Zupan's is open twenty-four hours a day.

I make a nuisance of myself at Zupan's. I want to know if the fish is farmed or wild, if the chicken is free-range, if the green beans are local. The fish clerk doesn't know. The produce stocker doesn't know. The head of the produce section comes, and he knows. It is August in Oregon's Willamette Valley, one of the most fertile and productive valleys in the country, and most of the produce is from California and farther away. Our local fruits and vegetables are bound by the ton for other climes.

Our local leader in natural foods has always been Nature's Fresh Northwest. Nature's started in 1976 as a small storefront selling only organic foods and gradually grew to a local chain of six stores. The original inventory slowly expanded over time until Nature's was selling everything from locally baked bread to meat, fish, wine, coffee, candles, makeup, toys, magazines, and ice cream. The prices have always been higher than local supermarkets, but I was happy to pay them when I could in order to support a locally owned business and the multiple small, alternative businesses whose products they sold.

A few years ago, Nature's was sold to General Nutrition Centers, Inc., for a healthy amount of money. (GNC owns more than 3,500 vitamin and supplement stores across the country.) Nature's didn't change too much with the sale. It still sells a lot of what is essentially "alternative" food. Many brands are made by small companies. Much of the meat is locally raised, and some is organic. Some of the fish is harvested from sustainable stocks. Some of the produce is organic. And prices are still high—alternatives like these have always come at a premium. But the whole picture put together makes less sense to me all the time. A lot of the food I see in stores like Nature's is heavily packaged and quite a bit of it is heavily processed and from dubious sources—especially the imported condiments and more exotic ingredients. Offering free-range chickens and turkeys raised without chemicals, hormones, or antibiotics is one thing, but Nature's sells shark, swordfish, and halibut, severely threatened fish long anathema to those concerned with sustainable stocks. The National Research Council recently reported that more than 80 percent of American fisheries are "fully exploited or overfished." But it didn't make headlines, and fish consumption, especially among baby boomers seeking low-fat food and micronutrients, continues apace. A new Nature's opened close to my home recently. By the door is a quote of John Muir's: "When one tugs at a single thing in nature, he finds it attached to the rest of the world." In the freezer cases are Stouffer's Lean Cuisine, on sale.

Even natural-foods stores are growing big beyond belief, big and bright and increasingly vertically integrated. GNC recently sold

Nature's to Wild Oats, at a $40 million profit. Wild Oats Markets, Inc., is the second-largest natural-foods chain in the country—with almost $400 million in annual sales. Last year Nature's closed its original little storefront and opened the first of what the company calls a "lifestyle" store. The new Nature's is a 40,000-square-foot megastore offering groceries, produce, complete ready-cooked meals for takeout, a restaurant, a cooking school, video entertainment, and the true alternative products of the 1990s: diet counseling, massages, facials, beauty salon makeovers, and a sauna.

Even cookbooks are a form of conglomerate now. The recent new edition of *Joy of Cooking* was written by many different people directed in part by a focus group. The quirky personality of Irma Rombauer has been wiped clean. Gone are the sweet-and-sour meatballs and the infamous tomato-soup mystery cake, gone are many of the helpful "About" sections of information. The whole book is a little fancy, and many of the recipes more time-consuming, expensive, and complex than Irma Rombauer's originals. They are also dead serious. Irma's grandson, Ethan, did a lot of the editing. He has Cordon Bleu experience and apparently none of Irma's fun-loving, "mistakes-were-made" spirit. Commenting on its new incarnation and the loss of Rombauer's "elegant turn of phrase," *Cook's Illustrated* mourned, "Sadly, the latest edition tells us that we are a professionally packaged consensus of opinion."

A new edition of *Betty Crocker's Picture Cook Book* was released in 1986, with new information on ethnic and international foods, a little on tofu, lots of chicken and seafood, salads and fresh vegetables, and nutrition notes. Back was the original Betty Crocker mission of teaching cooking techniques. Surveys showed that very few people learn how to cook at home anymore. By 1991, the cookbook edition put rice, pasta, beans, and produce in a central role. Meat had become part of the ensemble instead of the "star of the show."

The newest version of the cookbook, the eighth edition, was released in 1996. Words like *dredge* and *fold* were dropped, because hardly any readers know what they mean anymore. This edition emphasizes what Marcia Copeland calls "turbo flavors"—chilies and mustards and vinegars—to help satisfy the palate resigned to eating low-fat foods. An entire page is devoted to the difference between using butter, margarine, and vegetable oil spreads in recipes. The photo spreads are not pies, cakes, and dripping roasts—they are mounds of gourmet beans, Asian fruits, and fresh herbs. Of its 900 recipes, 150 have "light" versions alongside the original. There are no pigs in blankets anymore.

What I notice most in this latest Betty Crocker cookbook is the same thing I notice in *Joy of Cooking*—the utter lack of personality. There is a tremendous amount of information here, and I know without a doubt it's well-researched, carefully tested information. These recipes have been stretched, creased, folded, stapled, and mutilated in every possible way, and I'm sure each works just fine. But there is no heart, no literary style, no quirky voice or individuality. It is truly a computer-age cookbook—and a big seller. But General Mills also released a facsimile edition of the original book, my mother's 1950 *Betty Crocker's Picture Cook Book*, this past year because so many people had called wanting to get the recipes that "Mom used to make."

Time and again, Betty Crocker's portrait, like her book, has been updated to fit the times. In 1972, her image was supposed "to reflect the new roles women are accepting outside the home," but times changed and she had to be updated again in 1980, made both more "poised" and "softer." That didn't last, either. In 1986, when the sixties seemed so far away, a "more professional" Betty Crocker appeared, "approachable, friendly and confident; as comfortable in the board room as she is in the dining room." She even wore a floppy bow tie.

The newest portrait and the latest edition of the cookbook appeared in the seventy-fifth anniversary year of Betty Crocker's "birth." Painters, hairstylists, and makeup artists had always collaborated on her face, but the new image was a 1990s project from beginning to end. First, people were invited to nominate women who had the "spirit" of Betty Crocker—defined as commitment to family, "everyday" creativity, and, of course, pleasure in cooking. From the thousands of essays received, seventy-five women were chosen as "winners." Their photographs were then combined by computer with the 1986 portrait of Betty. (The work was done by the Lifestyle Software Group.) Then the computer picture was itself painted into the image of an "exceptionally knowledgeable, yet imminently approachable and genuinely caring" woman.

Now she is like us and not like us, as Betty Crocker was always supposed to be. She is still, always, in her mid-thirties, still Caucasian, trim but not athletic, neat, healthy. This is Woman at the end of the century. She is surprisingly like the woman real women were meant to become at the century's beginning. She is better than but not superior to other women, more experienced but not more worldly, serious and reliable but never cold, warm and caring but never silly, intelligent and curious but satisfied by the challenges of the domestic sphere, tasteful but not trendy, loving and kind but never stodgy.

Before I was born, in his history of the General Mills, James

Gray said that nobody really wanted to know if Betty Crocker was a living person. "The essence of Betty Crocker was—and is—reassurance," he wrote. "None of her followers has ever wanted to challenge her reality. She has fulfilled too deep a need."

I think she looks like an android one programming error away from mayhem. But I can't deny this portrait's perfect position in this time and place, where we rely on "virtual communities" for intimacy and having a cup of coffee with your best friend takes days of planning. Betty Crocker has her own Web site now. Nothing could be more appropriate for a millennial portrait of the imaginary housewife in a culture where the housewife barely exists than this ethnic stew of real human features turned pale and historyless. Nothing fits how we eat now better than a computer-generated woman without context or color. I'll bet *she's* the one who wrote the new cookbook.

APPLEBEE'S NEIGHBORHOOD GRILL AND BAR, with about 1,100 restaurants open in forty-eight states and five countries, is the largest of what are called "casual dining" chains in the United States. (Other chains in this category include Chili's, Olive Garden, Boston Market, and Cracker Barrel.) Applebee's has steadily consumed smaller dining chains over the last fifteen years, but part of its phenomenal success is due to clustering—the practice of opening several restaurants in a small enough area that each individual franchise will compete not with a Chili's or Boston Market but with another Applebee's. This both controls the attractive real estate in a given area and forces each management team to a new level of exposure within the company. When an Applebee's is getting beaten in the marketplace, often it's by another Applebee's.

Before he ran restaurants, the CEO of Applebee's, Lloyd Hill, was running the health-care company Kimberly. He learned about food on the job. When he tried to cut costs by eliminating garnishes, his managers protested because customers, they told him, consider garnishes a sign of food quality. Hill isn't really a restaurateur. He's a businessman, a "people" person, a manager able to disguise end-game competition in folksy phrases. He says he wants every employee to be able to say, " 'I am what I am, because of me.' " This philosophy is an excellent expression of the chain itself—meaningless, inarguable.

The Applebee's motto is "America's Favorite Neighbor." I first heard of Applebee's when I received an advertisement in the mail. It was a pamphlet on old-fashioned stock with a colorful pencil drawing: a grocery store on the sunny corner of Main Street, with distant mountains and green trees in the background. An old pickup truck loaded with red apples passes a bicycling boy and his golden retriever in the quiet street. "Applebee's," reads the headline, "Your Neighborhood Grill & Bar."

The homely setting is a manifestation of rootlessness, the foundering drift of our culture. We're a global village of virtual communities, and regional means what we see on television. (There are Web sites for individual Applebee's restaurants all over the country: Roanoke and Fountain Valley, California, and Portage, Minnesota. They're all really friendly Web sites.) *Wholesome, natural*, and *fresh* are all used up, so Applebee's works every variation of *local* and *home*. Local, regional, neighborhood, *yours*: They all mean not-from-somewhere-else. The neighborhood we want to live in is the place where everyone knows your name, just like they do on television. Applebee's is selling that big, happy neighborhood, a thousand village greens, all the same, all nice. When the waitress arrives at my table, the first thing she says is, "Have you ever been to an Applebee's before?" as though I might need instructions on how to proceed. And perhaps I do.

This strange cross-pollination of elements *is* Applebee's: a world where everyone is unique and no one stands out, where we're all the same and each person is entitled to his own special prize. The decor is intended to evoke the chunky shape of unreconstructed neighborhoods, the kind of unplanned but natural growth of organically developing communities. The clunkiness is also a controlled memory of past decades—its garage-sale texture is a shallow version of the immediate relationships people sought in funky cafés and food co-ops in the 1970s. There's a little basement-rec-room in it, a bit of messy-college-dorm-room. All the wacky bits and pieces are exactly the same from place to place—each Applebee's is a great deal like the next. Small elements shift around here and there, but the parts are identical. In the restaurant business, this carefully contrived mess is called "non-chain decor."

I first went to an Applebee's restaurant when I had to make dinner reservations for the nightmare assemblage of persons who make up a family reunion: two picky teenagers, a young man with a huge appetite, an elderly couple on strict low-fat diets, a woman with severe allergies, and a vegetarian. I took the crowd to Applebee's, without any idea of what we were getting into.

The place is crowded, impossibly nice. The service is mediocre at best, but also impossibly nice; the staff is made up entirely of handsome young people who seem to form a coed multiracial team of cheerleaders. I've returned several times, and it's always nice and the other customers always remind me of that same difficult combination:

There are young and pierced customers, old and gray customers, single people at the bar, families at the tables, white and black in alternating booths. An alien walking in off the street might suppose for a moment that we really are all one big, happy family.

Each area of the restaurant is a theme park of nostalgia, one melting almost invisibly into the next; memories and memorabilia, nostalgia and dreams. The wall of flight, opposite the astronaut wall, faces the firefighters' wall. Walking around, I find a baseball wall, a wall of boats, one for country music, a wall for rock and roll, one for golf, another for cars, another for cowboys—each represented by a busy collage of photographs, newspaper headlines, posters, and objects like canoe oars and baseball mitts and car bumpers. Seemingly unique pieces of history—evocative photographs, worn newspaper clippings, chipped baseball bats, cowboy lariats, and broken vinyl records—are reproduced again and again all over the country, more than a thousand times.

These images can't even be accused of showing breadth without depth, because there isn't any breadth. Applebee's declares a peculiarly narrow and shallow paradigm of nostalgia—white, middle-class, American nostalgia for physical prowess, classic beauty, manly strength, none of it true. In the "movie star/ Hollywood" section, there are 8 x 10 glamor shots of actors and actresses. In one corner, Bette Davis and Vivien Leigh cozy up cheek to cheek with Christina Applegate and Dana Delaney. They have been made equal, evened out in space and time and cultural merit.

Applebee's decor is history written by people who have never studied history. But they know a lot about marketing. They know how to make remembering an easy thing, because they know how uncomfortable real memory often is. They are selling a gestalt, a collage of comfortable invitations, a hodgepodge of apparently authentic and unique images. Nothing is coherent; these are the memories of amnesiacs. Here the profits are found in the curves, not the edges. There are no edges in Applebee's.

The food, one has to admit, is not bad—it is at least as good as McDonald's, as good as what a lot of people eat at home, certainly better than what a lot of us ate as children. As an ode to melting-pot assimilation, Applebee's is a triumph.

At Applebee's, themes come and go, and each theme comes with new entrees, appetizers, and drinks. The entrees are, to some extent, region-specific—a little Tex-Mex in one state, a little more Creole in another. But for the most part, a crazy quilt of tastes abound. Much of the menu has a finger-food approach: pizza sticks, Buffalo chicken wings, onion rings. The Santa Fe Sampler has nachos, a quesadilla, and jalapeño poppers. The Oriental Chicken Salad has "Oriental greens" and "crunchy chicken fingers." There is also Jambalaya Pasta and Chicken & Broccoli Pasta Alfredo, Tijuana "Philly" Steak Sandwich, Aztec Chicken Salad. These are the "neighborhood specialties," and since no neighborhood is specified, the implication is that this is *your* neighborhood. Enchiladas, Bourbon Street steak, fajitas, Caesar Pasta Combo, hamburgers, Gardenburgers—all part of the community. A fair number of dishes are labeled low-fat ("and fabulous!"). Others are swimming in cheese and oil. For dessert there are rich, gooey concoctions of whipped cream and chocolate and a "low-fat and fabulous" brownie "too good to be true." The bar serves made-up seasonal drinks like Hot Apple Rum and Crantinis and gorgeously fattened shakes of liqueurs and ice cream.

Just reading the menu at Applebee's makes me feel dislocated, its incongruous elements coming together in a dreamy logic. The logic dissolves the moment you awaken and are relieved to find that parallel lines don't really meet and Tuscan chicken doesn't really mean a "char-grilled Italian chicken breast served with Boboli® style croutons."

The food has been retouched just like the past: jalapeño poppers and Oriental greens equalized like movie stars and sitcom starlets, elevated or reduced until they flatten out to homogeneity, attenuated in meaning and flavor until they fit the buffet table of the democratic New World. In this postmodern future, movie stars and sitcom starlets really are the same, too—they are in our minds, because we can't remember a damned thing.

Applebee's serves a lot of chicken breast, of course. Chicken breast is the most inoffensive of meats, and except for profits, Applebee's purpose is inoffensiveness. There is almost nothing to react *to*, nothing to get offended *about*. The food is not good, but not bad, the service is not good, but not bad, and this is, as Betty Fussell pointed out, that magical world "where everybody is."

Remember rumaki—chicken livers and water chestnuts wrapped in bacon? Rumaki is one of the great twentieth-century fakes, a fictitious Chinese tidbit come from Hawaii by way of Trader Vic's. We can laugh at rumaki now. We laugh and then go out to eat at Applebee's, with its world food principles gone mad. All that is different between Mom's proud platter of rumaki and our Mesa Quesadillas is an overlay of ironic distance. Wink, wink—nudge, nudge. The "idealism" of the 1950s to which the Sterns unquestioningly refer has been replaced by a careful defense against hope. Happiness is what we're afraid of now. We are careful not to invest too much, we might be wrong—anything could happen, things change so fast. We are holding back as hard as we can, even as we lean forward into the future, into a tension pulling us apart.

WE HAVE IMAGINED INTO BEING A NEW FORM of intimacy, one that allows us to remain anonymous and still pretend to be seen. So many of us live so separately from one another now that chatting on a screen is preferable to our wounded solitude, our unwilling exile in a storm of stimulus. We are inundated by noise; we live in ever-shrinking family units. So it has been for a century—this world of planned divorce, absent fathers, and litigation for every scratch follows directly from a world where vacuum cleaners saved labor and the dinner hour disappeared into the commute. The millennial plague of depression is only our own neurasthenia, and still we speak about our sorrows as though they are something separate and outside ourselves, as though they could be fixed only that way.

Today's office worker is the logical and desired extension of 150 years of industrial and social change. He is stationed at a computer cubicle in a big company, electronically pushing parts of a giant economy around at a distance, clocking in and out, dressing much like everyone around him dresses. He eats distantly processed food that is a lot like the food a million other people are eating, food handed to him by a stranger at the hour dictated by the company. He can wear clothes from around the world, eat food his grandfather would never have imagined, get on an airplane during his carefully guarded vacation, and go almost anywhere he wants. Yet his life is extraordinarily immobile in a way; each choice is dictated, created, by others.

One of the essential marks of a modern life is that it is mediated, and we *all* are middlemen now. Little in our lives is begun, little finished. We are mediaries and we live between mediaries in indirect and dislocated relationships. This middle occupies so many layers that after a while there is little else to see—no end and no beginning, no cause and no effect, just the endless *processing* in between.

"Oh, I have plenty, I remind myself that night on the drive back to our summer home, a little red farmhouse in Vermont," wrote James Atlas in a *New Yorker* essay last year. "And I do: more than I could ever have imagined possible. A house in the country that I love, even if it still looks, from certain unforgiving angles, like one of those sharecroppers' shacks that Walker Evans photographed for 'Let Us Now Praise Famous Men.' A nice New York apartment, even if one of our children has to sleep in the maid's room. We go on vacation twice a year, even if I have to write a piece for *Travel & Leisure* to pay for it. . . . But do I have enough?"

Atlas is a modern man. Is he kidding? Perhaps a bit. But the hunger he feels is too true. Atlas considers his life in Manhattan to be essential to the artist he believes himself to be. The summer home is a necessity because the artist's life in Manhattan is so hard. He spends a remarkable number of hours at good restaurants and cocktail parties, because this is what writers in Manhattan are supposed to do. And throughout, he is almost breathless with the urge to consume and not simply to consume—to attend life ravenously, gluttonously, as though each day were a gargantuan medieval banquet and he is shouting with laughter as he wrestles a greasy joint of slightly gamy beef from a woman's slippery hand. We feast on stuff, space, privacy, and one another's bodies now in a cultural vomitorium, a built-in obsolescence of dissatisfaction.

At the beginning of this book, I quoted Massimo Montanari's observations of medieval Europe, where people's food choices "hinged on the at once clear and ambiguous idea of *quality*. . . . Expensive, elaborate and refined foods (those which only wealth and power could procure on a daily basis) were intended for noble stomachs, while coarse and common foods went into the stomachs of peasants." How much has really changed? *Quality* is the ultimate buzzword of our generation now, our public times: Whatever we do, whatever we wear, eat, buy, want, is based in our perception of quality. Our "expensive, elaborate and refined" foods are now more likely to be arugula and herb-crusted halibut than whole sheep and honey-drenched sweetmeats—but that's fashion, not change.

I walk through Zupan's and wonder when it will end. I try to buy fish from one of the few sustained fisheries left, and I look at the seafood counter and realize with a sinking feeling that most people don't care. Most people don't care where their food comes from, who grows, picks, catches, and prepares it. Life is hard; we can't track every unseen cost. We will eat the very last fish in the ocean. I know this. I believe this, and still I compromise. I buy time. I buy gratification. I rationalize. I deny. I turn away. I turn away.

Oh, we live in hell. There is something hellish and creepy in our prosperous luxury, our raw hunger, like some fiendish limbo. Too much is never enough. Perhaps we lost, if Americans ever had it, the ability to eat with understanding. More important, we lost the ability to tell the difference between excess and sufficiency, between what is enough and what is more than enough. Tomatoes were ruined because we wanted them all the time, and so with our lives: each single thing ruined because we want every thing at once.

Twisted by a strange and barbarically enhanced refinement, modern images of happiness are images of something rare, dainty, fastidious, and tough—guided adventure vacations breaking up the months of gracious living. Our hunger is voluptuous and dissolute, refinement merging into debauchery—but it is a debauchery complete with linen tablecloths and a fine Pinot noir.

At a writing workshop last summer, I asked my students to draw maps and pictures of a summer place they remembered. Over the course of an hour with crayons, they drew lovely pictures, almost all of them filled with water. In the water, along its banks, fertility. A big, deep mountain lake in rural British Columbia. The clear cove off Chesapeake Bay, teeming with crabs and swans. A neighborhood pond filled with frogs. A Sunday evening picnic table laid like a groaning board with berries and corn, framed by the serene laughter of unhurried, familiar adults. We showed our pictures and described the memories in them. The stories went like this. The shore of the hidden mountain lake has a big resort on it now. The crabs all got eaten and the swans are gone from the cove. The frog pond dried up and the frogs died and they built a subdivision. The garden vegetables, wild berries, the sweet preserved figs from the neighbor's trees—no more garden, no more trees.

Slowly the room filled with a terrible, tender melancholy, quiet and almost too hard to bear, an ache for all that was gone. Our rosy memories were partly false, of course. But they were also a little bit true.

We want what we remember of our childhood to return, or we want heartily to avoid what we remember. No difference. What we remember and what really occurred diverge in sometimes startling ways, and the truths we feel in our bones are often true whether they happened in fact or not. I want to be twelve again, swimming across a silent mountain lake; I want to be ten, sitting in the crotch of my grandmother's walnut tree, listening to the ratcheting of blue jays; I want to be nine, gathering acorns on a cold autumn day. Memory is like a randomly interrupted slide show of someone else's vacation, but that doesn't mean we don't recognize some of the places they've been.

Somehow Americans believed they could ruin the land without hurting their bodies, cure our bodies without helping our land. We are divorced from cause and effect, from the very notion of being divorced. A local fisherman complains about killer whales "stealing" the fish from his hulking nets. Loggers complain about how "wasteful" it is to let naturally downed trees decompose into soil. Farmers whose crops are planted in high desert demand compensation for their "right" to water when the rivers pumped out for irrigation run dry. The rest of us want our fish and wood and produce fresh and ready, too. Somehow we still manage to think these things aren't connected to our pain.

We drew our pictures that day in the living room of a big house in an expensive subdivision built on what once was primeval forest. There are no longer big, old trees here, only pretty parasitic birches and Kentucky bluegrass. We could hear the cars of the rapidly growing metropolis over the bubbling of the creek behind the house. Each person spoke, and between their words the room was still, bereft, and empty. We didn't have a thick, rich grief to share, the comforting syrup of grief when loss is sharp and near. These were old, enervated losses, dull as famine, and the words were lost along with the nerve.

That evening, I was driving with my friend Carlton, the student

who remembered hunkering down by the pond and catching tad-
poles. We were driving through city streets riddled with billboards
and power lines and neon just starting to glow in the pale, twilit
August sky, and Carlton said all at once, as though stricken by pain,
"Oh, these *days!*"

Earlier, he'd written a spontaneous two-minute composition
beginning with the line "Ah, bright wings" from a poem by Gerard
Manley Hopkins. From those few words he'd written a eulogy, and
couldn't read it aloud for his tears.

"I stand in the warm spray," he wrote, "waiting, but no more
words come . . . 'Ah, bright wings,' I say again, deliberately this
time, but if these words were once magic, their power is gone,
the gods they call to long dead or moved across the universe . . .
'Ah, bright wings,' just words, no gold, no light, no hint of moving air . . ."

We are, all of us, a Diaspora. But where is our homeland? The
exile from Eden is the Western archetype, the eternal search. It lasts
a lifetime, all the years marked with the hope of rescue, redemp-
tion, and reunion. We are refugees crossing a desert, gathering the
materials of the life we think we've lost.

"On days like these," Carlton finally said, "I'm inside and I look
out and I just see these days slipping by." These glorious days, which
once stretched timelessly before us, we children once so arrogant
and vigorous in our bright wings, by the lake, by the shore.

We drove on, under the August sky.

EPILOGUE

I SUGGESTED EARLY IN THIS BOOK THAT FEW Americans have experienced real hunger—the involuntary hunger most human beings have known, with regularity, throughout history. Even in its first few hours, hunger, like the guillotine, focuses the mind beautifully. We have created amazing institutions and systems to satisfy our endlessly inventive hunger, but we are insatiable; we can't be filled, can't be done. This is the danger, the gift, one of the secrets of food.

Food has always meant more than feeding. Food is bonding, sacrament, joy. A quotidian public delight. "A bon vivant is not just someone who enjoys eating and drinking," writes Bourdieu. "He is someone capable of entering into the generous and familiar—that is, both simple and free—relationship . . ." Generous and familiar, the eater and the eating alike. We have a very long history of treating food as a potent, holy, and mystically precious thing. The biggest marker of our modern life is that we have refused this and tried to make food a secular thing. Food matters so much. Why do we settle for so little?

What is the secret of food? Do you think I have it? I'm no more free of the tensions around us than you are. My relationship to food, this everyday need, has seemed endlessly complicated at times. To untangle it I needed to know my history, to know what distant wind has blown the small waves licking my feet. I looked far and I looked near—inward and outward. It has helped a lot to know the intimate and global dilemmas I'm within, to know how change has reached through space and time into my life.

It should be obvious by now that I think we are injured by too many choices—injured by getting what we want, in a way. For a lucky few of us, those of us doing well in America at the end of the millennium, anything is possible and so nothing seems to be enough. After all, we're taught every day not to turn anything down. For everyone else, faces pressed hungrily against the window, desire is bottomless, and change—well, change is awfully abrupt these days.

The secret of food, for me, is a steady walk through the middle of the cultural thicket, glancing only now and then to the extremes on either side. A little simplicity—local food, seasonal food, plain food. An apple. Good Oregon cheese on fresh bread, unadorned. But also a little indulgence, not money but time—a meal lasting for hours. A sacher torte made from scratch for a friend. Simmering, complex stews. A little of this, a little of that.

We do not reach for a cob of corn and remind ourselves that it is "the modeling of our first mother-father." We are more likely to calculate the calories in a little bit of butter. A little of this—concern. And a little of that—the sacred. We must be awake to really eat—awake to the world, to all that is more than the sum of its many parts. This doesn't mean spending every minute of our lives remembering the mother-father, but it does mean being able to do that now and then.

Certain things become impossible to eat when we understand the endless connections between land, planet, people. The cost, the losses, are too great, and too visible. Other things, single bites, become exquisitely dear.

Grandma's kuchen, fat-free brownies, oeufs à la neige aux framboises, Velveeta, or pad Thai—these distinctions don't matter as much as what we bring to them. As we learn to see into, and through, the infinite complexity of one plate of food, the false distinctions between us fall away.

So I come to balance, slowly, slowly, like a glass vase rocking dangerously on a table—almost falling, and gently coming to rest. To balance. In that balance, none of this is me, or my hunger. It's our hunger, and sharing it is the secret.

I go on retreat. It is winter, and the days are cold and tremblingly silent. We are awake before dawn in the December dark, awake long into the blanketing night. There is nothing to eat until three hours after rising, when we each have a bowl of oatmeal dribbled with sugar and a few raisins. I lean into the steam of my dark tea in the warming meditation hall, curl the first sip around my mouth in deep happiness. We work hard all day, and it is nothing like the wearing strain of other of my days, when there is always plenty from which to choose. Here, there is nothing to choose. The schedule never varies; work is assigned, seats and beds given, questions not asked.

I work in the kitchen, and move as silently as I can, as carefully as I can, without any distraction but the noise in my head, which is considerable at times. But it quiets as the week goes on. Then I am just chopping, just stirring. Just beginning over again. I go into warm rooms and out again into wind and blowing rain, into suddenly crisp, clear air broken by the shocking cry of a raven hidden in the pine tree nearby. That night I dip dark bread into kale soup, watching a pat of pale butter melt and the bread soak into the pine-green broth. And all is luminous. My cup is a rock of porcelain, my bowl a vessel of light. They are earthenware, wares of the earth, gifts, life's blessing. The tribe works, the tribe eats.

Now and then, these unforgettable joys. I close my eyes, take a breath. Vivid, unexpected delights in any given moment, for the taking, every day. There if I am willing. Sometimes this means careful attention—other times casual pleasure. Sometimes eating is just eating, and each thing I taste is the very best thing I've ever tasted—no more, no less. It is just eating, like sitting and walking, common miracles. I fill with gratitude, until gratitude itself is ordinary. "I have been so well nurtured throughout my life that I'm sure to die completely cured," said Fernand Point. What luck to eat well—and to believe that we deserve to eat well. What luck to be so very lucky. This is the real secret of food.

BIBLIOGRAPHY

ALLEN, BRIGID, ed. *Food: An Oxford Anthology.* New York: Oxford University Press, 1994.

BARTHES, ROLAND. *Empire of Signs,* trans. Richard Howard. New York: Hill & Wang, 1982.

————. "Toward a Psychosociology of Contemporary Food Consumption" (1961), in Robert Forster and Ranum Orest, eds., *Food and Drink in History,* vol. 5 of *Annales, Economies, Societes, Civilisations,* trans. Elborg Forster and Patricia M. Ranum. Baltimore: Johns Hopkins University Press, 1979.

BELASCO, WARREN J. *Appetite for Change: How the Counterculture Took on the Food Industry 1966–1988.* New York: Pantheon, 1989.

BERRY, WENDELL. *The Unsettling of America: Culture and Agriculture.* New York: Avon, 1977.

BOURDIEU, PIERRE. *Distinction: A Social Critique of the Judgement of Taste,* trans. Richard Nice. Cambridge, MA: Harvard University Press, 1984.

BRACKEN, PEG. *The I Hate to Cook Book.* New York: Harcourt, Brace, 1960.

————. *A Window Over the Sink: A Mainly Affectionate Memoir.* New York: Harcourt Brace Jovanovich, 1981.

BRAUDEL, FERNAND. *The Structures of Everyday Life: The Limits of the Possible,* vol.

1 of *Civilization and Capitalism 15th–18th Century,* trans. Sian Reynolds. New York: Harper & Row, 1979.

BROWN, DALE. *American Cooking.* New York: Time-Life Books, 1960.

CLAIBORNE, CRAIG. *A Feast Made for Laughter.* New York: Doubleday, 1982.

CLINE, SALLY. *Just Desserts: Women and Food.* London: Andre Deutsch, 1990.

COONTZ, STEPHANIE. *The Way We Really Are: Coming to Terms with America's Changing Families.* New York: Basic Books, 1997.

CORNELL, L. L. "Constructing a Theory of the Family: From Malinowski Through the Modern Nuclear Family to Production and Reproduction." *International Journal of Comparative Sociology* 31, no. 1–2 (1990).

COWAN, RUTH SCHWARTZ. *More Work for Mother: The Ironies of Household Technology from the Open Hearth to the Microwave.* New York: Basic Books, 1983.

COWARD, ROSALIND. *Female Desires: How They Are Sought, Bought and Packaged.* New York: Grove Weidenfeld, 1985.

CUMMINGS, RICHARD OSBURN. *The American and His Food: A History of Food Habits in the United States.* Chicago: University of Chicago Press, 1941.

DAVID, ELIZABETH. *Elizabeth David Classics: Mediterranean Food, French Country Cooking, Summer Cooking.* Newton, MA: Biscuit Books, 1998.

———. *South Wind Through the Kitchen.* New York: North Point Books, 1998.

DUSABLON, MARY ANNA. *America's Collectible Cookbooks: The History, the Politics, the Recipes.* Athens, OH: Ohio University Press, 1994.

ESCOFFIER, AUGUSTE. *The Escoffier Cookbook: A Guide to the Fine Art of French Cuisine.* New York: Crown, 1903, 1969.

FITCH, NOËL RILEY. *Appetite for Life: The Biography of Julia Child.* New York: Doubleday, 1997.

FOLBRE, NANCY. "Women on Their Own: Residential Independence in Massachusetts in 1880." *Continuity and Change* 6, no. 1 (1991): 87–105.

FOLBRE, NANCY, AND MARJORIE ABEL. "Women's Work and Women's Households: Gender Bias in the U.S. Census." *Social Research,* Autumn 1989.

FORTY, ADRIAN. *Objects of Desire: Design & Society from Wedgwood to IBM.* New York: Pantheon, 1986.

FRASER, LAURA. *Losing It: America's Obsession with Weight and the Industry That Feeds on It.* New York: Dutton, 1997.

FUSSELL, BETTY. *Masters of American Cookery: The American Food Revolution and the Cooks Who Shaped It.* New York: Times Books, 1983.

———. *The Story of Corn.* New York: Alfred A. Knopf, 1992.

GRAY, JAMES. *Business Without Boundary: The Story of General Mills.* Minneapolis: University of Minnesota Press, 1954.

GREEN, HARVEY. *The Uncertainty of Everyday Life: 1915–1945.* New York: HarperCollins, 1992.

HACKWOOD, F. W. *Good Cheer: The Romance of Food and Feasting.* New York: Sturgis & Walton Co., 1911.

HARVEY, BRETT. *The Fifties: A Women's Oral History.* New York: HarperCollins, 1993.

HAZLITT, W. CAREW. *Old Cookery Books and Ancient Cuisine.* London: Elliot Stock, 1886.

HESS, JOHN L. AND KAREN. *The Taste of America.* New York: Viking, 1977.

HIBBEN, SHEILA. *American Regional Cookery.* Boston: Little, Brown, 1946.

LASCH, CHRISTOPHER. *The Culture of Narcissism: American Life in an Age of Diminishing Expectations.* New York: W. W. Norton, 1978.

———. *Haven in a Heartless World.* New York: Basic Books, 1977.

LEARS, T. J. JACKSON. "From Salvation to Self-Realization: Advertising and the Therapeutic Roots of the Consumer Culture, 1880–1930," in Richard Wightman and T. J. Jackson Lears, eds., *The Culture of Consumption: Critical Essays in American History 1880–1980.* New York: Pantheon, 1983.

LEVENSTEIN, HARVEY A. *Paradox of Plenty: A Social History of Eating in Modern America.* New York: Oxford University Press, 1993.

———. *Revolution at the Table: The Transformation of the American Diet.* New York: Oxford University Press, 1988.

LOVEGREN, SYLVIA. *Fashionable Food: Seven Decades of Food Fads.* New York: Macmillan, 1995.

LUPTON, ELLEN. *Mechanical Brides: Women and Machines from Home to Office.* Princeton, NJ: Princeton Architectural Press, 1993.

LUPTON, ELLEN, AND J. ABBOTT MILLER. *The Bathroom, the Kitchen, and the Aesthetics of Waste: A Process of Elimination.* San Francisco: Chronicle Books, 1992.

MILLS, MARJORIE. *Cooking on a Ration: Food Is Still Fun.* Boston: Houghton Mifflin, 1943.

MINTZ, SIDNEY. *Tasting Food, Tasting Freedom: Excurions into Eating, Culture, and the Past.* Boston: Beacon Press, 1996.

MONTANARI, MASSIMO. *The Culture of Food,* trans. Carl Ipsen. Oxford: Blackwell, 1994.

PADDLEFORD, CLEMENTINE. *How America Eats.* New York: Scribner's, 1960.

PELLEGRINI, ANGELO. *Vintage Pellegrini: The Collected Wisdom of an American Buongustaio,* ed. Schuyler Ingle. Seattle: Sasquatch Books, 1991.

PENNY, PRUDENCE. *Prudence Penny Cook Book.* (*San Francisco Examiner,* 1939).

POINT, FERNAND. *Ma Gastronomie,* trans. Frank Kulla and Patricia Shannon Kulla. Wilton, CT: Lyceum Books, 1969.

POLIVY, JANET, AND PETER HERMAN. "Diagnosis and Treatment of Normal Eating." *Journal of Consulting and Clinical Psychology* 55, no. 5 (1987): 635−44.

———. "Dieting and Bingeing: A Causal Analysis." *American Psychologist* 40, no. 2 (February 1985): 193−201.

REVEL, JEAN-FRANÇOIS. *Culture and Cuisine: A Journey Through the History of Food,* trans. Helen R. Lane. New York: Da Capo Press, 1982.

ROOT, WAVERLEY, AND RICHARD DE ROCHEMONT. *Eating in America: A History.* Hopewell, NJ: Ecco Press, 1995.

RYBCZYNSKI, WITOLD. *Looking Around: A Journey Through Architecture.* New York: Viking, 1992.

SCHLISSEL, LILLIAN, BYRD GIBBENS, AND ELIZABETH HAMPTEN. *Far from Home: Families of the Westward Journey.* New York: Schocken Books, 1990.

SCHREMP, GERRY. *Kitchen Culture: Fifty Years of Food Fads.* New York: Pharos Books, 1991.

SCHWARTZ, HILLEL. *Never Satisfied: A Cultural History of Diets, Fantasies and Fat.* New York: The Free Press/Macmillan, 1986.

SEARS, BARRY. *The Zone: A Dietary Road Map.* New York: Regan Books, 1995.

SHEEHAN, MICHAEL M. "Choice of Marriage Partner in the Middle Ages: Development and Mode of Application of a Theory of Marriage," in *Studies in Medieval and Renaissance History,* vol. 1, ed. J. A. S. Evans and R. W. Unger. Vancouver: University of British Columbia Press, 1978.

SMITH, DANIEL SCOTT. "The Curious History of Theorizing About the History of the Western Nuclear Family." *Social Science History* 17, no. 3: 325−53.

SOKOLOV, RAYMOND. *Why We Eat What We Eat: How the Encounter Between the New World and the Old Changed the Way Everyone on the Planet Eats.* New York: Simon & Schuster, 1991.

STACEY, MICHELLE. *Consumed: Why Americans Love, Hate, and Fear Food.* New York: Touchstone, 1994.

STERN, JANE AND MICHAEL. *American Gourmet: Classic Recipes, Deluxe Delights, Flamboyant Favorites, and Swank "Company" Food from the '50s and '60s.* New York: HarperCollins, 1991.

————. *Square Meals: A Cookbook.* New York: Alfred A. Knopf, 1984.

TALBOT, MARGARET. "Les Très Riches Heures de Martha Stewart." *The New Republic,* May 13, 1996.

TANNAHILL, REAY. *Food in History.* New York: Three Rivers Press, 1988.

TEDLOCK, DENNIS, trans. *Popol Vuh: The Mayan Book of the Dawn of Life,* rev. ed. New York: Simon & Schuster, 1996.

VERRILL, A. HYATT. *Foods America Gave the World.* Boston: L. C. Page, 1937.

VISSER, MARGARET. *The Rituals of Dinner: The Origins, Evolution, Eccentricities, and Meaning of Table Manners.* New York: Grove Weidenfeld, 1991.

WATERS, ALICE. *Chez Panisse Menu Cookbook.* New York: Random House, 1982.

Portions of this book appeared in the past in altered form in *Antioch Review, Harper's, Mirabella, New York Times Magazine, Salon,* and *Saveur.*

ABOUT THE AUTHOR

Sallie Tisdale is the author of five books, including *Talk Dirty to Me*. A contributing editor at *Harper's* magazine, she has published numerous articles in *The New Yorker*, *Condé Nast Traveler*, *The New Republic*, *Esquire*, *Salon*, and *Vogue*. She is the recipient of an NEA fellowship, a James Phelan Award, a 1999 Pope Foundation fellowship for journalism, and three National Magazine Award nominations. She lives in Portland, Oregon.